www.wadsworth.com

www.wadsworth.com is the World Wide Web site for Thomson
Wadsworth and is your direct source to dozens of online
resources.

At www.wadsworth.com you can find out about supplements,
demonstration software, and student resources. You can also send
e-mail to many of our authors and preview new publications and
exciting new technologies.

www.wadsworth.com
Changing the way the world learns®

Founding Principles
of the
United States

Volume II Reader

Steven Bullock
University of Nebraska at Omaha

Carson Holloway
University of Nebraska at Omaha

EDITORS

THOMSON

™

WADSWORTH

Australia • Brazil • Canada • Mexico • Singapore
Spain • United Kingdom • United States

THOMSON

WADSWORTH

Founding Principles of the United States, Volume II Reader
Steven Bullock and Carson Holloway

Publisher: *Clark Baxter*
Acquisitions Editor: *Ashley Dodge*
Associate Development Editor: *Julie Yardley*
Editorial Assistant: *Lucinda Bingham*
Technology Project Manager: *Dave Lionetti*
Marketing Manager: *Lori Grebe Cook*
Marketing Assistant: *Teresa Jessen*
Marketing Communications Manager:
    Laurel Anderson
Senior Project Manager, Editorial Production:
    Kimberly Adams
Executive Art Director: *Maria Epes*

Print Buyer: *Rebecca Cross*
Permissions Editor: *Kiely Sisk*
Production Service: *Scratchgravel Publishing
    Services*
Copy Editor: *Mary Anne Shahidi*
Cover Designer: *Lisa Devenish*
Cover Image: *Patrick Henry addressing the Virginia
    Assembly/Art Resource, NY*
Cover Printer: *Malloy Incorporated*
Compositor: *Cadmus Professional Communications*
Printer: *Malloy Incorporated*

For more information about our products,
contact us at:
**Thomson Learning Academic
Resource Center
1-800-423-0563**

For permission to use material from this text
or product, submit a request online at
http://www.thomsonrights.com.

Any additional questions about
permissions can be submitted by email to
thomsonrights@thomson.com.

Library of Congress Control Number:
2005923111

ISBN 0-495-03002-3

**Thomson Higher Education
10 Davis Drive
Belmont, CA 94002-3098
USA**

Asia (including India)
Thomson Learning
5 Shenton Way
#01-01 UIC Building
Singapore 068808

Australia/New Zealand
Thomson Learning Australia
102 Dodds Street
Southbank, Victoria 3006
Australia

Canada
Thomson Nelson
1120 Birchmount Road
Toronto, Ontario M1K 5G4
Canada

UK/Europe/Middle East/Africa
Thomson Learning
High Holborn House
50–51 Bedford Row
London WC1R 4LR
United Kingdom

Latin America
Thomson Learning
Seneca, 53
Colonia Polanco
11560 Mexico
D.F. Mexico

Spain (including Portugal)
Thomson Paraninfo
Calle Magallanes, 25
28015 Madrid, Spain

Brief Contents

Contents

CHAPTER 4 Education   96

CHAPTER 5 Republican Government   129

CHAPTER 6 Limited Government   161

CHAPTER 7 Economic Liberty   193

Preface

By the time of the American Revolution, the Founding Fathers of the United States had already begun the task of forming a new nation that would be, to them, a beacon for others to follow. Even before the battles of Lexington and Concord, Enlightenment thought had permeated most of Western society and was beginning to influence the manner in which individuals perceived the world. The musings of Locke, Montesquieu, and Voltaire held tremendous sway over the intellectuals of Europe, though the rigid hierarchical and monarchical structures of most of those societies did not lend themselves to the adoption of Enlightenment ideals.

However, the American Founding Fathers, most of whom were intellectual descendants of Enlightenment thought in Europe, were not saddled with many of the same traditional constraints as found across the Atlantic. If one examines the writings and speeches of early American leaders or even the major documents of the founding era, a shocking consistency can be noted: virtually nothing new or unique can be found there. For example, Thomas Jefferson borrowed heavily from, among others, John Locke, in penning the Declaration of Independence and James Madison framed the Constitution with Montesquieu's *Spirit of Laws* as his guide. The United States, however, *was* the first nation founded on basic Enlightenment ideals. Although intellectuals in France, Scotland, and Germany quibbled over the details of theories and philosophic ambiguities, their American counterparts were intent on forming a nation that would place into practice what had been debated over the course of previous centuries.

Fast forward to September 11, 2001, when the United States endured harrowing terrorist attacks on symbols of American economic prosperity and military might that caused many to evaluate the exact nature of American citizenship. As days and months passed after the attack, questions arose, such as: "Why do the terrorists hate us so much?" Such inquiries subsequently led to heated debate about terrorism, the role of the United States in a global community, and, most importantly, the fundamental values of American society. Thus, these books have been compiled with the purpose of identifying the founding principles of the United States and illuminating the evolution of those principles since the American Revolution. The seven principles that are examined in each volume include: equality, virtue, religion, education, republican government, limited government, and economic liberty.

These principles are not intended to be comprehensive but, instead, focus on the essential components that the editors believe have most profoundly impacted the development of American society.

Acknowledgments

We would like to thank the following reviewers for their valuable input:

Leslie M. Alexander, The Ohio State University

Lesley J. Gordon, University of Akron, Ohio

Murray A. Rubinstein, Baruch College–The City University of New York

Sean Taylor, Minnesota State University, Moorhead

William Benton Whisenhunt, College of Dupage

Introduction to Volume II

Following the end of Reconstruction, which concluded the most divisive period in American history, the founding principles of the United States continued to evolve separately and distinctly. Issues such as the expansion of industry, increased immigration, and the perceived moral decline of society all contributed to the adjustment and realignment of America's founding ideals, especially during the course of the twentieth century.

Chapter 1: Equality

Chapter 1 covers the development of America's understanding of equality over the last 100 years and more. A good deal of attention is given to the question of race. The readings trace the Supreme Court's embrace and later rejection of the "separate but equal" doctrine, and the subsequent argument over the effort to prohibit racial discrimination in "public accommodations." In addition, excerpts from a recent Supreme Court case, *Grutter* v. *Bollinger* (2003), are used to illustrate the debate over affirmative action, or racial preferences. As in Volume I, the question of the equality of men and women is also covered, and readings are included on the Equal Rights Amendment and the Supreme Court's use of the "equal protection" clause of the Fourteenth Amendment to prohibit certain kinds of discrimination against women.

Chapter 2: Virtue

By the turn of the twentieth century, the term "virtue" had largely been replaced in the American lexicon by "morality" and, as seen in the readings in this chapter, these two terms were significantly different. American society became notably more accepting of behavior that had been deemed unacceptable in previous generations, and living modestly eroded even as an ideal. Also, as the twentieth century progressed, many Americans became concerned that a main quality of republican virtue promoted by the founders—the sublimation of self-interest for the benefit of others—had lost its appeal.

Chapter 3: Religion

The selections included here trace the development of two persistent conflicts related to religion's role in modern America: the tension between the rights of religious minorities and the authority of the majority to enact its preferences in law; and the tension between a desire to recognize, sometimes officially, the importance of religion to America's public life and the desire to maintain a separation between church and state. These debates continue today, as evidenced by the recent constitutional dispute over the inclusion of the words "under God" in the Pledge of Allegiance.

Chapter 4: Education

The decades following the Civil War were years of enormous expansion and change in the field of education. Into the twentieth century the founders' dream of maintaining an educational system that identified and fostered talent, regardless of class or social standing, was beginning to materialize. The selections for this chapter detail the major obstacles for realizing this dream, including racism, apathy, lack of academic rigor, and a disconnection between the needs of society and the direction of education.

Chapter 5: Republican Government

The development of America's understanding of republican government is taken up in Chapter 5, which pays particular attention to the expansion of the franchise in the latter half of our nation's history. Thus selections cover the direct election of senators, the extension of the suffrage to women and those at least 18 years old, and the effort to make good the promise of the Fifteenth Amendment through the Voting Rights Act of 1965. In addition, readings illustrate the modern Supreme Court's application of the "equal protection" clause to the right to vote, including the controversial *Bush* v. *Gore* case arising from the disputed 2000 election.

Chapter 6: Limited Government

Chapter 6 deals with America's persistent commitment to, but changing understanding of, limited government. The readings follow how the Supreme Court has often modified its account of Federalism and individual rights in relation to new and challenging situations, such as the Great Depression and the Cold War. As in Volume I, we include readings on the challenge of adhering to limited government in time of war. Moreover, a number of selections also illustrate the controversies arising from the Court's recognition of a constitutional right to privacy or personal liberty such as the freedom to have an abortion or engage in homosexual conduct.

Chapter 7: Economic Liberty

The period from the Civil War to the contemporary era was characterized by enormous economic expansion and a drifting away from the economic liberty envisioned by most of the Founding Fathers to a state of regulated capitalism. Most importantly, this economic environment embraced the acquisition of goods well beyond the point of necessity and, in some cases, well beyond the point of comprehension. The readings in this chapter detail the emergence of wide economic disparities in the United States along with many of the primary issues that arose from the unfettered capitalism around the turn of the twentieth century to the increasingly regulated American economy since that time.

CHAPTER 1

Equality

1

President Chester Arthur: State of the Union Message (1881)

Here President Arthur urges a new solution to the "Indian problem." Native Americans, he argues, should be brought under the protection of American law. At the same time, they should be offered individual plots of private property in order to encourage them to adopt agriculture and abandon their traditional tribal life. These recommendations were incorporated into the Dawes Act of 1887. President Arthur's approach to the question illustrates the ambivalence of American whites' attitude toward the equality of Native Americans: on the one hand, seeking to apply the principle of equality to them as individuals, but, on the other, refusing to recognize their tribal way of life as worthy of preservation.

Prominent among the matters which challenge the attention of Congress at its present session is the management of our Indian affairs. While this question has been a cause of trouble and embarrassment from the infancy of the Government, it is but recently that any effort has been made for its solution at once serious, determined, consistent, and promising success.

It has been easier to resort to convenient makeshifts for tiding over temporary difficulties than to grapple with the great permanent problem, and accordingly the easier course has almost invariably been pursued.

It was natural, at a time when the national territory seemed almost illimitable and contained many millions of acres far outside the bounds of civilized settlements, that a policy should have been initiated which more than aught else has been the fruitful source of our Indian complications.

I refer, of course, to the policy of dealing with the various Indian tribes as separate nationalities, of relegating them by treaty stipulations to the occupancy of immense reservations in the West, and of encouraging them to live a savage life, undisturbed by any earnest and well-directed efforts to bring them under the influences of civilization.

The unsatisfactory results which have sprung from this policy are becoming apparent to all.

As the white settlements have crowded the borders of the reservations, the Indians, sometimes contentedly and sometimes against their will, have been transferred to other hunting grounds, from which they have again been dislodged whenever their new-found homes have been desired by the adventurous settlers.

These removals and the frontier collisions by which they have often been preceded have led to frequent and disastrous conflicts between the races.

It is profitless to discuss here which of them has been chiefly responsible for the disturbances whose recital occupies so large a space upon the pages of our history.

We have to deal with the appalling fact that though thousands of lives have been sacrificed and hundreds of millions of dollars expended in the attempt to solve the Indian problem, it has until within the past few years seemed scarcely nearer a solution than it was half a century ago. But the Government has of late been cautiously but steadily feeling its way to the adoption of a policy which has already produced gratifying results, and which, in my judgment, is likely, if Congress and the Executive accord in its support, to relieve us ere long from the difficulties which have hitherto beset us.

For the success of the efforts now making to introduce among the Indians the customs and pursuits of civilized life and gradually to absorb them into the mass of our citizens, sharing their rights and holden to their responsibilities, there is imperative need for legislative action.

My suggestions in that regard will be chiefly such as have been already called to the attention of Congress and have received to some extent its consideration.

First. I recommend the passage of an act making the laws of the various States and Territories applicable to the Indian reservations within their borders and extending the laws of the State of Arkansas to the portion of the Indian Territory not occupied by the Five Civilized Tribes.

The Indian should receive the protection of the law. He should be allowed to maintain in court his rights of person and property. He has repeatedly begged for this privilege. Its exercise would be very valuable to him in his progress toward civilization.

Second. Of even greater importance is a measure which has been frequently recommended by my predecessors in office, and in furtherance of which several bills have been from time to time introduced in both Houses of Congress. The enactment of a general law permitting the allotment in severalty, to such Indians, at least, as desire it, of a reasonable quantity of land secured to them by patent, and for their own protection made inalienable for twenty or twenty-five years, is demanded for their present welfare and their permanent advancement.

In return for such considerate action on the part of the Government, there is reason to believe that the Indians in large numbers would be persuaded to sever their tribal relations and to engage at once in agricultural pursuits. Many of them realize the fact that their hunting days are over and that it is now for their best interests to conform their manner of life to the new order of things. By no greater inducement than the assurance of permanent title to the soil can they be led to engage in the occupation of tilling it.

The well-attested reports of their increasing interest in husbandry justify the hope and belief that the enactment of such a statute as I recommend would be at once attended with gratifying results. A resort to the allotment system would have a direct and powerful influence in dissolving the tribal bond, which is so prominent a feature of savage life, and which tends so strongly to perpetuate it.

Third. I advise a liberal appropriation for the support of Indian schools, because of my confident belief that such a course is consistent with the wisest economy.

Even among the most uncultivated Indian tribes there is reported to be a general and urgent desire on the part of the chiefs and older members for the education of their children. It is unfortunate, in view of this fact, that during the past year the means which have been at the command of the Interior Department for the purpose of Indian instruction have proved to be utterly inadequate.

The success of the schools which are in operation at Hampton, Carlisle, and Forest Grove should not only encourage a more generous provision for the support of those institutions, but should prompt the establishment of others of a similar character.

They are doubtless much more potent for good than the day schools upon the reservation, as the pupils are altogether separated from the surroundings of savage life and brought into constant contact with civilization.

2

Justice Joseph Bradley: Opinion of the Court in *The Civil Rights Cases* (1883)

In the Civil Rights Act of 1875, Congress prohibited certain kinds of businesses from discriminating against African Americans in the services they provided. A number of persons violated the law and were accordingly indicted. They challenged the constitutionality of the law, however, and the question came before the Supreme Court. In the following excerpt from the Court's opinion, Justice Bradley argues that Congress has no power to prevent such business discrimination, but only to correct discrimination carried out by the state governments.

[The law's effect] is to declare that in all inns, public conveyances, and places of amusement, colored citizens, whether formerly slaves or not, and citizens of other races, shall have the same accommodations and privileges in all inns, public conveyances, and places of amusement, as are enjoyed by white citizens; and vice versa. . . . .

Has congress constitutional power to make such a law? Of course, no one will contend that the power to pass it was contained in the constitution before the adoption of the last three amendments. The power is sought, first, in the Fourteenth Amendment. . . .

The first section of the Fourteenth Amendment, which is the one relied on, after declaring who shall be citizens of the United States, and of the several states, is prohibitory in its character, and prohibitory upon the states. It declares that "no state shall make or enforce any law which shall abridge the privileges or immunities of citizens of the United States; nor shall any state deprive any person of life, liberty, or property without due process of law; nor deny to any person within its jurisdiction the equal protection of the laws." It is state action of a particular character that is prohibited. Individual invasion of individual rights is not the subject matter of the amendment. It has a deeper and broader scope. It nullifies and makes void all state legislation, and state action of every kind, which impairs the privileges and immunities of citizens of the United States, or which injures them in life, liberty, or property without due process of law, or which denies to any of them the equal protection of the laws. It not only does this, but . . . the last section of the amendment invests congress with power to enforce it by appropriate legislation. To enforce what? To enforce the prohibition. To adopt appropriate legislation for correcting the effects of such prohibited state law and state acts, and thus to render them effectually null, void, and innocuous. This is the legislative power conferred upon congress, and this is the whole of it. . . .

An inspection of the law shows that it makes no reference whatever to any supposed or apprehended violation of the Fourteenth Amendment on the part of the states. It is not predicated on any such view. It proceeds *ex directo* to declare that certain acts committed by individuals shall be deemed offenses, and shall be prosecuted and punished by proceedings in the courts of the United States. It does not profess to be corrective of any constitutional wrong committed by the states; it does not make its operation to depend upon any such wrong committed. . . . In other words, it steps into the domain of local jurisprudence, and lays down rules for the conduct of individuals in society towards each other, and imposes sanctions for the enforcement of those rules, without referring in any manner to any supposed action of the state or its authorities.

If this legislation is appropriate for enforcing the prohibitions of the amendment, it is difficult to see where it is to stop. Why may not Congress, with equal show of authority, enact a code of laws for the enforcement and vindication of all rights of life, liberty, and property? If it is supposable that the states may deprive persons of life, liberty, and property without due process of law (and the amendment itself does suppose this), why should not Congress proceed at once to prescribe due process of law for the protection of every one of these fundamental rights, in every possible case, as well as to prescribe equal privileges in inns, public conveyances, and theaters? The truth is that the implication of a power to legislate in this manner is based upon the assumption that if the states are forbidden to legislate or act in a particular way on a particular subject, and power is conferred upon Congress to enforce the prohibition, this gives congress power to legislate generally upon that subject, and not merely power to provide modes of redress against such state legislation or action. The assumption is certainly unsound. It is repugnant to the Tenth Amendment of the Constitution, which declares that powers not delegated to the United States by the Constitution, nor prohibited by it to the states, are reserved to the states respectively or to the people. . . . .

But the power of congress to adopt direct and primary, as distinguished from corrective, legislation on the subject in hand, is sought, in the second place, from the Thirteenth Amendment, which abolishes slavery. This amendment declares "that neither slavery, nor involuntary servitude, except as a punishment for crime, whereof the party shall have been duly convicted, shall exist within the United States, or any place subject to their jurisdiction;" and it gives Congress power to enforce the amendment by appropriate legislation. . . .

It is true that slavery cannot exist without law any more than property in lands and goods can exist without law, and therefore the Thirteenth Amendment may be regarded as nullifying all state laws which establish or uphold slavery. But it has a reflex character also, establishing and decreeing universal civil and political freedom throughout the United States; and it is assumed that the power vested in Congress to enforce the article by appropriate legislation, clothes Congress with power to pass all laws necessary and proper for abolishing all badges and incidents of slavery in the United Stated; and upon this assumption it is claimed that this is sufficient authority for declaring by law that all persons shall have equal accommodations and privileges in all inns, public conveyances, and places of public amusement; the argument being that the denial of such equal accommodations and privileges is in itself a subjection to a species of servitude within the meaning of the amendment. Conceding the major proposition to be true, that that Congress has a right to enact all necessary and proper laws for the obliteration and prevention of slavery, with all its badges and incidents, is the minor proposition also true, that the denial to any person of admission to the accommodations and privileges of an inn, a public conveyance, or a theater, does subject that person to any form of servitude, or tend to fasten upon him any badge of slavery? If it does not, then power to pass the law is not found in the Thirteenth Amendment.

The only question under the present head, therefore, is, whether the refusal to any persons of the accommodations of an inn, or a public conveyance, or a place of public amusement, by an individual, and without any sanction or support from any state law or regulation, does inflict upon such persons any manner of servitude, or form of slavery, as those terms are understood in this country? . . . Can the act of a mere individual, the owner of the inn, the public conveyance, or place of amusement, refusing the accommodation, be justly regarded as imposing any badge of slavery or servitude upon the applicant, or only as inflicting an ordinary civil injury, properly cognizable by the laws of the state, and presumably subject to redress by those laws until the contrary appears?

After giving to these questions all the consideration which their importance demands, we are forced to the conclusion that such an act of refusal has nothing to do with slavery or involuntary servitude, and that if it is violative of any right of the party, his redress is to be sought under the laws of the state; or, if those laws are adverse to his rights and do not protect him, his remedy will be found in the corrective legislation which Congress has adopted, or may adopt, for counteracting the effect of state laws, or state action, prohibited by the Fourteenth Amendment. It would be running the slavery argument into the ground to make it apply to every act of discrimination which a person may see fit to make as to the guests he will entertain, or as to the people he will take into his coach or cab or car, or admit to his concert or theater, or deal with in other matters of intercourse or business. . . .

On the whole, we are of opinion that no countenance of authority for the passage of the law in question can be found in either the Thirteenth or Fourteenth Amendment of the Constitution; and no other ground of authority for its passage being suggested, it must necessarily be declared void, at least so far as its operation in the several states is concerned.

3

Frederick Douglass:
Speech on *The Civil Rights Cases* (1883)

Douglass, a former slave who had escaped to freedom, was an important figure in the abolition movement prior to the Civil War. After the war he continued as a prominent advocate for the equal rights of African Americans. In the following passages he criticizes the Supreme Court's decision in The Civil Rights Cases, *arguing that it deprived the government of a reasonable power to protect the rights of all its citizens and threatened to endanger the republic by depriving America of the friendship of its African American population.*

We have been, as a class, grievously wounded, wounded in the house of our friends, and this wound is too deep and too painful for ordinary measured speech. . . .

The cause which has brought us here tonight is neither common nor trivial. Few events in our national history have surpassed it in magnitude, importance and significance. It has swept over the land like a moral cyclone, leaving moral desolation in its track.

We feel it, as we felt the furious attempt, years ago, to force the accursed system of slavery upon the soil of Kansas, the enactment of the Fugitive Slave Bill, the repeal of the Missouri Compromise, the Dred Scott decision. I look upon it as one more shocking development of that moral weakness in high places which has attended the conflict between the spirit of liberty and the spirit of slavery from the beginning, and I venture to predict that it will be so regarded by after-coming generations.

Far down the ages, when men shall wish to inform themselves as to the real state of liberty, law, religion and civilization in the United States at this juncture of our history, they will overhaul the proceedings of the Supreme Court, and read the decision declaring the Civil Rights Bill unconstitutional and void.

From this they will learn more than from many volumes, how far we have advanced, in this year of grace, from barbarism toward civilization. . . .

To come a little nearer to the case now before us. The Supreme Court of the United States, in the exercise of its high and vast constitutional power, has suddenly and unexpectedly decided that the law intended to secure to colored people the civil rights guaranteed to them by the following provision of the Constitution of the United States, is unconstitutional and void. Here it is:

"No State," says the 14th Amendment, "shall make or enforce any law which shall abridge the privileges or immunities of citizens of the United States; nor shall any State deprive any person of life, liberty, or property without due process of law; nor deny any person within its jurisdiction the equal protection of the laws." . . .

What will be said here tonight, will be spoken, I trust, more in sorrow than in anger, more in a tone of regret than of bitterness.

We cannot, however, overlook the fact that though not so intended, this decision has inflicted a heavy calamity upon seven millions of the people of this country, and left them naked and defenseless against the action of a malignant, vulgar, and pitiless prejudice.

It presents the United States before the world as a Nation utterly destitute of power to protect the rights of its own citizens upon its own soil.

It can claim service and allegiance, loyalty and life, of them, but it cannot protect them against the most palpable violation of the rights of human nature, rights to secure which, governments are established. It can tax their bread and tax their blood, but has no protecting power for their persons. Its National power extends only to the District of Columbia, and the Territories—where the people have no votes, and where the land has no people. All else is subject to the States. In the name of common sense, I ask, what right have we to call ourselves a Nation, in view of this decision, and this utter destitution of power?

In humiliating the colored people of this country, this decision has humbled the Nation. It gives to a South Carolina, or a Mississippi, railroad conductor, more power than it gives to the National Government. He may order the wife of the Chief Justice of the United States into a smoking-car full of hirsute men and compel her to go and listen to the coarse jests of a vulgar crowd. It gives to a hotel-keeper who may, from a prejudice born of the rebellion, wish to turn her out at midnight into the darkness of the storm, power to compel her to go. In such a case, according to this decision of the Supreme Court, the National Government has no right to interfere. She must take her claim for protection and redress, not to the Nation, but to the State, and when the State, as I understand it, declares there is upon its Statute book, no law for her protection, the function and power of the National Government is exhausted, and she is utterly without redress.

Bad, therefore, as our case is under this decision, the evil principle affirmed by the court is not wholly confined to or spent upon persons of color. The wife of Chief Justice Waite—I speak of respectfully—is protected today, not by law, but solely by the accident of her color. So far as the law of the land is concerned, she is in the same condition as that of the humblest colored woman in the Republic. The difference between colored and white, here, is, that the one, by reason of color, needs legal protection, and the other, by reason of color, does not need protection. It is nevertheless true, that manhood is insulted, in both cases. No man can put a chain about the ankle of his fellow man, without at last finding the other end of it fastened about his own neck.

The lesson of all the ages on this point is, that a wrong done to one man, is a wrong done to all men. It may not be felt at the moment, and the evil day may be long delayed, but so sure as there is a moral government of the universe, so sure will the harvest of evil come.

Color prejudice is not the only prejudice against which a Republic like ours should guard. The spirit of caste is dangerous everywhere. There is the prejudice of the rich against the poor, the pride and prejudice of the idle dandy against the hard handed working man. There is, worst of all, religious prejudice; a prejudice which has stained a whole continent with blood. It is, in fact, a spirit infernal, against which every enlightened man should wage perpetual war. Perhaps no class of our fellow citizens has carried this prejudice against color to a point more extreme and dangerous than have our Catholic Irish fellow citizens, and yet no people on the face of the earth have been more relentlessly persecuted and oppressed on account of race and religion, than the Irish people.

But in Ireland, persecution has at last reached a point where it reacts terribly upon her persecutors. England today is reaping the bitter consequences of her injustice and oppression. Ask any man of intelligence to-day, "What is the chief source of England's weakness?" "What has reduced her to the rank of a second-class power?" and the answer will be "Ireland!" Poor, ragged, hungry, starving and oppressed as she is, she is strong enough to be a standing menace to the power and glory of England.

Fellow citizens! We want no black Ireland in America. We want no aggrieved class in America. Strong as we are without the Negro, we are stronger with him than without him. The power and friendship of seven millions of people scattered all over the country, however humble, are not to be despised. . . .

I am not here, in this presence, to discuss the constitutionality or unconstitutionality of this decision of the Supreme Court. The decision may or may not be constitutional. That is a question for lawyers, and not for laymen, and there are lawyers on this platform as learned, able, and eloquent as any who have appeared in this case before the Supreme Court, or as any in the land. To these I leave the exposition of the Constitution; but I claim the right to remark upon a strange and glaring inconsistency with former decisions, in the action of the court on this Civil Rights Bill. It is a new departure, entirely out of the line of the precedents and decisions of the Supreme Court at other times and in other directions where the rights of colored men were concerned. It has utterly ignored and rejected the force and application of object and intention as a rule of interpretation. It has construed the Constitution in defiant disregard of what was the object and intention of the adoption of the Fourteenth Amendment. It has made no account whatever of the intention and purpose of Congress and the President in putting the Civil Rights' Bill upon the Statute Book of the Nation. It has seen fit in this case, affecting a weak and much-persecuted people, to be guided by the narrowest and most restricted rules of legal interpretation. It has viewed both the Constitution and the law with a strict regard to their letter, but without any generous recognition of their broad and liberal spirit. . . .

It used to be thought that the whole was more than a part; that the greater included the less, and that what was unconstitutional for a State to do was equally unconstitutional for an individual member of a State to do. What is a State, in the absence of the people who compose it? Land, air and water. That is all. As individuals, the people of the State of South Carolina may stamp out the rights of the Negro wherever they please, so long as they do not do so as a State. All the parts can violate the Constitution, but the whole cannot. It is not the act itself, according to this decision, that is unconstitutional. The unconstitutionality of the case depends wholly upon the party committing the act. If the State commits it, it is wrong, if the citizen of the State commits it, it is right.

O consistency, thou art indeed a jewel! What does it matter to a colored citizen that a State may not insult and outrage him, if a citizen of a State may? The effect upon him is the same, and it was just this effect that the framers of the Fourteenth Amendment plainly intended by that article to prevent. . . .

4

Justice Henry Billings Brown: Opinion of the Court in *Plessy* v. *Ferguson* (1896)

After the Civil War, the nation amended the Constitution in order to secure a greater equality between the races. The Thirteenth Amendment abolished slavery, and the Fourteenth forbade the states to deny to persons within their jurisdiction the "equal protection of the laws." Nevertheless, many states continued to enact laws that discriminated against African Americans. In this case the Supreme Court considered the constitutionality of a Louisiana law requiring racial segregation of railroad passengers. When Plessy was charged with a violation of the law, he contended that it violated the Thirteenth and Fourteenth Amendments. The Court, however, upheld the law, and thus embraced the notion that the Constitution allows state governments to require "separate but equal" facilities for the races.

This case turns upon the constitutionality of an act of the general assembly of the state of Louisiana, passed in 1890, providing for separate railway carriages for the white and colored races. . . .

The constitutionality of this act is attacked upon the ground that it conflicts both with the thirteenth amendment of the constitution, abolishing slavery, and the fourteenth amendment, which prohibits certain restrictive legislation on the part of the states.

1. That it does not conflict with the thirteenth amendment, which abolished slavery and involuntary servitude, except as punishment for crime, is too clear for argument. Slavery implies involuntary servitude, a state of bondage; the ownership of mankind as a chattel, or, at least, the control of the labor and services of one man for the benefit of another, and the absence of a legal right to the disposal of his own person, property, and services. This amendment was said in the *Slaughter-House Cases* (1873) to have been intended primarily to abolish slavery, as it had been previously known in this country, and that it equally forbade Mexican peonage or the Chinese coolie trade, when they amounted to slavery or involuntary servitude, and that the use of the word "servitude" was intended to prohibit the use of all forms of involuntary slavery, of whatever class or name. It was intimated, however, in that case, that this amendment was regarded by the statesmen of that day as insufficient to protect the colored race from certain laws which had been enacted in the Southern states, imposing upon the colored race onerous disabilities and burdens, and curtailing their rights in the pursuit of life, liberty, and property to such an extent that their freedom was of little value; and that the fourteenth amendment was devised to meet this exigency. . . .

2. By the fourteenth amendment . . . the states are forbidden from making or enforcing any law which shall abridge the privileges or immunities of citizens of the United States, or shall deprive any person of life, liberty, or property without due process of law, or deny to any person within their jurisdiction the equal protection of the laws. . . .

The object of the amendment was undoubtedly to enforce the absolute equality of the two races before the law, but, in the nature of things, it could not have been intended to abolish distinctions based upon color, or to enforce social, as distinguished from political, equality, or a commingling of the two races upon terms unsatisfactory to either. Laws permitting, and even requiring, their separation, in places where they are liable to be brought into contact, do not necessarily imply the inferiority of either race to the other, and have been generally, if not universally, recognized as within the competency of the state legislatures in the exercise of their police power. The most common instance of this is connected with the establishment of separate schools for white and colored children, which have been held to be a valid exercise of the legislative power even by courts of states where the political rights of the colored race have been longest and most earnestly enforced.

One of the earliest of these cases is that of *Roberts* v. *City of Boston* . . . in which the supreme judicial court of Massachusetts held that the general school committee of Boston had power to make provision for the instruction of colored children in separate schools established exclusively for them, and to prohibit their attendance upon the other schools. "The great principle," said Chief Justice Shaw, "advanced by the learned and eloquent advocate for the plaintiff [Mr. Charles Sumner], is that, by the constitution and laws of Massachusetts, all persons, without distinction of age or sex, birth or color, origin or condition, are equal before the law. . . . But, when this great principle comes to be applied to the actual and various conditions of persons in society, it will not warrant the assertion that men and women are legally clothed with the same civil and political powers, and that children and adults are legally to have the same functions and be subject to the same treatment; but only that the rights of all, as they are settled and regulated by law, are equally entitled to the paternal consideration and protection of the law for their maintenance and security." It was held that the powers of the committee extended to the establishment of separate schools for children of different ages, sexes and colors. . . . Similar laws have been enacted by congress under its general power of legislation over the District of Columbia as well as by the legislatures of many of the states, and have been generally, if not uniformly, sustained by the courts.

Laws forbidding the intermarriage of the two races may be said in a technical sense to interfere with the freedom of contract, and yet have been universally recognized as within the police power of the state. . . .

So far, then, as a conflict with the fourteenth amendment is concerned, the case reduces itself to the question whether the statute of Louisiana is a reasonable regulation, and with respect to this there must necessarily be a large discretion on the part of the legislature. In determining the question of reasonableness, it is at liberty to act with reference to the established usages, customs, and traditions of the people, and with a view to the promotion of their comfort, and the preservation of the public peace and good order. Gauged by this standard, we cannot say that a law which authorizes or even requires the separation of the two races in public conveyances is unreasonable, or more obnoxious to the fourteenth amendment than the acts of congress requiring separate schools for colored children in the District of Columbia, the constitutionality of which does not seem to have been questioned, or the corresponding acts of state legislatures.

We consider the underlying fallacy of the plaintiff's argument to consist in the assumption that the enforced separation of the two races stamps the colored race with a badge of inferiority. If this be so, it is not by reason of anything found in the act, but solely because the colored race chooses to put that construction upon it. The argument necessarily assumes that if, as has been more than once the case, and is not unlikely to be so again, the colored race should become the dominant power in the state legislature, and should enact a law in precisely similar terms, it would thereby relegate the white race to an inferior position. We imagine that the white race, at least, would not acquiesce in this assumption. The argument also assumes that social prejudices may be overcome by legislation, and that equal rights cannot be secured to the negro except by an enforced commingling of the two races. We cannot accept this proposition. If the two races are to meet upon terms of social equality, it must be the result of natural affinities, a mutual appreciation of each other's merits, and a voluntary consent of individuals. . . .

5

Chief Justice Earl Warren: Opinion of the Court in *Brown* v. *Board of Education* (1954)

In this landmark case the Supreme Court unanimously repudiated the "separate but equal" doctrine of Plessy v. Ferguson. In some earlier decisions the Court had struck down schemes of segregation on the grounds that the separate facilities provided for African Americans were not truly equal to those provided for whites. Here for the first time the Court held that separate facilities are inherently unequal. The decision declared unconstitutional racial segregation in public education, and it marked the beginning of the end of all government-sanctioned segregation.

In each of the cases, minors of the Negro race, through their legal representatives, seek the aid of the courts in obtaining admission to the public schools of their community on a nonsegregated basis. In each instance, they had been denied admission to schools attended by white children under laws requiring or permitting segregation according to race. This segregation was alleged to deprive the plaintiffs of the equal protection of the laws under the Fourteenth Amendment. In each of the cases other than the Delaware case, a three-judge federal district court denied relief to the plaintiffs on the so-called "separate but equal" doctrine announced by this Court in *Plessy* v. *Ferguson*. Under that doctrine, equality of treatment is accorded when the races are provided substantially equal facilities, even though these facilities be separate. . . .

The plaintiffs contend that segregated public schools are not "equal" and cannot be made "equal," and that hence they are deprived of the equal protection of the laws. Because of the obvious importance of the question presented, the Court took jurisdiction. Argument was heard in the 1952 Term, and reargument was heard this Term on certain questions propounded by the Court. . . .

In the first cases in this Court construing the Fourteenth Amendment, decided shortly after its adoption, the Court interpreted it as proscribing all state-imposed discriminations against the Negro race. The doctrine of "separate but equal" did not make its appearance in this Court until 1896 in the case of *Plessy* v. *Ferguson* involving not education but transportation. American courts have since labored with the doctrine for over half a century. . . . In more recent cases, all on the graduate school level, inequality was found in that specific benefits enjoyed by white students were denied to Negro students of the same educational qualifications. In none of these cases was it necessary to re-examine the doctrine to grant relief to the Negro plaintiff. And in *Sweatt* v. *Painter* (1950) the Court expressly reserved decision on the question whether *Plessy* v. *Ferguson* should be held inapplicable to public education.

In the instant cases, that question is directly presented. Here, unlike *Sweatt* v. *Painter*, there are findings below that the Negro and white schools involved have been equalized, or are being equalized, with respect to buildings, curricula, qualifications and salaries of teachers, and other "tangible" factors. Our decision, therefore, cannot turn on merely a comparison of these tangible factors in the Negro and white schools involved in each of the cases. We must look instead to the effect of segregation itself on public education.

In approaching this problem, we cannot turn the clock back to 1868 when the Amendment was adopted, or even to 1896 when *Plessy* v. *Ferguson* was written. We must consider public education in the light of its full development and its present place in American life throughout the Nation. Only in this way can it be determined if segregation in public schools deprives these plaintiffs of the equal protection of the laws.

Today, education is perhaps the most important function of state and local governments. Compulsory school attendance laws and the great expenditures for education both demonstrate our recognition of the importance of education to our democratic society. It is required in the performance of our most basic public responsibilities, even service in the armed forces. It is the very foundation of good citizenship. Today it is a principal instrument in awakening the child to cultural values, in preparing him for later professional training, and in helping him to adjust normally to his environment. In these days, it is doubtful that any child may reasonably be expected to succeed in life if he is denied the opportunity of an education. Such an opportunity, where the state has undertaken to provide it, is a right which must be made available to all on equal terms.

We come then to the question presented: Does segregation of children in public schools solely on the basis of race, even though the physical facilities and other "tangible" factors may be equal, deprive the children of the minority group of equal educational opportunities? We believe that it does.

In *Sweatt* v. *Painter*, in finding that a segregated law school for Negroes could not provide them equal educational opportunities, this Court relied in large part on "those qualities which are incapable of objective measurement but which make for greatness in a law school." In *McLaurin* v. *Oklahoma State Regents* (1950) the Court, in requiring that a Negro admitted to a white graduate school be treated like all other students, again resorted to intangible considerations: ". . . his ability to study, to engage in discussions and exchange views with other students, and, in general, to learn his profession." Such considerations apply with added force to children in grade and high schools. To separate them from others of similar age and qualifications solely because of their race generates a feeling of inferiority as to their status in the community that may affect their hearts and minds in a way unlikely ever to be undone. The effect of this separation on their educational opportunities was well stated by a finding in the Kansas case by a court which nevertheless felt compelled to rule against the Negro plaintiffs:"Segregation of white and colored children in public schools has a detrimental effect upon the colored children. The impact is greater when it has the sanction of the law; for the policy of separating the races is usually interpreted as denoting the inferiority of the negro group. A sense of inferiority affects the motivation of a child to learn. Segregation with the sanction of law, therefore, has a tendency to [retard] the educational and mental development of negro children and to deprive them of some of the benefits they would receive in a racial[ly] integrated school system."

Whatever may have been the extent of psychological knowledge at the time of *Plessy* v. *Ferguson*, this finding is amply supported by modern authority. Any language in *Plessy* v. *Ferguson* contrary to this finding is rejected.

We conclude that in the field of public education the doctrine of "separate but equal" has no place. Separate educational facilities are inherently unequal. Therefore, we hold that the plaintiffs and others similarly situated for whom the actions have been brought are, by reason of the segregation complained of, deprived of the equal protection of the laws guaranteed by the Fourteenth Amendment.

6

President John F. Kennedy: Speech on Civil Rights (1963)

In this speech, President Kennedy refers to steps, such as calling out the National Guard, that the federal government took to overcome southern resistance to desegregation ordered by the federal courts. Like the civil rights movement of the time, however, Kennedy also calls for a greater measure of equality between the races. Thus he asks Congress to pass laws forbidding certain forms of discrimination by individual citizens. Specifically, he urges Congress to disallow discrimination in "public accommodations"—that is, privately owned businesses that serve the public, such as theaters, hotels, and restaurants. Provisions of this nature were included in the Civil Rights Act of 1964, and they represent the nation's attempt to realize not only equality before the law but also some measure of social equality.

This afternoon, following a series of threats and defiant statements, the presence of Alabama National Guardsmen was required on the University of Alabama to carry out the final and unequivocal order of the United States District Court of the Northern District of Alabama. That order called for the admission of two clearly qualified young Alabama residents who happened to have been born Negro.

That they were admitted peacefully on the campus is due in good measure to the conduct of the students of the University of Alabama, who met their responsibilities in a constructive way.

I hope that every American, regardless of where he lives, will stop and examine his conscience about this and other related incidents. This Nation was founded by men of many nations and backgrounds. It was founded on the principle that all men are created equal, and that the rights of every man are diminished when the rights of one man are threatened.

Today we are committed to a worldwide struggle to promote and protect the rights of all who wish to be free. And when Americans are sent to Viet-Nam or West Berlin, we do not ask for whites only. It ought to be possible, there-fore, for American students of any color to attend any public institution they select without having to be backed up by troops.

It ought to be possible for American consumers of any color to receive equal service in places of public accommodation, such as hotels and restaurants and theaters and retail stores, without being forced to resort to demonstrations in the street, and it ought to be possible for American citizens of any color to register to vote in a free election without interference or fear of reprisal.

It ought to be possible, in short, for every American to enjoy the privileges of being American without regard to his race or his color. In short, every American ought to have the right to be treated as he would wish to be treated, as one would wish his children to be treated. But this is not the case. . . .

This is not a sectional issue. Difficulties over segregation and discrimina-tion exist in every city, in every State of the Union, producing in many cities a rising tide of discontent that threatens the public safety. Nor is this a partisan issue. In a time of domestic crisis men of good will and generosity should be able to unite regardless of party or politics. This is not even a legal or legisla-tive issue alone. It is better to settle these matters in the courts than on the streets, and new laws are needed at every level, but law alone cannot make men see right.

We are confronted primarily with a moral issue. It is as old as the scriptures and is as clear as the American Constitution.

The heart of the question is whether all Americans are to be afforded equal rights and equal opportunities, whether we are going to treat our fellow Americans as we want to be treated. If an American, because his skin is dark, cannot eat lunch in a restaurant open to the public, if he cannot send his chil-dren to the best public school available, if he cannot vote for the public offi-cials who will represent him, if, in short, he cannot enjoy the full and free life which all of us want, then who among us would be content to have the color of his skin changed and stand in his place? Who among us would then be con-tent with the counsels of patience and delay?

One hundred years of delay have passed since President Lincoln freed the slaves, yet their heirs, their grandsons, are not fully free. They are not yet freed from the bonds of injustice. They are not yet freed from social and economic oppression. And this Nation, for all its hopes and all its boasts, will not be fully free until all its citizens are free. . . .

Next week I shall ask the Congress of the United States to act, to make a commitment it has not fully made in this century to the proposition that race has no place in American life or law. The Federal judiciary has upheld that proposition in the conduct of its affairs, including the employment of Federal personnel, the use of Federal facilities, and the sale of federally financed housing.

But there are other necessary measures which only the Congress can provide, and they must be provided at this session. The old code of equity law under which we live commands for every wrong a remedy, but in too many communities, in too many parts of the country, wrongs are inflicted on Negro citizens and there are no remedies at law. Unless the Congress acts, their only remedy is in the street.

I am, therefore, asking the Congress to enact legislation giving all Americans the right to be served in facilities which are open to the public— hotels, restaurants, theaters, retail stores, and similar establishments.

This seems to me to be an elementary right. Its denial is an arbitrary indignity that no American in 1963 should have to endure, but many do.

I have recently met with scores of business leaders urging them to take voluntary action to end this discrimination and I have been encouraged by their response, and in the last 2 weeks over 75 cities have seen progress made in desegregating these kinds of facilities. But many are unwilling to act alone, and for this reason, nationwide legislation is needed if we are to move this problem from the streets to the courts.

I am also asking the Congress to authorize the Federal Government to participate more fully in lawsuits designed to end segregation in public education. We have succeeded in persuading many districts to desegregate voluntarily. Dozens have admitted Negroes without violence. Today a Negro is attending a State-supported institution in every one of our 50 States, but the pace is very slow.

Too many Negro children entering segregated grade schools at the time of the Supreme Court's decision nine years ago will enter segregated high schools this fall, having suffered a loss which can never be restored. The lack of an adequate education denies the Negro a chance to get a decent job.

The orderly implementation of the Supreme Court decision, therefore, cannot be left solely to those who may not have the economic resources to carry the legal action or who may be subject to harassment.

Other features will also be requested, including greater protection for the right to vote. But legislation, I repeat, cannot solve this problem alone. It must be solved in the homes of every American in every community across our country. . . .

This is one country. It has become one country because all of us and all the people who came here had an equal chance to develop their talents.

We cannot say to 10 percent of the population that you can't have that right; that your children cannot have the chance to develop whatever talents they have; that the only way that they are going to get their rights is to go into the streets and demonstrate. I think we owe them and we owe ourselves a better country than that.

7

Senator Barry Goldwater:
Speech on the 1964 Civil Rights Act (1964)

Senator Goldwater, who unsuccessfully sought the presidency as the Republican candidate in 1964, here explains his opposition to the 1964 Civil Rights Act. He contends that the federal government has no constitutional authority to regulate the discriminatory behavior of private individuals, and that the government's attempt to do so will result in an unacceptable intrusion into the private lives of citizens. His constitutional argument is similar to that by which the Supreme Court had struck down federal antidiscrimination laws in The Civil Rights Cases *of 1883. The 1964 Civil Rights Act was challenged in the federal courts on the basis of such arguments, but the Supreme Court discarded its earlier understanding and upheld the constitutionality of the law.*

There have been few, if any, occasions when the searching of my conscience and the re-examination of my views of our constitutional system have played a greater part in the determination of my vote than they have on this occasion.

I am unalterably opposed to discrimination or segregation on the basis of race, color, or creed, or on any other basis; not only with my words, but more importantly my actions through the years have repeatedly demonstrated the sincerity of my feeling in this regard.

This is fundamentally a matter of the heart. Our problems of discrimination can never be cured by laws alone; but I would be the first to agree that laws can help—laws carefully considered and weighed in an atmosphere of dispassion, in the absence of political demagoguery, and in the light of fundamental constitutional principles. . . .

I realize fully that the Federal government has a responsibility in the field of civil rights, but it would serve no purpose at this juncture to review my position as to just where that Federal responsibility appropriately lies. I supported the civil rights bills which were enacted in 1957 and 1960, and my public utterances during the debates on those measures and since reveal clearly the areas in which I feel the Federal responsibility lies and Federal legislation on this subject can be both effective and appropriate. Many of those areas are encompassed in this bill, and to that extent I favor it.

I wish to make myself perfectly clear. The two portions of this bill to which I have constantly and consistently voiced objections, and which are of such overriding significance that they are determinative of my vote on the entire measure, are those which would embark the Federal government on a regulatory course of action with regard to private enterprise in the area of so-called "public accommodations" and in the area of employment—to be more specific, Titles II and VII of the bill.

I find no constitutional basis for the exercise of Federal regulatory authority in either of these two areas; and I believe the attempted usurpation of such power to be a grave threat to the very essence of our basic system of government, namely, that of a constitutional republic in which fifty sovereign states have reserved to themselves and to the people those powers not specifically granted to the central or Federal government.

If it is the wish of the American people that the Federal government should be granted the power to regulate in these two areas and in the manner contemplated by this bill, then I say that the Constitution should be so amended by the people as to authorize such action in accordance with the procedures for amending the Constitution which that great document itself prescribes.

I say further that for this great legislative body to ignore the Constitution and the fundamental concepts of our governmental system is to act in a manner which could ultimately destroy the freedom of all American citizens, including the freedoms of the very persons whose feelings and whose liberties are the major subject of this legislation.

My basic objection to this measure is, therefore, constitutional. But, in addition, I would like to point out to my colleagues in the Senate and to the people of America, regardless of their race, color, or creed, the implications involved in the enforcement of regulatory legislation of this sort. To give genuine effect to the prohibitions of this bill will require the creation of a Federal police force of mammoth proportions.

It also bids fair to result in the development of an "informer" psychology in great areas of our national life—neighbors spying on neighbors, workers spying on workers, businessmen spying on businessmen, where those who would harass their fellow citizens for selfish and narrow purposes will have ample inducement to do so. These, the Federal police force and an "informer" psychology, are the hallmarks of the police state and landmarks in the destruction of a free society.

I repeat again: I am unalterably opposed to discrimination of any sort and I believe that though the problem is fundamentally one of the heart, some law can help—but not law that embodies features like these, provisions which fly in the face of the Constitution and which require for their effective execution the creation of a police state. And so, because I am unalterably opposed to the destruction of our great system of government and the loss of our God-given liberties, I shall vote "No" on this bill.

The vote will be reluctantly cast, because I had hoped to be able to vote "Yea" on this measure as I have on the civil rights bills which have preceded it; but I cannot, in good conscience to the oath that I took when assuming office, cast my vote in the affirmative. With the exception of Titles II and VII, I could whole-heartedly support this bill; but with their inclusion, not measurably improved by the compromise version we have been working on, my vote must be "No."

If my vote is misconstrued, let it be, and let me suffer its consequences. Just let me be judged in this by the real concern I have voiced here and not by words that others may speak or by what others may say about what I think.

8

Senator Edward Brooke: Speech in Favor of the Equal Rights Amendment (1972)

The Equal Rights Amendment provides that "Equality of Rights under the law shall not be denied or abridged by the United States or any State on account of sex." The amendment was introduced in and considered by every Congress from 1923 to 1972, when it finally passed. Here Senator Brooke, a Republican from Massachusetts and the first elected African American senator since Reconstruction, defends the amendment as necessary to redress the legal, social, and economic inequalities suffered by American women.

The amendment . . . gives the women of this country the personal magna carta they have sought for so long. They seek nothing more than equality. They deserve no less.

Women now outnumber men; they comprise 53 percent of our population. But despite their number, despite their suffrage, the doors of equal opportunity have been shut to them since before the American revolution. In State after State—instance after instance—the law itself discriminates against them: here, women cannot own property or do business without their husband's— and in some cases the court's—consent. There, a woman cannot get a loan at a bank, sign a lease or invest her own money without her husband's consent. Millions of women in the labor force do not receive social security benefits equal to their payments into the fund if their husband also receives social security. The women who serve in the military do not receive housing allowances and health benefits for their dependents. Women can be, and are, sentenced to far harsher prison terms for an offense which would earn a much lighter sentence if committed by a man.

Many of the laws which "protect" women did, in fact, perform that necessary function 50, 60, or 70 years ago when the sweatshop and the blatant exploitation of women and children were a reality. Tens of thousands of those women were immigrants, newly arrived in this country, unfamiliar with our laws, and desperate for income to support themselves and their families. Unions were in their infant stage, almost impotent. Wages and hours legislation had not been enacted for all our people. Government, at every level, had to throw its weight into the scales as the ally of women and children who had no vote and were powerless to protect themselves.

What was designed to liberate and succor, generations ago, shackles today.

The growth of unions, the economic floor which wages and hours legislation has placed under all workers, an alert media and the public conscience now make most of these unnecessary. They are, in fact, a roadblock to the realization of the equal-pay-for-equal-work concept.

The statistics condemn the status quo: On an average, families with male heads had an income of $7,783 in 1969; families with female heads had an average income of $4,007. Only 3 percent of workingwomen earn more than $10,000 per year; yet 26 percent of workingmen earn over $10,000 per year.

One hunts through the professions—business, industry—in vain, for enlightenment in regard to the status of women. Look at education, for example.

Women in the teaching profession are consistently relegated to the less demanding, lower paying positions as elementary and secondary school teachers. Only 10 percent of women college teachers attain the rank of full professor, while 50 percent of male teachers do so. Women average $576 less per year at the rank of assistant professor; $742 less per year as associate professors; and $1,119 less per year as full professors. Yet 91 percent of all the women in this country with Ph.D.'s are working today—81 percent of them full time.

I wish I could exempt my own profession, the law, from this indictment. I cannot. It is no accident that there are so few women judges. Or that so few women lawyers become partners in the prestigious, affluent law firms of this country.

Mr. President, it is time to call a halt. It is time for Congress to redress the balance. The adoption of this amendment would help to do that.

There are some ancillary benefits for men which will flow from the enactment of this amendment—paying alimony to a woman who is self-supporting will become a thing of the past. Men will also inherit and enjoy the same protection which is now afforded to women in business and industry.

But what of the women who desire no change in their present status? Women who want to be mothers and housewives rather than "breadwinners." Women who have always been dependent upon a husband's earned income, retirement pay or survivor's benefits. Women who do not want to invest or own property in their own name.

Those women can rest easy. Those who prefer or elect to retain the status quo may do so. But for most of the 42 percent of American women who are in the work force in some capacity, for the many millions of American women who are single and self-supporting or who are the sole support of other dependents, this amendment guarantees new opportunity and that most elementary but elusive status: equality.

No longer will they be denied the opportunity to hold a job simply because they are women. No longer will they be denied loans, access to housing or other benefits solely on the grounds that they are women. Equal rights for women is long overdue. I applaud this amendment and support its passage.

9

Senator James Buckley: Speech Against the Equal Rights Amendment (1972)

Senator Buckley of New York was unusual in that he was elected neither as a Republican nor a Democrat but as the candidate of the Conservative Party of the state. He served in the Senate from 1971 to 1977 and later was a judge on the United States Court of Appeals, D.C. Circuit. Here he argues against the Equal Rights Amendment on the grounds that it could result in an absolute equality of the sexes that would destroy certain traditional deferences accorded only to women. Although this line of argument failed in the Congress, which passed the amendment, it was taken up by conservative activists who were able to prevent a sufficient number of states from ratifying the amendment. Thus the Equal Rights Amendment never became part of the Constitution.

I find myself in full agreement with the finding that there still exists in our country a discrimination against women which cannot be justified and which ought not to be tolerated. As to this I feel there is virtually no disagreement either within the Senate or within the United States as a whole. The argument, therefore, concerns only the question of how best to redress these legitimate grievances.

In America today we find three factors which affect the relative rights, prerogatives, duties, immunities, and obligations of men and women. Some of these are cultural, others social, and the balance are economic. I speak of distinctions based on sex, deferences conferred because of sex, and discrimination which is predicated on sex. Only the last, I submit, is the proper target of the amendment now under consideration and of the enormous effort by the women of America to redress their longstanding and legitimate grievances. Yet the proposed equal rights amendment would have the inevitable effect of obliterating all of these differences—these distinctions, deferences, and discriminations—in the name of an abstract equality [without regard to] whether they in fact infringe upon the substantive rights of women.

It is because of this—because, quite specifically, of my deep respect for women—that I cannot support the amendment; and I cannot support it because whatever the intentions of its sponsors, I think we will inevitably find it tugged and twisted and extended far beyond the limits of commonsense and reason. I am opposed to the proposed amendment because, in its attempt to eliminate discrimination against women, it will inevitably strike down those distinctions and those deferences which our society now extends to women. It seems to me that the discriminations which all of us want to see ended can be more effectively accomplished in other ways, as I shall discuss later in my remarks.

Now I recognize that many militants regard the deferences and distinctions which are embedded in our social customs as discriminatory per se.

Yet, if in fact these customs and attitudes do not penalize women, I cannot see why we should abandon them. Yet that is precisely what would happen to many of our existing conventions based on the analyses given by the proponents themselves. . . .

One of the most immediate and obvious results of the amendment would be to make women equally subject to being drafted into military service as men. . . . Quite frankly, I cannot see why we should adopt a constitutional amendment which would preclude American society from determining that the obligation to serve in the infantry and other combat forces will be restricted to men. I cannot, for the life of me, see where this distinction would relegate women to the category of "second class citizens." . . .

Mr. President, this entire discussion and debate rests at bottom on certain assumptions about the meaning of the word "equality."

It is a word of singularly elusive meaning, and it is therefore incumbent upon Congress, in passing on this proposal, to make as clear as it possibly can just what is intended. . . .

It is here, I must confess, that in seeking to limit the ambiguity of the word "equality" to an irreducible minimum, I find the proponents of the measure to be less than fully enlightening. From the outset, proponents of the amendment both within Congress and without, have oscillated between two conflicting interpretations of the amendment's central purpose. Even now, on the eve of the vote, they seem uncertain as to which understanding ought to operate as the controlling intent.

The first interpretation, which derives from what might be called the "unisex" approach to the problem, holds in effect that any legal classification based on sex would be per se unconstitutional. The second interpretation, seeking to avoid the necessary rigidities of a per se rule, holds that sexual classifications are valid provided that they are applied equally to both sexes. . . .

The [first] view would, presumably, obliterate all distinctions based on sex; whereas the [second] view would, presumably, tend in the direction of "separate but equal." But it is not at all easy to say. It was the [first] view, presumably, which prompted the Coast Guard recently to promulgate regulations to allow female members of a ship's crew to use washroom and toilet facilities that are also used by male members of a crew. The [second] view, presumably, would permit separate facilities. But, again, it is not easy to say which view ought to be thought of as controlling the intention of Congress. But if the intention of Congress is ambiguous with respect to something so ludicrous as washrooms and toilet facilities how can we expect the courts to find clarity of intention with respect to a whole host of genuine and important problems of construction that may arise once this amendment is passed? I pity the judges who will be obliged to wallow through the legislative history of this proposal in search of clarity where there is none, vainly trying to pin Congress down where Congress has deliberately sought to be evasive. . . .

At the root of this ambiguity is a fundamental confusion between so-called equal rights—which is itself a problematic concept, as I suggested earlier—and so-called women's rights. The former tends in the direction of, and if some proponents of the measure are to be believed, actually embraces the idea of sameness and would therefore tend to obliterate altogether any legal distinctions based on sex. The latter, rightly understood, seeks to eliminate only those laws which discriminate against women and which relegate them to an inferior legal status. If the latter concept were the controlling intention of the proponents, and if it were certain that the courts would implement that intention and refrain from indulging the excesses of "unisex," I would gladly support an amendment designed to accomplish that goal. But I am convinced, Mr. President, that the present amendment is not so limited, and I am further convinced that adequate remedies exist today to correct the inequities which are the appropriate targets for a women's rights amendment. The most important of these, of course, is the 14th Amendment. In the past, some have doubted whether that amendment could be used as an effective vehicle for the elimination of unreasonable classifications based on sex. But the Supreme Court last December clearly opened the door to future litigation to test the constitutionality of all such classifications. . . .

Title VII of the Civil Rights Act of 1964 . . . provides yet another powerful tool for the relief of women discriminated against in the field of employment. Litigation under the 14th amendment and under Title VII seems to me to provide adequate remedies for the great majority of cases in which women are relegated to an inferior legal status. . . .

Litigation under existing constitutional and statutory provisions would have another advantage, one that is to my mind the most important of all. It is that litigation, proceeding as it does from case A to case B to case C until a rule of reasonable applicability is framed, is more likely to protect the interests of those women who want and need protection. This is something that very much needs talking about, although given the passions which animate the women's liberation movement it has for the most part been so far ignored.

The most conspicuous and outspoken representatives of the women's liberation movement have a habit of talking as if they were the duly appointed guardians of the women of America. Whether the women of America want or need this kind of guardianship, however, is another matter altogether. I am unaware of any plebiscite granting representative authority to the women's liberation movement from the women of America, nor am I aware of any demonstrable indication that the women of America approve of what their self-appointed guardians would have delivered up for them. On the contrary . . . in the only detailed poll taken on the subject, the overwhelming majority of those polled revealed a singular indifference, if not hostility, toward the more obvious legal consequences that would flow from the passage of the equal rights amendment. Fully 77 percent of American women opposed equal treatment with respect to military service; 83 percent opposed the idea that a wife should be the breadwinner if she were a better wage earner than her husband; and 69 percent opposed the idea that a woman should pay alimony if she has money and her husband does not.

Yet . . . if the equal rights amendment were to be ratified, women would be drafted and could be required to serve in combat; States would be barred from imposing greater liability for support on a husband than on a wife merely because of his sex; criminal sanctions for failure to support one's family could not be sustained where only the male is liable for such support; and obligation of alimony could be placed upon either spouse. Such changes in the law may bring joy to the hearts of the women's liberation movement, but they are not necessarily in the interests of most American women.

10

Justice Ruth Bader Ginsburg: Opinion of the Court in *U.S.* v. *Virginia* (1996)

The failure of the Equal Rights Amendment did not simply leave the government free to discriminate on the basis of sex. As Senator Buckley observed, the Supreme Court has held that the "equal protection" clause of the Fourteenth Amendment, which was initially intended to protect the rights of the recently freed slaves, also forbids laws that unreasonably discriminate on account of sex. Justice Ginsburg was nominated by President Clinton in 1993 and is the second woman to be elevated to the Supreme Court. Her opinion for the Court in this case finds that the State of Virginia violated the principle of equal protection by its policy of admitting only men to the Virginia Military Institute (VMI).

[D]oes Virginia's exclusion of women from the educational opportunities provided by VMI—extraordinary opportunities for military training and civilian leadership development—deny to women "capable of all of the individual activities required of VMI cadets" the equal protection of the laws guaranteed by the Fourteenth Amendment? . . .

The Fourth Circuit initially held that Virginia had advanced no state policy by which it could justify, under equal protection principles, its determination "to afford VMI's unique type of program to men and not to women." Virginia challenges that . . . ruling and asserts two justifications in defense of VMI's exclusion of women. First, the Commonwealth contends, "single-sex education provides important educational benefits," and the option of single-sex education contributes to "diversity in educational approaches." Second, the Commonwealth argues, "the unique VMI method of character development and leadership training," the school's adversative approach, would have to be modified were VMI to admit women. We consider these two justifications in turn.

Single-sex education affords pedagogical benefits to at least some students, Virginia emphasizes, and that reality is uncontested in this litigation. Similarly, it is not disputed that diversity among public educational institutions can serve the public good. But Virginia has not shown that VMI was established, or has been maintained, with a view to diversifying, by its categorical exclusion of women, educational opportunities within the State. . . .

Neither recent nor distant history bears out Virginia's alleged pursuit of diversity through single-sex educational options. In 1839, when the State established VMI, a range of educational opportunities for men and women was scarcely contemplated. Higher education at the time was considered dangerous for women; reflecting widely held views about women's proper place, the Nation's first universities and colleges—for example, Harvard in Massachusetts, William and Mary in Virginia—admitted only men. VMI was not at all novel in this respect: In admitting no women, VMI followed the lead of the State's flagship school, the University of Virginia, founded in 1819. . . .

Virginia eventually provided for several women's seminaries and colleges. Farmville Female Seminary became a public institution in 1884. Two women's schools, Mary Washington College and James Madison University, were founded in 1908; another, Radford University, was founded in 1910. By the mid-1970's, all four schools had become coeducational.

Debate concerning women's admission as undergraduates at the main university continued well past the century's midpoint. Familiar arguments were rehearsed. If women were admitted, it was feared, they "would encroach on the rights of men; there would be new problems of government, perhaps scandals; the old honor system would have to be changed; standards would be lowered to those of other coeducational schools; and the glorious reputation of the university, as a school for men, would be trailed in the dust."

Ultimately, in 1970, "the most prestigious institution of higher education in Virginia," the University of Virginia, introduced coeducation and, in 1972, began to admit women on an equal basis with men. . . .

In sum, we find no persuasive evidence in this record that VMI's male-only admission policy "is in furtherance of a state policy of 'diversity.' " No such policy, the Fourth Circuit observed, can be discerned from the movement of all other public colleges and universities in Virginia away from single-sex education. . . . A purpose genuinely to advance an array of educational options, as the Court of Appeals recognized, is not served by VMI's historic and constant plan—a plan to "affor[d] a unique educational benefit only to males." However "liberally" this plan serves the State's sons, it makes no provision whatever for her daughters. That is not equal protection.

Virginia next argues that VMI's adversative method of training provides educational benefits that cannot be made available, unmodified, to women. Alterations to accommodate women would necessarily be "radical," so "drastic," Virginia asserts, as to transform, indeed "destroy," VMI's program. Neither sex would be favored by the transformation, Virginia maintains: Men would be deprived of the unique opportunity currently available to them; women would not gain that opportunity because their participation would "eliminat[e] the very aspects of [the] program that distinguish [VMI] from . . . other institutions of higher education in Virginia."

The District Court forecast from expert witness testimony, and the Court of Appeals accepted, that coeducation would materially affect "at least these three aspects of VMI's program—physical training, the absence of privacy, and the adversative approach." And it is uncontested that women's admission would require accommodations, primarily in arranging housing assignments and physical training programs for female cadets. It is also undisputed, however, that "the VMI methodology could be used to educate women." The District Court even allowed that some women may prefer it to the methodology a women's college might pursue. "[S]ome women, at least, would want to attend [VMI] if they had the opportunity," the District Court recognized, and "some women," the expert testimony established, "are capable of all of the individual activities required of VMI cadets." The parties, furthermore, agree that "some women can meet the physical standards [VMI] now impose[s] on men." In sum, as the Court of Appeals stated, "neither the goal of producing citizen soldiers" . . . "nor VMI's implementing methodology is inherently unsuitable to women." . . .

It may be assumed, for purposes of this decision, that most women would not choose VMI's adversative method. As Fourth Circuit Judge Motz observed, however, in her dissent from the Court of Appeals' denial of rehearing en banc, it is also probable that "many men would not want to be educated in such an environment." Education, to be sure, is not a "one size fits all" business. The issue, however, is not whether "women—or men—should be forced to attend VMI"; rather, the question is whether the State can constitutionally deny to women who have the will and capacity, the training and attendant opportunities that VMI uniquely affords.

The notion that admission of women would downgrade VMI's stature, destroy the adversative system and, with it, even the school, is a judgment hardly proved, a prediction hardly different from other "self-fulfilling prophec[ies]" once routinely used to deny rights or opportunities. When women first sought admission to the bar and access to legal education, concerns of the same order were expressed. . . . Women's successful entry into the federal military academies, and their participation in the Nation's military forces, indicate that Virginia's fears for the future of VMI may not be solidly grounded. The State's justification for excluding all women from "citizen-soldier" training for which some are qualified, in any event, cannot rank as "exceedingly persuasive," as we have explained and applied that standard. . . .

. . . VMI's mission [is] to produce "citizen-soldiers," individuals "imbued with love of learning, confident in the functions and attitudes of leadership, possessing a high sense of public service, advocates of the American democracy and free enterprise system, and ready . . . to defend their country in time of national peril."

Surely that goal is great enough to accommodate women, who today count as citizens in our American democracy equal in stature to men. Just as surely, the State's great goal is not substantially advanced by women's categorical exclusion, in total disregard of their individual merit, from the State's premier "citizen-soldier" corps. Virginia, in sum, "has fallen far short of establishing the 'exceedingly persuasive justification'" that must be the solid base for any gender-defined classification. . . .

A prime part of the history of our Constitution, historian Richard Morris recounted, is the story of the extension of constitutional rights and protections to people once ignored or excluded. VMI's story continued as our compre-hension of "We the People" expanded. There is no reason to believe that the admission of women capable of all the activities required of VMI cadets would destroy the Institute rather than enhance its capacity to serve the "more per-fect Union."

11

Justice Antonin Scalia: Dissenting Opinion in *U.S.* v. *Virginia* (1996)

Justice Scalia was nominated by President Reagan in 1986 and is the first Italian American elevated to the Supreme Court. In his dissenting opinion he contends that VMI's policy did not violate the "equal protection" clause and that the Court's finding otherwise imperils all single-sex education that is supported by government funds.

Today the Court shuts down an institution that has served the people of the Commonwealth of Virginia with pride and distinction for over a century and a half. To achieve that desired result, it rejects (contrary to our established practice) the factual findings of two courts below, sweeps aside the precedents of this Court, and ignores the history of our people. As to facts: it explicitly rejects the finding that there exist "gender-based developmental differences" supporting Virginia's restriction of the "adversative" method to only a men's institution, and the finding that the all-male composition of the Virginia Military Institute (VMI) is essential to that institution's character. As to prece-dent: it drastically revises our established standards for reviewing sex-based classifications. And as to history: it counts for nothing the long tradition, enduring down to the present, of men's military colleges supported by both States and the Federal Government.

Much of the Court's opinion is devoted to deprecating the closed-mindedness of our forebears with regard to women's education. . . . Closed-minded they were—as every age is, including our own, with regard to matters it cannot guess, because it simply does not consider them debatable. The virtue of a democratic system with a First Amendment is that it readily enables the peo-ple, over time, to be persuaded that what they took for granted is not so, and to change their laws accordingly. That system is destroyed if the smug assur-ances of each age are removed from the democratic process and written into the Constitution. So to counterbalance the Court's criticism of our ancestors, let me say a word in their praise: they left us free to change. The same cannot be said of this most illiberal Court, which has embarked on a course of inscrib-ing one after another of the current preferences of the society (and in some cases only the counter-majoritarian preferences of the society's law-trained elite) into our Basic Law. Today it enshrines the notion that no substantial educational value is to be served by an all-men's military academy—so that the decision by the people of Virginia to maintain such an institution denies equal protection to women who cannot attend that institution but can attend others. Since it is entirely clear that the Constitution of the United States— the old one—takes no sides in this educational debate, I dissent. . . .

. . . [I]t is my view that "when a practice not expressly prohibited by the text of the Bill of Rights bears the endorsement of a long tradition of open, widespread, and unchallenged use that dates back to the beginning of the Republic, we have no proper basis for striking it down," *Rutan v. Republican Party of Illinois* (1990) (Scalia, J., dissenting). The same applies . . . to a practice asserted to be in violation of the post-Civil War Fourteenth Amendment.

The all-male constitution of VMI comes squarely within such a governing tradition. Founded by the Commonwealth of Virginia in 1839 and continuously maintained by it since, VMI has always admitted only men. And in that regard it has not been unusual. For almost all of VMI's more than a century and a half of existence, its single-sex status reflected the uniform practice for government-supported military colleges. Another famous Southern institution, The Citadel, has existed as a state-funded school of South Carolina since 1842. And all the federal military colleges—West Point, the Naval Academy at Annapolis, and even the Air Force Academy, which was not established until 1954—admitted only males for most of their history. Their admission of women in 1976 (upon which the Court today relies), came not by court decree, but because the people, through their elected representatives, decreed a change. In other words, the tradition of having government-funded military schools for men is as well rooted in the traditions of this country as the tradition of sending only men into military combat. The people may decide to change the one tradition, like the other, through democratic processes; but the assertion that either tradition has been unconstitutional through the centuries is not law, but politics-smuggled-into-law.

And the same applies, more broadly, to single-sex education in general, which, as I shall discuss, is threatened by today's decision with the cut-off of all state and federal support. Government-run nonmilitary educational institutions for the two sexes have until very recently also been part of our national tradition. . . . These traditions may of course be changed by the democratic decisions of the people, as they largely have been.

Today, however, change is forced upon Virginia, and reversion to single-sex education is prohibited nationwide, not by democratic processes but by order of this Court. Even while bemoaning the sorry, bygone days of "fixed notions" concerning women's education, the Court favors current notions so fixedly that it is willing to write them into the Constitution of the United States by application of custom-built "tests." This is not the interpretation of a Constitution, but the creation of one. . . .

It is beyond question that Virginia has an important state interest in providing effective college education for its citizens. That single-sex instruction is an approach substantially related to that interest should be evident enough from the long and continuing history in this country of men's and women's colleges. But beyond that, as the Court of Appeals here stated: "That single-gender education at the college level is beneficial to both sexes is a fact established in this case."

The evidence establishing that fact was overwhelming—indeed, "virtually uncontradicted" in the words of the court that received the evidence. As an initial matter, Virginia demonstrated at trial that "[a] substantial body of contemporary scholarship and research supports the proposition that, although males and females have significant areas of developmental overlap, they also have differing developmental needs that are deep-seated." While no one questioned that for many students a coeducational environment was nonetheless not inappropriate, that could not obscure the demonstrated benefits of single-sex colleges. . . .

But besides its single-sex constitution, VMI is different from other colleges in another way. It employs a "distinctive educational method," sometimes referred to as the "adversative, or doubting, model of education." "Physical rigor, mental stress, absolute equality of treatment, absence of privacy, minute regulation of behavior, and indoctrination in desirable values are the salient attributes of the VMI educational experience." No one contends that this method is appropriate for all individuals; education is not a "one size fits all" business. Just as a State may wish to support junior colleges, vocational institutes, or a law school that emphasizes case practice instead of classroom study, so too a State's decision to maintain within its system one school that provides the adversative method is "substantially related" to its goal of good education. Moreover, it was uncontested that "if the state were to establish a women's VMI-type [i.e., adversative] program, the program would attract an insufficient number of participants to make the program work," and it was found by the District Court that if Virginia were to include women in VMI, the school "would eventually find it necessary to drop the adversative system altogether." Thus, Virginia's options were an adversative method that excludes women or no adversative method at all.

There can be no serious dispute that, as the District Court found, single-sex education and a distinctive educational method "represent legitimate contributions to diversity in the Virginia higher education system." As a theoretical matter, Virginia's educational interest would have been best served (insofar as the two factors we have mentioned are concerned) by six different types of public colleges—an all-men's, an all-women's, and a coeducational college run in the "adversative method," and an all-men's, an all-women's, and a coeducational college run in the "traditional method." But as a practical matter, of course, Virginia's financial resources, like any State's, are not limitless, and the Commonwealth must select among the available options. Virginia thus has decided to fund, in addition to some 14 coeducational 4-year colleges, one college that is run as an all-male school on the adversative model: the Virginia Military Institute. . . .

Under the constitutional principles announced and applied today, single-sex public education is unconstitutional. By going through the motions of applying a balancing test—asking whether the State has adduced an "exceedingly persuasive justification" for its sex-based classification—the Court creates the illusion that government officials in some future case will have a clear shot at justifying some sort of single-sex public education. . . .

In any event, regardless of whether the Court's rationale leaves some small amount of room for lawyers to argue, it ensures that single-sex public education is functionally dead. The costs of litigating the constitutionality of a single-sex education program, and the risks of ultimately losing that litigation, are simply too high to be embraced by public officials. Any person with standing to challenge any sex-based classification can haul the State into federal court and compel it to establish by evidence (presumably in the form of expert testimony) that there is an "exceedingly persuasive justification" for the classification. . . . No state official in his right mind will buy such a high-cost, high-risk lawsuit by commencing a single-sex program. The enemies of single-sex education have won; by persuading only seven Justices (five would have been enough) that their view of the world is enshrined in the Constitution, they have effectively imposed that view on all 50 States.

12

Justice Sandra Day O'Connor: Opinion of the Court in *Grutter* v. *Bollinger* (2003)

Some Americans believe that the full realization of our commitment to equality requires the use of affirmative action, or racial preferences, to aid members of groups that have faced official discrimination in the past. In this case the Supreme Court considered the use of such preferences in higher education, upholding the constitutionality of the University of Michigan's consideration of race in admitting students to its law school. Justice O'Connor, the author of the Court's opinion, was appointed to the Court by President Reagan and is the first woman to be elevated to the Supreme Court.

This case requires us to decide whether the use of race as a factor in student admissions by the University of Michigan Law School is unlawful. . . .

The hallmark of that policy is its focus on academic ability coupled with a flexible assessment of applicants' talents, experiences, and potential "to contribute to the learning of those around them." The policy requires admissions officials to evaluate each applicant based on all the information available in the file, including a personal statement, letters of recommendation, and an essay describing the ways in which the applicant will contribute to the life and diversity of the Law School. In reviewing an applicant's file, admissions officials must consider the applicant's undergraduate grade point average (GPA) and Law School Admissions Test (LSAT) score because they are important (if imperfect) predictors of academic success in law school. . . .

The policy makes clear, however, that even the highest possible score does not guarantee admission to the Law School. Nor does a low score automatically disqualify an applicant. Rather, the policy requires admissions officials to look beyond grades and test scores to other criteria that are important to the Law School's educational objectives. So-called "soft" variables such as "the enthusiasm of recommenders, the quality of the undergraduate institution, the quality of the applicant's essay, and the areas and difficulty of undergraduate course selection" are all brought to bear in assessing an "applicant's likely contributions to the intellectual and social life of the institution."

The policy aspires to "achieve that diversity which has the potential to enrich everyone's education and thus make a law school class stronger than the sum of its parts." The policy does not restrict the types of diversity contributions eligible for "substantial weight" in the admissions process, but instead recognizes "many possible bases for diversity admissions." The policy does, however, reaffirm the Law School's longstanding commitment to . . . "racial and ethnic diversity with special reference to the inclusion of students from groups which have been historically discriminated against, like African-Americans, Hispanics and Native Americans, who without this commitment might not be represented in our student body in meaningful numbers." By enrolling a "'critical mass' of [underrepresented] minority students," the Law School seeks to "ensur[e] their ability to make unique contributions to the character of the Law School."

The Equal Protection Clause provides that no State shall "deny to any person within its jurisdiction the equal protection of the laws." Because the Fourteenth Amendment "protect[s] *persons*, not *groups*," all "governmental action based on race—a *group* classification long recognized as in most circumstances irrelevant and therefore prohibited—should be subjected to detailed judicial inquiry to ensure that the *personal* right to equal protection of the laws has not been infringed." . . . It follows from that principle that "government may treat people differently because of their race only for the most compelling reasons." . . .

With these principles in mind, we turn to the question whether the Law School's use of race is justified by a compelling state interest. Before this Court, as they have throughout this litigation, respondents assert only one justification for their use of race in the admissions process: obtaining "the educational benefits that flow from a diverse student body." . . .

Today, we hold that the Law School has a compelling interest in attaining a diverse student body. . . .

As part of its goal of "assembling a class that is both exceptionally academically qualified and broadly diverse," the Law School seeks to "enroll a 'critical mass' of minority students." The Law School's interest is not simply "to assure within its student body some specified percentage of a particular group merely because of its race or ethnic origin." That would amount to outright racial balancing, which is patently unconstitutional. Rather, the Law School's concept of critical mass is defined by reference to the educational benefits that diversity is designed to produce.

These benefits are substantial. As the District Court emphasized, the Law School's admissions policy promotes "cross-racial understanding," helps to break down racial stereotypes, and "enables [students] to better understand persons of different races." These benefits are "important and laudable," because "classroom discussion is livelier, more spirited, and simply more enlightening and interesting" when the students have "the greatest possible variety of backgrounds." . . .

In addition to the expert studies and reports entered into evidence at trial, numerous studies show that student body diversity promotes learning outcomes, and "better prepares students for an increasingly diverse workforce and society, and better prepares them as professionals."

These benefits are not theoretical but real, as major American businesses have made clear that the skills needed in today's increasingly global marketplace can only be developed through exposure to widely diverse people, cultures, ideas, and viewpoints. What is more, high-ranking retired officers and civilian leaders of the United States military assert that, "[b]ased on [their] decades of experience," a "highly qualified, racially diverse officer corps . . . is essential to the military's ability to fulfill its principle mission to provide national security." . . .

We have repeatedly acknowledged the overriding importance of preparing students for work and citizenship, describing education as pivotal to "sustaining our political and cultural heritage" with a fundamental role in maintaining the fabric of society. This Court has long recognized that "education . . . is the very foundation of good citizenship." For this reason, the diffusion of knowledge and opportunity through public institutions of higher education must be accessible to all individuals regardless of race or ethnicity. . . . Effective participation by members of all racial and ethnic groups in the civic life of our Nation is essential if the dream of one Nation, indivisible, is to be realized.

Moreover, universities, and in particular, law schools, represent the training ground for a large number of our Nation's leaders. Individuals with law degrees occupy roughly half the state governorships, more than half the seats in the United States Senate, and more than a third of the seats in the United States House of Representatives. The pattern is even more striking when it comes to highly selective law schools. A handful of these schools accounts for 25 of the 100 United States Senators, 74 United States Courts of Appeals judges, and nearly 200 of the more than 600 United States District Court judges.

In order to cultivate a set of leaders with legitimacy in the eyes of the citizenry, it is necessary that the path to leadership be visibly open to talented and qualified individuals of every race and ethnicity. All members of our heterogeneous society must have confidence in the openness and integrity of the educational institutions that provide this training. As we have recognized, law schools "cannot be effective in isolation from the individuals and institutions with which the law interacts." Access to legal education (and thus the legal profession) must be inclusive of talented and qualified individuals of every race and ethnicity, so that all members of our heterogeneous society may participate in the educational institutions that provide the training and education necessary to succeed in America. . . .

In summary, the Equal Protection Clause does not prohibit the Law School's narrowly tailored use of race in admissions decisions to further a compelling interest in obtaining the educational benefits that flow from a diverse student body.

13

Justice Clarence Thomas: Dissenting Opinion in *Grutter* v. *Bollinger* (2003)

Justice Thomas was appointed in 1991 and became the second African American elevated to the Supreme Court, replacing the first, Thurgood Marshall, who had retired that same year. He argues that affirmative action violates the principle of equality and, in addition, that it may harm those it is intended to benefit.

Frederick Douglass, speaking to a group of abolitionists almost 140 years ago, delivered a message lost on today's majority:

> [I]n regard to the colored people, there is always more that is benevolent, I perceive, than just, manifested towards us. What I ask for the negro is not benevolence, not pity, not sympathy, but simply *justice*. The American people have always been anxious to know what they shall do with us. . . . I have had but one answer from the beginning. Do nothing with us! Your doing with us has already played the mischief with us. Do nothing with us! If the apples will not remain on the tree of their own strength, if they are worm-eaten at the core, if they are early ripe and disposed to fall, let them fall! . . . And if the negro cannot stand on his own legs, let him fall also. All I ask is, give him a chance to stand on his own legs! Let him alone! . . . [Y]our interference is doing him positive injury.

Like Douglass, I believe blacks can achieve in every avenue of American life without the meddling of university administrators. Because I wish to see all students succeed whatever their color, I share, in some respect, the sympathies of those who sponsor the type of discrimination advanced by the University of Michigan Law School. The Constitution does not, however, tolerate institutional devotion to the status quo in admissions policies when such devotion ripens into racial discrimination. . . .

No one would argue that a university could set up a lower general admission standard and then impose heightened requirements only on black applicants. Similarly, a university may not maintain a high admission standard and grant exemptions to favored races. The Law School, of its own choosing, and for its own purposes, maintains an exclusionary admissions system that it knows produces racially disproportionate results. Racial discrimination is not a permissible solution to the self-inflicted wounds of this elitist admissions policy. . . .

The Constitution abhors classifications based on race, not only because those classifications can harm favored races or are based on illegitimate motives, but also because every time the government places citizens on racial registers and makes race relevant to the provision of burdens or benefits, it demeans us all. . . .

I believe what lies beneath the Court's decision today are the benighted notions that one can tell when racial discrimination benefits (rather than hurts) minority groups and that racial discrimination is necessary to remedy general societal ills. This Court's precedents supposedly settled both issues, but clearly the majority still cannot commit to the principle that racial classifications are *per se* harmful and that almost no amount of benefit in the eye of the beholder can justify such classifications.

. . . I must contest the notion that the Law School's discrimination benefits those admitted as a result of it. . . . [N]owhere in any of the filings in this Court is any evidence that the purported "beneficiaries" of this racial discrimination prove themselves by performing at (or even near) the same level as those students who receive no preferences.

The silence in this case is deafening to those of us who view higher education's purpose as imparting knowledge and skills to students, rather than a communal, rubber-stamp, credentialing process. The Law School is not looking for those students who, despite a lower LSAT score or undergraduate grade point average, will succeed in the study of law. The Law School seeks only a façade—it is sufficient that the class looks right, even if it does not perform right. . . .

While these students may graduate with law degrees, there is no evidence that they have received a qualitatively better legal education (or become better lawyers) than if they had gone to a less "elite" law school for which they were better prepared. And the aestheticists will never address the real problems facing "underrepresented minorities," instead continuing their social experiments on other people's children.

Beyond the harm the Law School's racial discrimination visits upon its test subjects, no social science has disproved the notion that this discrimination "engender[s] attitudes of superiority or, alternatively, provoke[s] resentment among those who believe that they have been wronged by the government's use of race." "These programs stamp minorities with a badge of inferiority and may cause them to develop dependencies or to adopt an attitude that they are 'entitled' to preferences."

It is uncontested that each year, the Law School admits a handful of blacks who would be admitted in the absence of racial discrimination. Who can differentiate between those who belong and those who do not? The majority of blacks are admitted to the Law School because of discrimination, and because of this policy all are tarred as undeserving. This problem of stigma does not depend on determinacy as to whether those stigmatized are actually the "beneficiaries" of racial discrimination. When blacks take positions in the highest places of government, industry, or academia, it is an open question today whether their skin color played a part in their advancement. The question itself is the stigma—because either racial discrimination did play a role, in which case the person may be deemed "otherwise unqualified," or it did not, in which case asking the question itself unfairly marks those blacks who would succeed without discrimination. . . .

For the immediate future . . . the majority has placed its *imprimatur* on a practice that can only weaken the principle of equality embodied in the Declaration of Independence and the Equal Protection Clause. "Our Constitution is color-blind, and neither knows nor tolerates classes among citizens." *Plessy* v. *Ferguson* (1896) (Harlan, J., dissenting).

DISCUSSION QUESTIONS FOR CHAPTER 1

1. Explain President Arthur's approach to the "Indian problem." What is the proper way for the government to respect the equality of Native Americans?

2. Contrast the conclusions reached by the Supreme Court in *Plessy* v. *Ferguson* and *Brown* v. *Board of Education*. Is government-enforced separation of the races compatible with the American principle of equality and the Constitution?

3. Compare the positions of Justice Bradley and Frederick Douglass on the issues raised in *The Civil Rights Cases*, and those of President Kennedy and Senator Goldwater regarding the Civil Rights Act of 1964. Should the government be understood to have the power to remedy discriminatory business practices and private discrimination? Or does such a power lead to an overly intrusive federal bureaucracy? What would be the social consequences if the government failed to address nongovernmental discrimination?

4. Explain the differences between Senators Brooke and Buckley regarding the Equal Rights Amendment. Do social and economic inequalities between men and women require that the Constitution be amended to remedy them, or would such a move prevent the government from making reasonable distinctions between the sexes?

5. Contrast the views of Justices Ginsburg and Scalia in *U.S.* v. *Virginia*. Is government-funded single-sex education a violation of the principle of equality?

6. Contrast the views of Justices O'Connor and Thomas regarding the issues in *Grutter* v. *Bollinger*. Is affirmative action a violation of America's commitment to equality of opportunity, or is it a reasonable way to achieve the educational benefits that come from diversity in higher education?

CHAPTER 2

$$\Longrightarrow\!\!\!\!\!\Longrightarrow\!\!\!\times\!\!\Longleftarrow\!\!\!\!\!\Longleftarrow$$

Virtue

1

Frances E. Willard: "Social Purity Work" (1887)

By the late nineteenth century, Victorian culture in the United States was both broad and deep in its influence on American society. Hundreds of temperance, social purity, and personal improvement organizations thrived during the era, virtually all formed with the goal, reflected in the following two readings, of improving the virtue and moral character of Americans. The first reading, an article by the president of the Women's Christian Temperance Union, Frances Willard, sets forth the guidelines for two social purity organizations and also includes a petition to Congress requesting that laws against the exploitation of women be strengthened. The second reading, composed by socialite activist Grace Dodge, the first national president of the YWCA, addresses the classical republican virtue of simplicity and fortitude, urging young women to be judicious in their spending but also diligent in their occupational efforts.

. . .[W]hat are now our plans? They involve some points that are now. As before, we have grouped the work under three heads: Preventive, Reformatory and Legislative.

Under the first our effort will be chiefly to carry forwards the plans of the White Cross Societies. These are given at length in the "White Cross Manual," which we have just brought out, and which is for sale at our Headquarters, 161 LaSalle Street, Chicago.

THE WHITE CROSS SOCIETY

is formed on men alone. No woman or girl has ever, in any land been made a member. It is not a secret society, but it very simply organized, and has no admission fee. Each member takes the following fivefold obligation:

I ——
PROMISE BY THE HELP OF GOD

1. *To treat all women with respect, and endeavor to protect them from wrong and degradation.*

2. *To endeavor to put down all indecent language and coarse jests.*

3. *To maintain the law of purity as equally binding upon men and women.*

4. *To endeavor to spread these principles among my companions, and to try and help my younger brothers.*

5. *To use every possible means to fulfill the command, "Keep THYSELF pure. . . ."*

THE WHITE SHIELD

is the name chosen for the women's pledge, which is as follows, and was unanimously adopted by the Minneapolis Convention:

I ——
PROMISE BY THE HELP OF GOD

1. *To uphold the law of purity as equally binding upon men and women.*

2. *To be modest in language, behavior and dress.*

3. *To avoid all conversation, reading, pictures and amusements which may put impure thoughts into my mind.*

4. *To guard the purity of others, especially of the young.*

5. *To strive after the special blessing promised to THE PURE IN HEART. . . .*

PETITION

To the Senate and House of Representatives:

The increasing and alarming frequency of assaults upon women, and the frightful indignities to which even little girls are subject, have become the shame of our boasted civilization.

A study of the Statutes has revealed their utter failure to meet the demands of that newly-awakened public sentiment which requires better legal protection of womanhood and girlhood.

Therefore we, men and women of ——, State of ——, do most earnestly appeal to you to enact such statutes as shall provide for the adequate punishment of crimes against women and girls. We also urge that the age at which a girl can legally consent to her own ruin be raised to at least eighteen years; and we call attention to the disgraceful fact that protection of the person is not placed by our laws upon so high a plane as protection of the purse.

The United States Congress will be appealed to by similar petitions at the present session. A Bill to meet the requirements of these petitions has been prepared, with the advice of the best legal minds and of thoughtful men and women well qualified to deal with this difficult subject. This bill has been sent to every State and Territory, except those which have already passed the desired laws.

The term "age of consent" has been much objected to by white ribbon women, and it is suggested—after taking legal advice—that "age of protection" meets the [need] and is less objectionable.

We reiterate the urgent request to *each local union* [for] the appointment of a Superintendent of the Department for the Promotion of Social Purity. . . .

2

Grace H. Dodge: "Working and Saving" (1887)

Dear Girls:

We are all workers—busy bodies; and I think there is not one of us who could not say, "It seems as if a woman's work was never done." Some of us have home cares, and from the making of the fire before six o'clock until nine or ten at night, when the children or family are in bed, we have few idle moments. We find so much to do even in our small rooms or houses. Others of us are due at seven o'clock at factory or shop, and have eight or nine hours of manual work, with only lunch time off. When we get home, if there is no housework there is sewing or planning for clothes, and if we find time for any recreation or fun, we are wondrous busy up to a late hour. Again, there are some of us who use our fingers, and as dressmakers it is sew, sew, sew, until we get tired of needles and thread. Still there are among us those who have brain work combined with hand effort, and as teachers, telegraph operators, stenographers, clerks, or bearing still heavier responsibility, we come to night tired both in body and in mind. Some are ashamed of being called workingwomen, but why should we be? Is it not a grand thing to be a worker, and to have ability to work? Nowadays hundreds of girls are proud of being workers who might stay at home and be supported by father or mother. They wish to feel able to care for themselves. No honest work degrades us, rather uplifts and strengthens us. I like to feel myself a worker, and to count as true friends many who labor from early to late in shop or factory. . . .

When we are at home we serve for love, from a sense of duty, but when we go out from home into any position we expect to serve for more than these things—for *money*.

Here, then, are the two points of our letter today—Work, Money; serving, and the wage received for said service. . . .

First. Set your mind on the work, whatever it is, feeling it is necessary and cannot be shirked.

Second. When the mind is fixed and it is to be done, try and take a cheery view of the work. There are two words which are often used, "Don't worry." Apply them to the work to be done, and put after them, "over it."

Third. Endeavor by system and order to simplify the work. Bring your brains to it and try to lighten it by planning for it. . . .

Fourth. Put your heart into your work. . . .

Fifth. Do the work as well as you can, and try and take pride in the doing.

Sixth. Make the work yours for the time being, and even if it is done for others, feel it your own, and show interest in it.

Seventh. Quiet, slow work usually tells better in the long run than that done with rapid, spasmodic effort. . . .

Eighth. It is hardly necessary to add the thought of faithful, thorough work. No one will ever succeed or be advanced who does not do earnest, true work. I have heard it said that one reason why women cannot compare with men as "wage-earners" is, that they do not do faithful, thorough work, for they do not think of work as a life pursuit, but rather as a necessary means of tiding over those years before they marry, and have some man to do the money-earning for them.

Girls, I would not like to think this true, but rather to feel that we women are so anxious to become skillful, thorough workers that we at all times are doing our utmost to fit ourselves for that duty which is ours. Happy women also, for we realize that we must work, and are doing the best we can in a cheery, earnest manner.

3

Margaret Sanger: Sex and Birth Control (1914)

The early twentieth century witnessed a number of radical social movements in the United States, one of which included evolving sexual mores. Women's rights crusader Margaret Sanger, who had earlier worked in overpopulated immigrant neighborhoods as a health-care worker, led a controversial movement to allow women access to contraception. In the following reading, Sanger addresses the right of women to have control over their own bodies and laments what she feels is the prudish nature of society.

. . . In this present chaos of sex atmosphere it is difficult for the girl of this uncertain age to know just what to do or really what constitutes clean living without prudishness. All this slushy talk about white slavery, the man painted and described as a hideous vulture pouncing down upon the young, pure and innocent girl, drugging her through the medium of grape juice and lemonade

Source: From Margaret Sanger, "No Gods No Masters," *Women Rebel*, March 1914.

and then dragging her off to his foul den for other men equally as vicious to feed and fatten on her enforced slavery—surely this picture is enough to sicken and disgust every thinking woman and man, who has lived even a few years past the adolescent age. Could any more repulsive and foul conception of sex be given to adolescent girls as a preparation for life than this picture that is being perpetuated by the stupidly ignorant in the name of "sex education"!

If it were possible to get the truth from girls who work in prostitution today, I believe most of them would tell you that the first sex experience was with a sweetheart or through the desire for a sweetheart or something impelling within themselves, the nature of which they knew not, neither could they control. Society does not forgive this act when it is based upon the natural impulses and feelings of a young girl. It prefers the other story of the grape juice procurer which makes it easy to shift the blame from its own shoulders, to cast the stone and to evade the unpleasant facts that it alone is responsible for. It sheds sympathetic tears over white slavery, holds the often mythical procurer up as a target, while in reality it is supported by the misery it engenders.

If, as reported, there are approximately 35,000 women working as prostitutes in New York City alone, is it not sane to conclude that some force, some living, powerful, social force is at play to compel these women to work at a trade which involves police persecution, social ostracism and the constant danger of exposure to venereal diseases. From my own knowledge of adolescent girls and from sincere expressions of women working as prostitutes inspired by mutual understanding and confidence I claim that the first sexual act of these so-called wayward girls is partly given, partly desired yet reluctantly so because of the fear of the consequences together with the dread of lost respect of the man. These fears interfere with mutuality of expression—the man becomes conscious of the responsibility of the set and often refuses to see her again, sometimes leaving the town and usually denouncing her as having been with "other fellows." His sole aim is to throw off responsibility. The same uncertainty in these emotions is experienced by girls in marriage in as great a proportion as in the unmarried. After the first experience the life of a girl varies. All these girls do not necessarily go into prostitution. They have had an experience which has not "ruined" them, but rather given them a larger vision of life, stronger feelings and a broader understanding of human nature. . . .

Is there any reason why women should not receive clean, harmless, scientific knowledge on how to prevent conception? Everybody is aware that the old, stupid fallacy that such knowledge will cause a girl to enter into prostitution has long been shattered. Seldom does a prostitute become pregnant. Seldom does the girl practicing promiscuity become pregnant. The woman of the upper middle class have all available knowledge and implements to prevent conception. The woman of the lower middle class is struggling for this knowledge. She tries various methods of prevention, and after a few years of experience plus medical advice succeeds in discovering some method suitable to her individual self. The woman of the people is the only one left in ignorance of this information. Her neighbors, relatives and friends tell her stories of special devices and the success of them all. They tell her also of the blood-sucking men with M. D. after their names who perform operations for the price of so-and-so. But the working woman's purse is thin. It's far cheaper to have a baby, "though God knows what it will do after it gets here." Then, too, all other classes of women live in places where there is at least a semblance of privacy and sanitation. It is easier for them to care for themselves whereas the large majority of the women of the people have no bathing or sanitary conveniences. This accounts too for the fact that the higher the standard of living, the more care can be taken and fewer children result. No plagues, famine or wars could ever frighten the capitalist class so much as the universal practice of the prevention of conception. On the other hand no better method could be utilized for increasing the wages of the workers.

As is well known, a law exists forbidding the imparting of information on this subject, the penalty being several years' imprisonment. Is it not time to defy this law!

MARRIAGE

. . . Marriage laws abrogate the freedom of woman by enforcing upon her a continuous sexual slavery and a compulsory motherhood.

Marriage laws have been dictated and dominated by the Church always and ever upon the unquestionable grounds of the wisdom of the Bible.

A man and woman who under a natural condition avow their love for each other should be immediately qualified by this to give expression to their love or to perpetuate the race without the necessity of a public declaration. A reciprocal, spontaneous voluntary declaration of love and mutual feelings by a man and woman is the expression of Nature's desires. Were it not natural it would not be so and being natural it is right.

The marriage institution viewed from the light of human experience and the demands of the individual has proven a failure. Statistical reports show that one out of every twelve marriages in the United States has resulted in a divorce—which does not include the thousands of women who want divorces—but on account of the Church and conventions are restrained from obtaining them. Nor does it mention the thousands of women too poor to obtain the price to set in motion the ponderous machinery of the divorce courts. The divorce courts give us only a hint of the dissatisfaction and unhappiness underlying the institution of marriage.

Superstition; blind following; unthinking obedience on the part of working women; together with the pretence, hypocrisy and sham morality of the women of the middle class have been the greatest obstacles in the obtaining of woman's freedom.

Every change in social life is accomplished only by a struggle. Rebel women of the world must fight for the freedom to harmonize their actions with the natural desires of their being, for their deeds are but the concrete expressions of their thoughts. . . .

4

Theodore Roosevelt:
"Duties of American Citizenship" (1883)

Theodore Roosevelt was the leading proponent of his era of cultivating an active citizenry that could improve the state of affairs both nationally and internationally. An ardent imperialist, Roosevelt felt that being an American, and everything symbolized by that status, obligated citizens to become informed and active while also exhibiting the desirable qualities of fortitude, loyalty, and willingness to sacrifice. Throughout the following speech, given before he had garnered a significant national reputation, Roosevelt extols primarily the importance of character, reflecting the four classical virtues of prudence, temperance, justice, and fortitude.

. . . [F]or what I wish to talk of is the attitude of the American citizen in civic life. It ought to be axiomatic in this country that every man must devote a reasonable share of his time to doing his duty in the political life of the community. No man has a right to shirk his political duties under whatever plea of pleasure or business; and while such shirking may be pardoned in those of small means it is entirely unpardonable in those among whom it is most common—in the people whose circumstances give them freedom in the struggle for life. In so far as the community grows to think rightly, it will likewise grow to regard the young man of means who shirks his duty to the State in time of peace as being only one degree worse than the man who thus shirks it in time of war. A great many of our men in business, or of our young men who are bent on enjoying life (as they have a perfect right to do if only they do not sacrifice other things to enjoyment), rather plume themselves upon being good citizens if they even vote; yet voting is the very least of their duties. Nothing worth gaining is ever gained without effort. You can no more have freedom without striving and suffering for it than you can win success as a banker or a lawyer without labor and effort, without self-denial in youth and the display of a ready and alert intelligence in middle age. The people who say that they have not time to attend to politics are simply saying that they are unfit to live in a free community. Their place is under a despotism; or if they are content to do nothing but vote, you can take despotism tempered by an occasional plebiscite, like that of the second Napoleon. In one of Lowell's magnificent stanzas about the Civil War he speaks of the fact which his countrymen were then learning, that freedom is not a gift that tarries long in the hands of cowards: nor yet does it tarry long in the hands of the sluggard and the idler, in the hands of the man so much absorbed in the pursuit of pleasure or in the pursuit of gain, or so much wrapped up in his own easy home life as to be unable to take his part in the rough struggle with his fellow men for political supremacy. If freedom is worth having, if the right of self-government is a valuable right, then the one and the other must be retained exactly as our forefathers acquired them, by labor, and especially by labor in organization, that is in combination with our fellows who have the same interests and the same principles. We should not accept the excuse of the business man who attributed his failure to the fact that his social duties were so pleasant and engrossing that he had no time left for work in his office; nor would we pay much heed to his further statement that he did not like business anyhow because he thought the morals of the business community by no means what they should be, and saw that the great successes were most often won by men of the Jay Gould stamp. It is just the same way with politics. It makes one feel half angry and half amused, and wholly contemptuous, to find men of high business or social standing in the community saying that they really have not got time to go to ward meetings, to organize political clubs, and to take a personal share in all the important details of practical politics; men who further urge against their going the fact that they think the condition of political morality low, and are afraid that they may be required to do what is not right if they go into politics.

The first duty of an American citizen, then, is that he shall work in politics; his second duty is that he shall do that work in a practical manner; and his third is that it shall be done in accord with the highest principles of honor and justice. Of course, it is not possible to define rigidly just the way in which the work shall be made practical. Each man's individual temper and convictions must be taken into account. To a certain extent his work must be done in accordance with his individual beliefs and theories of right and wrong. To a yet greater extent it must be done in combination with others, he yielding or modifying certain of his own theories and beliefs so as to enable him to stand on a common ground with his fellows, who have likewise yielded or modified certain of their theories and beliefs. There is no need of dogmatizing about independence on the one hand or party allegiance on the other. There are occasions when it may be the highest duty of any man to act outside of parties and against the one with which he has himself been hitherto identified; and there may be many more occasions when his highest duty is to sacrifice some of his own cherished opinions for the sake of the success of the party which he on the whole believes to be right. I do not think that the average citizen, at least in one of our great cities, can very well manage to support his own party all the time on every issue, local and otherwise; at any rate if he can do so he has been more fortunately placed than I have been. On the other hand, I am fully convinced that to do the best work people must be organized; and of course an organization is really a party, whether it be a great organization covering the whole nation and numbering its millions of adherents, or an association of citizens in a particular locality, banded together to win a certain specific victory, as, for instance, that of municipal reform. Somebody has said that a racing-yacht, like a good rifle, is a bundle of incompatibilities; that you must get the utmost possible sail power without sacrificing some other quality if you really do get the utmost sail power, that, in short you have got to make more or less of a compromise on each in order to acquire the dozen things needful; but, of course, in making this compromise you must be very careful

for the sake of something unimportant not to sacrifice any of the great principles of successful naval architecture. Well, it is about so with a man's political
work. He has got to preserve his independence on the one hand; and on the
other, unless he wishes to be a wholly ineffective crank, he has got to have
some sense of party allegiance and party responsibility, and he has got to realize that in any given exigency it may be a matter of duty to sacrifice one quality, or it may be a matter of duty to sacrifice the other. . . .

Finally, the man who wishes to do his duty as a citizen in our country must
be imbued through and through with the spirit of Americanism. I am not saying this as a matter of spread-eagle rhetoric: I am saying it quite soberly as a
piece of matter-of-fact, common-sense advice, derived from my own experience of others. Of course, the question of Americanism has several sides. If a
man is an educated man, he must show his Americanism by not getting misled
into following out and trying to apply all the theories of the political thinkers
of other countries, such as Germany and France, to our own entirely different
conditions. He must not get a fad, for instance, about responsible government;
and above all things he must not, merely because he is intelligent, or a college
professor well read in political literature, try to discuss our institutions when
he has had no practical knowledge of how they are worked. Again, if he is a
wealthy man, a man of means and standing, he must really feel, not merely
affect to feel, that no social differences obtain save such as a man can in some
way himself make by his own actions. People sometimes ask me if there is not
a prejudice against a man of wealth and education in ward politics. I do not
think that there is, unless the man in turn shows that he regards the facts of his
having wealth and education as giving him a claim to superiority aside from
the merit he is able to prove himself to have in actual service. Of course, if he
feels that he ought to have a little better treatment than a carpenter, a plumber,
or a butcher, who happens to stand beside him, he is going to be thrown out
of the race very quickly, and probably quite roughly; and if he starts in to
patronize and elaborately condescend to these men he will find that they resent
this attitude even more. Do not let him think about the matter at all. Let him
go into the political contest with no more thought of such matters than a college boy gives to the social standing of the members of his own and rival teams
in a hotly contested football match. As soon as he begins to take an interest in
politics (and he will speedily not only get interested for the sake of politics,
but also take a good healthy interest in playing the game itself—an interest
which is perfectly normal and praise-worthy, and to which only a prig would
object), he will begin to work up the organization in the way that will be most
effective, and he won't care a rap about who is put to work with him, save in
so far as he is a good fellow and an efficient worker. There was one time that
a number of men who think as we do here to-night (one of the number being
myself) got hold of one of the assembly districts of New York, and ran it in
really an ideal way, better than any other assembly district has ever been run
before or since by either party. We did it by hard work and good organization;
by working practically, and yet by being honest and square in motive and
method: especially did we do it by all turning in as straight-out Americans

without any regard to distinctions of race origin. Among the many men who did a great deal in organizing our victories was the son of a Presbyterian cler-gyman, the nephew of a Hebrew rabbi, and two well-known Catholic gentle-men. We also had a Columbia College professor (the stroke-oar of a university crew), a noted retail butcher, and the editor of a local German paper, various brokers, bankers, lawyers, bricklayers and a stone-mason who was particularly useful to us, although on questions of theoretic rather than applied politics he had a decidedly socialistic turn of mind. . . .

In facing the future and in striving, each according to the measure of his individual capacity, to work out the salvation of our land, we should be neither timid pessimists nor foolish optimists. We should recognize the dangers that exist and that threaten us: we should neither overestimate them nor shrink from them, but steadily fronting them should set to work to overcome and beat them down. Grave perils are yet to be encountered in the stormy course of the Republic—perils from political corruption, perils from individual laziness, indolence and timidity, perils springing from the greed of the unscrupulous rich, and from the anarchic violence of the thriftless and turbulent poor. There is every reason why we should recognize them, but there is no reason why we should fear them or doubt our capacity to overcome them, if only each will, according to the measure of his ability, do his full duty, and endeavor so to live as to deserve the high praise of being called a good American citizen.

5

Calvin Coolidge: Speech to the State Senate of Massachusetts (1914)

One of simplest and most reserved presidents in history, Calvin Coolidge was a great believer in personal responsibility and individual action. As with most of the Founding Fathers 150 years earlier, Coolidge did not envision a cumbersome federal government that attempted to legislate morality. In the following speech, given after his election as the chief executive of the Massachusetts state senate, the future president reiterates his desire for a voluntarily virtuous citizenry and suggests that Americans should have faith in their fellow man to make proper decisions.

Honorable Senators:

I thank you—with gratitude for the high honor given, with appreciation for the solemn obligations assumed—I thank you.

This commonwealth is one. We are all members of one body. The welfare of the weakest and the welfare of the most powerful are inseparably bound together. Industry cannot flourish if labor languishes. Transportation cannot prosper if manufactures decline. The general welfare cannot be provided for in any one act, but it is well to remember that the benefit of one is the benefit of all, and the neglect of one is the neglect of all. The suspension of one man's dividends is the suspension of another man's pay envelope.

Men do not make laws. They do but discover them. Laws must be justified by something more than the will of the majority. They must rest on the eternal foundation of righteousness. That state is most fortunate in its form of government which has the aptest instruments for the discovery of laws. The latest, most modern, and nearest perfect system that statesmanship has devised is representative government. Its weakness is the weakness of us imperfect human beings who administer it. Its strength is that even such administration secures to the people more blessings than any other system ever produced. No nation has discarded it and retained liberty. Representative government must be preserved.

Courts are established, not to determine the popularity of a cause, but to adjudicate and enforce rights. No litigant should be required to submit his case to the hazard and expense of a political campaign. No judge should be required to seek or receive political rewards. The courts of Massachusetts are known and honored wherever men love justice. Let their glory suffer no diminution at our hands. The electorate and judiciary cannot combine. A hearing means a hearing. When the trial of causes goes outside the court room, Anglo-Saxon constitutional government ends.

The people cannot look to legislation generally for success. Industry, thrift, character, are not conferred by act or resolve. Government cannot relieve from toil. It can provide no substitute for the rewards of service. It can, of course, care for the defective and recognize distinguished merit. The normal must care for themselves. Self-government means self-support.

Man is born into the universe with a personality that is his own. He has a right that is founded upon the constitution of the universe to have property that is his own. Ultimately, property rights and personal rights are the same thing. The one cannot be preserved if the other be violated. Each man is entitled to his rights and the rewards of his service be they never so large or never so small.

History reveals no civilized people among whom there were not a highly educated class, and large aggregations of wealth, represented usually by the clergy and the nobility. Inspiration has always come from above. Diffusion of learning has come down from the university to the common school—the kindergarten is last. No one would now expect to aid the common school by abolishing higher education.

It may be that the diffusion of wealth works in an analogous way. As the little red schoolhouse is built in the college, it may be that the fostering and protection of large aggregations of wealth are the only foundation on which to build the prosperity of the whole people. Large profits mean large pay rolls. But profits must be the result of service performed. In no land are there so many and such large aggregations of wealth as here; in no land do they perform larger service; in no land will the work of a day bring so large a reward in material and spiritual welfare. Have faith in Massachusetts. In some unimportant detail some other States may surpass her, but in the general results, there is no place on earth where the people secure, in a larger measure, the blessings of organized government, and nowhere can those functions more properly be termed self-government.

Do the day's work. If it be to protect the rights of the weak, whoever objects, do it. If it be to help a powerful corporation better to serve the people, whatever the opposition, do that. Expect to be called a stand-patter, but don't be a stand-patter. Expect to be called a demagogue, but don't be a demagogue. Don't hesitate to be as revolutionary as science. Don't hesitate to be as reactionary as the multiplication table. Don't expect to build up the weak by pulling down the strong. Don't hurry to legislate. Give administration a chance to catch up with legislation. We need a broader, firmer, deeper faith in the people—a faith that men desire to do right, that the Commonwealth is founded upon a righteousness which will endure, a reconstructed faith that the final approval of the people is given not to demagogues, slavishly pandering to their selfishness, merchandising with the clamor of the hour, but to statesmen, ministering to their welfare, representing their deep, silent, abiding convictions.

Statutes must appeal to more than material welfare. Wages won't satisfy, be they never so large. Nor houses; nor lands; nor coupons, though they fall thick as the leaves of autumn. Man has a spiritual nature. Touch it, and it must respond as the magnet responds to the pole. To that, not to selfishness, let the laws of the Commonwealth appeal. Recognize the immortal worth and dignity of man. Let the laws of Massachusetts proclaim to her humblest citizen, performing the most menial task, the recognition of his manhood, the recognition that all men are peers, the humblest with the most exalted, the recognition that all work is glorified. Such is the path to equality before the law. Such is the foundation of liberty under the law. Such is the sublime revelation of man's relation to man—Democracy.

6

Hollywood's Motion Picture Production Code (1930)

By the 1920s the term "virtue" in America had largely been replaced in the national lexicon with various derivatives of the expression "morality." Because of the inordinate impact on American culture of fields such as art, literature, theatre and, especially, film, many Americans of the era became concerned about the negative impact that such productions might have on public morality. With few previous, strict guidelines to follow regarding acceptable on-screen content, the Association of Motion Picture Producers adopted the Motion Picture Production Code in 1930, outlined in the following, to ensure uniform measures of decency were followed.

General Principles
1. No picture shall be produced which will lower the moral standards of those who see it. Hence the sympathy of the audience should never be thrown to the side of crime, wrongdoing, evil or sin.

2. Correct standards of life, subject only to the requirements of drama and entertainment, shall be presented.

3. Law, natural or human, shall not be ridiculed, nor shall sympathy be created or its violation.

Particular Applications

I. Crimes Against the Law

These shall never be presented in such a way as to throw sympathy with the crime as against law and justice or to inspire others with a desire for imitation.

1. *Murder*

   a. The technique of murder must be presented in a way that will not inspire imitation.

   b. Brutal killings are not to be presented in detail.

   c. Revenge in modern times shall not be justified.

2. *Methods of Crime* should not be explicitly presented.

   a. Theft, robbery, safe-cracking, and dynamiting of trains, mines, buildings, etc., should not be detailed in method.

   b. Arson must be subject to the same safeguards.

   c. The use of firearms should be restricted to essentials.

   d. Methods of smuggling should not be presented.

3. *Illegal drug traffic* must never be presented.

4. *The use of liquor* in American life, when not required by the plot or for proper characterization will not be shown.

II. Sex

The sanctity of the institution of marriage and the home shall be upheld. Pictures shall not infer that low forms of sex relationship are the accepted or common thing.

1. *Adultery,* sometimes necessary plot material, must not be explicitly treated, or justified, or presented attractively.

2. *Scenes of Passion*

   a. They should not be introduced when not essential to the plot.

   b. Excessive and lustful kissing, lustful embraces, suggestive postures and gestures, are not to be shown.

   c. In general passion should so be treated that these scenes do not stimulate the lower and baser element.

3. *Seduction or Rape*

   a. They should never be more than suggested, and only when essential for the plot, and even then never shown by explicit method.

   b. They are never the proper subject for comedy.

4. *Sex perversion* or any inference to it is forbidden.

5. *White-slavery* shall not be treated.

6. *Miscegenation* (sex relationships between the white and black races) is forbidden.

7. *Sex hygiene* and venereal diseases are not subjects for motion pictures.

8. Scenes of *actual child birth,* in fact or in silhouette, are never to be presented.

9. *Children's sex organs* are never to be exposed.

III. Vulgarity
The treatment of low, disgusting, unpleasant, though not necessarily evil, subjects should be subject always to the dictates of good taste and a regard for the sensibilities of the audience.

IV. Obscenity
Obscenity in word, gesture, reference, song, joke, or by suggestion (even when likely to be understood only by part of the audience) is forbidden.

V. Profanity
Pointed profanity (this includes the words, God, Lord, Jesus, Christ—unless used reverently—Hell, S.O.B. damn, Gawd), or every other profane or vulgar expression, however used, is forbidden.

VI. Costume
1. *Complete nudity* is never permitted. This includes nudity in fact or in silhouette, or any lecherous or licentious notice thereof by other characters in the picture.

2. *Undressing scenes* should be avoided, and never used save where essential to the plot.

3. *Indecent or undue exposure* is forbidden.

4. *Dancing costumes* intended to permit undue exposure or indecent movements in the dance are forbidden.

VII. Dances
1. Dances suggesting or representing sexual actions or indecent passion are forbidden.

2. Dances which emphasize indecent movements are to be regarded as obscene.

VIII. Religion
1. No film or episode may throw ridicule on any religious faith.

2. *Ministers of religion* in their character as ministers of religion should not be used as comic characters or as villains.

3. *Ceremonies* of any definite religion should be carefully and respectfully handled.

IX. Locations
The treatment of bedrooms must be governed by good taste and delicacy.

X. National Feelings

    1. *The use of the Flag* shall be consistently respectful.

    2. *The history,* institutions, prominent people and citizenry of other nations shall be represented fairly.

XI—Titles

Salacious, indecent, or obscene titles shall not be used.

XII. Repellent Subjects

The following subjects must be treated within the careful limits of good taste:

    1. *Actual hangings* or electrocutions as legal punishments for crime.

    2. *Third Degree* methods.

    3. *Brutality* and possible gruesomeness.

    4. *Branding* of people or animals.

    5. *Apparent cruelty* to children or animals.

    6. *The sale of women* or a woman selling her virtue.

    7. *Surgical operations.*

7

John Kenneth Galbraith: *The Affluent Society* (1958)

As mentioned previously, the replacement of "virtue" with "morality" as a standard code of conduct was essentially complete even before World War II. The two terms are largely synonymous, though significant differences do exist. Embedded in the definition of classical virtue is temperance, or moderation, in all areas of one's life, whereas morality does not necessarily contain such a provision. Post–World War II America witnessed the almost complete abandonment of a simplistic lifestyle as a collective ideal. To be sure, Americans from earlier generations lived to excess and the consumption of unnecessary goods increased steadily from the founding era and beyond. However, as noted by the economist John Kenneth Galbraith in the following reading, by the 1950s Americans were in an unprecedented period of prosperity, yet poverty still existed in the United States. Recognizing this prosperity and the embrace of a material culture, Galbraith characterizes the seemingly uncaring reaction to the persistence of poverty as a "disgrace."

The final problem of the productive society is what it produces. This manifests itself in an implacable tendency to provide an opulent supply of some things and a niggardly yield of others. This disparity carries to the point where it is a cause of social discomfort and social unhealth. The line which divides our area

Source: Excerpt from *The Affluent Society* by John Kenneth Galbraith. Copyright © 1958, renewed 1986 by John Kenneth Galbraith. Reprinted by permission of Houghton Mifflin Company. All rights reserved.

of wealth from our area of poverty is roughly that which divides privately produced and marketed goods and services from publicly rendered services. . . .

In the years following World War II, the papers of any major city—those of New York were an excellent example—told daily of the shortages and shortcomings in the elementary municipal and metropolitan services. The schools were old and overcrowded. The police force was under strength and underpaid. The parks and playgrounds were insufficient. Streets and empty lots were filthy, and the sanitation staff was underequipped and in need of men. Access to the city by those who work there was uncertain and painful and becoming more so. Internal transportation was overcrowded, unhealthful and dirty. So was the air. . . .

The discussion of this public poverty competed, on the whole successfully, with the stories of ever-increasing opulence in privately produced goods. The Gross National Product was rising. So were retail sales. So was personal income. Labor productivity had also advanced. The automobiles that could not be parked were being produced at an expended rate. The children, though without schools, subject in the playgrounds to the affectionate interest of adults with odd tastes, and disposed to increasingly imaginative forms of delinquency, were admirably equipped with television sets. We had difficulty finding storage space for the great surpluses of food despite a national disposition to obesity. Food was grown and packaged under private auspices. The care and refreshment of the mind, in contrast with the stomach, was principally in the public domain. Our colleges and universities were severely overcrowded and underprovided, and the same was true of mental hospitals.

The contrast was and remains evident not alone to those who read. The family which takes its mauve and cerise, air-conditioned, power steered and power-braked automobile out for a tour passes through cities that are badly paved, made hideous by litter, blighted buildings, billboards, and posts for wires that should long since have been put underground. They pass on into a countryside that has been rendered largely invisible by commercial art. . . . They picnic on exquisitely packaged food from a portable icebox by a polluted stream and go on to spend the night at a park which is a menace to public health and morals. Just before dozing off on an air mattress, beneath a nylon tent, amid the stench of decaying refuse, they may reflect vaguely on the curious unevenness of their blessings. Is this, indeed, the American genius? . . .

An affluent society, that is also both compassionate and rational, would not doubt, secure to all who needed it the minimum income essential for decency and comfort. . . .

To eliminate poverty efficiently we should invest more than proportionately in the children of the poor community. It is there that high quality schools, strong health services, special provision for nutrition and recreation are most needed to compensate for the very low investment which families are able to make in their own offspring. . . .

Much can be done to treat those characteristics which cause people to reject or be rejected by the modern industrial society. Educational deficiencies can be overcome. Mental deficiencies can be treated. Physical handicaps can be remedied. The limiting factor is not knowledge of what can be done. Overwhelmingly it is our failure to invest in people. . . .

Poverty—grim, degrading, and ineluctable—is not remarkable in India. For few the fate is otherwise. But in the United States the survival of poverty is remarkable. We ignore it because we share with all societies at all times the capacity for not seeing what we do not wish to see. Anciently this has enabled the nobleman to enjoy his dinner while remaining oblivious to the beggars around his door. In our own day it enables us to travel in comfort through south Chicago and the South. But while our failure to notice can be explained, it cannot be excused. "Poverty," Pitt exclaimed, "is no disgrace but it is damned annoying." In the contemporary United States it is not annoying but it is a disgrace.

8

The Port Huron Statement (1962)

The "long 60s" (the 1960s and early 1970s) witnessed the greatest social upheaval in modern American history in response to real and perceived injustices. In many ways the activist movements of the 1960s were rooted in an attempt to recapture the lost virtues of the past while maintaining a decidedly progressive path towards equality and justice. In the famous Port Huron Statement that follows, the Students for a Democratic Society lament the fact that American culture does not promote the evaluation of individuals based on the strength of their character but instead relies on superficial means of assessment such as material possessions and test scores. Note, as well, the concerns relating to the disengagement of Americans from society—a common theme in post-1960s cultural discourse.

AWAKENING OF A GENERATION

We are people of this generation, bred in at least modest comfort, housed now in universities, looking uncomfortably to the world we inherit.

When we were kids the United States was the wealthiest and strongest country in the world; the only one with the atom bomb, the least scarred by modern war, an initiator of the United Nations that we thought would distribute Western influence throughout the world. Freedom and equality for each individual, government of, by, and for the people—these American values we found good, principles by which we could live as men. Many of us began maturing in complacency.

As we grew, however, our comfort was penetrated by events too troubling to dismiss. . . .

Not only did tarnish appear on our image of American virtue, not only did disillusion occur when the hypocrisy of American ideals was discovered, but we began to sense that what we had originally seen as the American Golden Age was actually the decline of an era. The worldwide outbreak of revolution against colonialism and imperialism, the entrenchment of totalitarian states, the menace of war, overpopulation, international disorder, supertechnology— these trends were testing the tenacity of our own commitment to democracy and freedom and our abilities to visualize their application to a world in upheaval. . . .

For most Americans, all crusades are suspect, threatening. The fact that each individual sees apathy in his fellows perpetuates the common reluctance to organize for change. The dominant institutions are complex enough to blunt the minds of their potential critics, and entrenched enough to swiftly dissipate or entirely repel the energies of protest and reform, thus limiting human expectancies. Then, too, we are a materially improved society, and by our own improvements we seem to have weakened the case for further change.

Some would have us believe that Americans feel contentment amidst prosperity—but might it not better be called a glaze above deeply felt anxieties about their role in the new world? And if these anxieties produce a developed indifference to human affairs, do they not as well produce a yearning to believe that there is an alternative to the present, that something can be done to change circumstances in the school, the workplaces, the bureaucracies, the government? It is to this latter yearning, at once the spark and engine of change, that we direct our present appeal. . . .

Human relationships should involve fraternity and honesty. Human interdependence is contemporary fact; human brotherhood must be willed, however, as a condition of future survival and as the most appropriate form of social relations. Personal links between man and man are needed, especially to go beyond the partial and fragmentary bonds of function that bind men only as worker to worker, employer to employee, teacher to student, American to Russian.

Loneliness, estrangement, isolation describe the vast distance between man and man today. These dominant tendencies cannot be overcome by better personnel management, nor by improved gadgets, but only when a love of man overcomes the idolatrous worship of things by man. As the individualism we affirm is not egoism, the selflessness we affirm is not self-elimination. On the contrary, we believe in generosity of a kind that imprints one's unique individual qualities in the relation to other men, and to all human activity. Further, to dislike isolation is not to favor the abolition of privacy; the latter differs from isolation in that it occurs or is abolished according to individual will.

We would replace power rooted in possession, privilege, or circumstance by power and uniqueness rooted in love, reflectiveness, reason, and creativity. As a social system we seek the establishment of a democracy of individual participation, governed by two central aims: that the individual share in those social decisions determining the quality and direction of his life; that society be organized to encourage independence in men and provide the media for their common participation. . . .

Almost no students value activity as citizens. Passive in public, they are hardly more idealistic in arranging their private lives: Gallup concludes they will settle for "low success, and won't risk high failure." There is not much willingness to take risks (not even in business), no setting of dangerous goals, no real conception of personal identity except one manufactured in the image of others, no real urge for personal fulfillment except to be almost as successful as the very successful people.

Attention is being paid to social status (the quality of shirt collars, meeting people, getting wives or husbands, making solid contacts for later on); much, too, is paid to academic status (grades, honors, the med school rat race). But neglected generally is real intellectual status, the personal cultivation of the mind. "Students don't even give a damn about the apathy," one has said.

Apathy toward apathy begets a privately constructed universe, a place of systematic study schedules, two nights each week for beer, a girl or two, and early marriage; a framework infused with personality, warmth, and under control, no matter how unsatisfying otherwise. Under these conditions university life loses all relevance to some. Four hundred thousand of our classmates leave college every year. The accompanying "let's pretend" theory of student extracurricular affairs validates student government as a training center for those who want to live their lives in political pretense, and discourages initiative from the more articulate, honest, and sensitive students. The bounds and style of controversy are delimited before controversy begins. The university "prepares" the student for "citizenship" through perpetual rehearsals and, usually, through emasculation of what creative spirit there is in the individual. The academic life contains reinforcing counterparts to the way in which extracurricular life is organized. . . .

The desperation of people threatened by forces about which they know little and of which they can say less; the cheerful emptiness of people "giving up" all hope of changing things; the faceless ones polled by Gallup who listed "international affairs" fourteenth on their list of "problems" but who also expected thermonuclear war in the next few years; in these and other forms, Americans are in withdrawal from public life, from any collective effort at directing their own affairs.

Some regard these national doldrums as a sign of healthy approval of the established order—but is it approval by consent or manipulated acquiescence? Others declare that the people are withdrawn because compelling issues are fast disappearing—perhaps there are fewer bread lines in America, but is Jim Crow gone, is there enough work and work more fulfilling, is world war a diminishing threat, and what of the revolutionary new peoples? Still others think the national quietude is a necessary consequence of the need for elites to resolve complex and specialized problems of modern industrial society— but then, why should business elites help decide foreign policy, and who controls the elites anyway, and are they solving mankind's problems? Others, finally, shrug knowingly and announce that full democracy never worked anywhere in the past—but why lump qualitatively different civilizations together, and how can a social order work well if its best thinkers are skeptics, and is man really doomed forever to the domination of today?

There are now convincing apologies for the contemporary malaise. While the world tumbles toward the final war, while men in other nations are trying desperately to alter events, while the very future qua future is uncertain—America is without community impulse, without the inner momentum necessary for an age when societies cannot successfully perpetuate themselves by their military weapons, when democracy must be viable because of its quality of life, not its quantity of rockets.

9

Richard Nixon: Acceptance Speech at the Republican National Convention (1968)

The 1960s and 1970s were difficult times for Americans who embraced a collective identity and shared the views of the Founding Fathers that citizens should sacrifice their own self-interest for the benefit of society as a whole. As individualism became more prevalent during the postmodernist cultural upheavals, many Americans withdrew as active participants in society. To some, apathy, inconsiderate behavior, and immorality all caused Americans to divide rather than unite. The pair of readings that follow, though written by two individuals with disparate personalities, reflect many of these concerns. In his acceptance speech at the Republican National Convention shortly before he was elected to the White House, future President Nixon questions the direction of the United States, whereas President Carter's famous "Malaise" speech echoes the sentiments of the New Left of the 1960s.

. . . As we look at America, we see cities enveloped in smoke and flame. We hear sirens in the night. We see Americans dying on distant battlefields abroad. We see Americans hating each other; fighting each other; killing each other at home. And as we see and hear these things, millions of Americans cry out in anguish.

Did we come all this way for this?

Did American boys die in Normandy, and Korea, and in Valley Forge for this? . . .

America is in trouble today not because her people have failed but because her leaders have failed. And what America needs are leaders to match the greatness of her people. And this great group of Americans, the forgotten Americans, and others know that the great question Americans must answer by their votes in November is this: Whether we shall continue for four more years the policies of the last five years.

And this is their answer and this is my answer to that question.

When the strongest nation in the world can be tied down for four years in a war in Vietnam with no end in sight; when the richest nation in the world can't manage its own economy; when the nation with the greatest tradition of the rule of law is plagued by unprecedented lawlessness; when a nation that has been known for a century for equality of opportunity is torn by unprecedented racial violence; and when the President of the United States cannot travel abroad or to any major city at home without fear of a hostile demonstration—then it's time for new leadership for the United States of America. . . .

The American Revolution was a shining example of freedom in action which caught the imagination of the world. Today, too often, America is an example to be avoided and not followed. A nation that can't keep the peace at home won't be trusted to keep the peace abroad. A President who isn't treated with respect at home will not be treated with respect abroad. A nation which can't manage its own economy can't tell others how to manage theirs. If we are to restore prestige and respect for America abroad, the place to begin is at home in the United States of America. My friends, we live in an age of revolution in America and in the world. And to find the answers to our problems, let us turn to a revolution, a revolution that will never grow old. The world's greatest continuing revolution, the American Revolution. . . .

Because, my friends, let this message come through clear from what I say tonight. Time is running out for the merchants of crime and corruption in American society. The wave of crime is not going to be the wave of the future in the United States of America. We shall re-establish freedom from fear in America so that America can take the lead in re-establishing freedom from fear in the world. . . .

I see a day when Americans are once again proud of their flag. When once again at home and abroad, it is honored as the world's greatest symbol of liberty and justice.

I see a day when the President of the United States is respected and his office is honored because it is worthy of respect and worthy of honor.

I see a day when every child in this land, regardless of his background, has a chance for the best education our wisdom and schools can provide, and an equal chance to go just as high as his talents will take him.

I see a day when life in rural America attracts people to the country, rather than driving them away.

I see a day when we can look back on massive breakthroughs in solving the problems of slums and pollution and traffic which are choking our cities to death.

I see a day when our senior citizens and millions of others can plan for the future with the assurance that their government is not going to rob them of their savings by destroying the value of their dollars.

I see a day when we will again have freedom from fear in America and freedom from fear in the world.

I see a day when our nation is at peace and the world is at peace and everyone on earth—those who hope, those who aspire, those who crave liberty—will look to America as the shining example of hopes realized and dreams achieved. . . .

My fellow Americans, the long dark night for America is about to end. The time has come for us to leave the valley of despair and climb the mountain so that we may see the glory of the dawn—a new day for America, and a new dawn for peace and freedom in the world.

10

President Jimmy Carter: The "Malaise" Speech (1979)

. . . [A]fter listening to the American people I have been reminded again that all the legislation in the world can't fix what's wrong with America. So, I want to speak to you first tonight about a subject even more serious than energy or inflation. I want to talk to you right now about a fundamental threat to American democracy. I do not mean our political and civil liberties. They will endure. And I do not refer to the outward strength of America, a nation that is at peace tonight everywhere in the world, with unmatched economic power and military might.

The threat is nearly invisible in ordinary ways. It is a crisis that strikes at the very heart and soul and spirit of our national will. We can see this crisis in the growing doubt about the meaning of our own lives and in the loss of a unity of purpose for our Nation.

The erosion of our confidence in the future is threatening to destroy the social and the political fabric of America. . . .

In a nation that was proud of hard work, strong families, close-knit communities, and our faith in God, too many of us now tend to worship self-indulgence and consumption. Human identity is no longer defined by what one does, but by what one owns. But we've discovered that owning things and consuming things does not satisfy our longing for meaning. We've learned that piling up material goods cannot fill the emptiness of lives which have no confidence or purpose.

The symptoms of this crisis of the American spirit are all around us. For the first time in the history of our country a majority of our people believe that the next five years will be worse than the past five years. Two-thirds of our people do not even vote. The productivity of American workers is actually dropping, and the willingness of Americans to save for the future has fallen below that of all other people in the Western world.

As you know, there is a growing disrespect for government and for churches and for schools, the news media, and other institutions. This is not a message of happiness or reassurance, but it is the truth and it is a warning. These changes did not happen overnight. They've come upon us gradually over the last generation, years that were filled with shocks and tragedy.

We were sure that ours was a nation of the ballot, not the bullet, until the murders of John Kennedy and Robert Kennedy and Martin Luther King, Jr. We were taught that our armies were always invincible and our causes were always just, only to suffer the agony of Vietnam. We respected the Presidency as a place of honor until the shock of Watergate. . . .

We simply must have faith in each other, faith in our ability to govern ourselves, and faith in the future of this Nation. Restoring that faith and that confidence to America is now the most important task we face. It is a true challenge of this generation of Americans. . . .

We are at a turning point in our history. There are two paths to choose. One is a path I've warned about tonight, the path that leads to fragmentation and self-interest. Down that road lies a mistaken idea of freedom, the right to grasp for ourselves some advantage over others. That path would be one of constant conflict between narrow interests ending in chaos and immobility. It is a certain route to failure.

All the traditions of our past, all the lessons of our heritage, all the promises of our future point to another path, the path of common purpose and the restoration of American values. That path leads to true freedom for our Nation and ourselves. . . .

Little by little we can and we must rebuild our confidence. We can spend until we empty our treasuries, and we may summon all the wonders of science. But we can succeed only if we tap our greatest resources—America's people, America's values, and America's confidence.

I have seen the strength of America in the inexhaustible resources of our people. In the days to come, let us renew that strength in the struggle for an energy-secure nation.

In closing, let me say this: I will do my best, but I will not do it alone. Let your voice be heard. Whenever you have a chance, say something good about our country. With God's help and for the sake of our Nation, it is time for us to join hands in America. Let us commit ourselves together to a rebirth of the American spirit. Working together with our common faith we cannot fail.

Thank you and goodnight.

11

President George W. Bush: Speech to Congress (2001)

The terrorist attacks against America on September 11, 2001, shocked and frightened many citizens as no event had done before. The destruction of the World Trade Center towers and the attack on the Pentagon eliminated the umbrella of safety that the United States had long enjoyed in contrast to much of the rest of the world. In the following reading, President George W. Bush addresses Congress shortly after the incident, highlighting the virtues of the American people and vowing to persevere.

Mr. Speaker, Mr. President Pro Tempore, members of Congress, and fellow Americans:

In the normal course of events, Presidents come to this chamber to report on the state of the Union. Tonight, no such report is needed. It has already been delivered by the American people. We have seen it in the courage of passengers, who rushed terrorists to save others on the ground—passengers like an exceptional man named Todd Beamer. And would you please help me to welcome his wife, Lisa Beamer, here tonight.

We have seen the state of our Union in the endurance of rescuers, working past exhaustion. We have seen the unfurling of flags, the lighting of candles, the giving of blood, the saying of prayers—in English, Hebrew, and Arabic. We have seen the decency of a loving and giving people who have made the grief of strangers their own.

My fellow citizens, for the last nine days, the entire world has seen for itself the state of our Union—and it is strong.

Tonight we are a country awakened to danger and called to defend freedom. Our grief has turned to anger, and anger to resolution. Whether we bring our enemies to justice, or bring justice to our enemies, justice will be done.

I thank the Congress for its leadership at such an important time. All of America was touched on the evening of the tragedy to see Republicans and Democrats joined together on the steps of this Capitol, singing "God Bless America." And you did more than sing; you acted, by delivering $40 billion to rebuild our communities and meet the needs of our military.

Speaker Hastert, Minority Leader Gephardt, Majority Leader Daschle and Senator Lott, I thank you for your friendship, for your leadership and for your service to our country. . . .

Americans are asking: What is expected of us? I ask you to live your lives, and hug your children. I know many citizens have fears tonight, and I ask you to be calm and resolute, even in the face of a continuing threat.

I ask you to uphold the values of America, and remember why so many have come here. We are in a fight for our principles, and our first responsibility is to live by them. No one should be singled out for unfair treatment or unkind words because of their ethnic background or religious faith. . . .

I ask your continued participation and confidence in the American economy. Terrorists attacked a symbol of American prosperity. They did not touch its source. America is successful because of the hard work, and creativity, and enterprise of our people. These were the true strengths of our economy before September 11th, and they are our strengths today. . . .

After all that has just passed—all the lives taken, and all the possibilities and hopes that died with them—it is natural to wonder if America's future is one of fear. Some speak of an age of terror. I know there are struggles ahead, and dangers to face. But this country will define our times, not be defined by them. As long as the United States of America is determined and strong, this will not be an age of terror; this will be an age of liberty, here and across the world.

Great harm has been done to us. We have suffered great loss. And in our grief and anger we have found our mission and our moment. Freedom and fear are at war. The advance of human freedom—the great achievement of our time, and the great hope of every time—now depends on us. Our nation— this generation—will lift a dark threat of violence from our people and our future. We will rally the world to this cause by our efforts, by our courage. We will not tire, we will not falter, and we will not fail.

It is my hope that in the months and years ahead, life will return almost to normal. We'll go back to our lives and routines, and that is good. Even grief recedes with time and grace. But our resolve must not pass. Each of us will remember what happened that day, and to whom it happened. We'll remember the moment the news came—where we were and what we were doing. Some will remember an image of a fire, or a story of rescue. Some will carry memories of a face and a voice gone forever.

And I will carry this: It is the police shield of a man named George Howard, who died at the World Trade Center trying to save others. It was given to me by his mom, Arlene, as a proud memorial to her son. This is my reminder of lives that ended, and a task that does not end.

I will not forget this wound to our country or those who inflicted it. I will not yield; I will not rest; I will not relent in waging this struggle for freedom and security for the American people.

The course of this conflict is not known, yet its outcome is certain. Freedom and fear, justice and cruelty, have always been at war, and we know that God is not neutral between them.

Fellow citizens, we'll meet violence with patient justice—assured of the rightness of our cause, and confident of the victories to come. In all that lies before us, may God grant us wisdom, and may He watch over the United States of America.

Thank you.

12

Attorney General Edwin Meese: Report on Pornography (1986)

Largely the result of legal challenges by individuals such as Larry Flynt, the proliferation of pornography in the United States during the 1970s and 1980s resulted in massive social movements to combat such trends. Feminist organizations as well as other groups concerned about the deterioration of morality in America aligned together in mostly unsuccessful attempts to ban pornography on the basis that it was harmful to the general welfare. Issued during the Reagan presidency by Attorney General Edwin Meese, his report on pornography outlines some of the most convincing arguments for outlawing sexually explicit materials.

That this is a "harm" we think undisputable, on several grounds. First, those who "perform" in current pornography are, as a group, extremely young, ignorant, confused, and exploited; as we have discussed in our examination of their situations, they very frequently cannot be said to have given an informed consent to their use. Second, even when such consent exists, such performances, where they are given in exchange for money, are inseparable from prostitution, and degrade the performers in exactly the same ways as prostitutes are injured by their profession. Neither of these concerns applies, by contrast to the making of noncommercial, sexually explicit films for use in education or sex therapy—arenas where the reputations of performers are unlikely to be damaged.

Quite apart from injury to the performers, though, we believe that injury occurs to society as a whole from such performances, injury that may best be described as the blurring of legitimate boundaries for public dialogue on sexuality. Where no reticence is allowed, where only the act of sex is regarded as an authentic statement about its meaning, most citizens can be expected to withdraw, rather than enter the discussion. Reducing the general sense that some aspects of every person's sexual life are so unique as to deserve special deference means, we think, that many will all the more militantly seek to shut out any dialogue on sexuality all together. The virulent, devastating divisiveness over sex education in the public schools is, we think, a symptom of the fears that can arise from this destruction of the sense of boundaries.

Now against all of this what proof is offered that the taboo of sexual privacy should be dismissed with regard to filmed pornography?

Some argue, convincingly enough, that such pornography expresses an idea, if no more elaborate an idea than an attack on sexual privacy itself. Yet that is hardly an argument against the "harm" we have discussed, for ideas can be as harmful as, indeed more harmful than a wide variety of more concrete afflictions. Others contend that the extreme reticence on sexual matters practiced by our society in the past was repressive of and injurious to healthy sexuality. That is also, so far as it goes, true enough. But do we need to pay other people to copulate for us on film in order to discuss sexuality freely?

Surely the case for that need has not been made with even minimal rigor. And even if it had been made, we remain convinced, as we said above, that as many of us are silenced in the resulting dialogue as are given voice. Indeed, after a year of witnessing the grotesque sexism of commercial pornography, we now have begun to understand what Catherine MacKinnon, Andrea Dworkin, and others meant when they told us that pornography "silences" women.

Photographic pornography silences and it also degrades. With the exception of noncommercial material produced for educational or therapeutic purposes, it exploits some human beings in violation of some of mankind's deepest instincts about the privacy of sexual conduct. The "right of the Nation and of the States to maintain a decent society," recognized in dissent by Chief Justice Warren and by a majority of the Supreme Court since 1973, largely means only this: some aspects of American life, and of American sexual behavior, deserve special protection from intrusion, public display, and commercial mass-marketing. Mr. Shaw—and the sex industry—to the contrary notwithstanding, Americans do know the value of privacy. And it is a value that commercial pornography deeply offends.

13

President and Nancy Reagan:
Speech on the "War Against Drugs" (1986)

By President Ronald Reagan's second term many urban areas across the country had been transformed into veritable killing fields. Increases in the use of drugs such as crack cocaine had begun to devastate inner city neighborhoods with rival gangs competing to control the illegal drug trade. In the passionate address included here, both President and Nancy Reagan highlight some of the most detrimental aspects of drug abuse and extol Americans to resist the temptation of drugs by remaining temperate in their private conduct.

. . . Drugs are menacing our society. They're threatening our values and undercutting our institutions. They're killing our children.

From the beginning of our administration, we've taken strong steps to do something about this horror. Tonight I can report to you that we've made much progress. Thirty-seven Federal agencies are working together in a vigorous national effort, and by next year our spending for drug law enforcement will have more than tripled from its 1981 levels. We have increased seizures of illegal drugs. Shortages of marijuana are now being reported. Last year alone over 10,000 drug criminals were convicted and nearly $250 million of their assets were seized by the DEA, the Drug Enforcement Administration.

And in the most important area, individual use, we see progress. In 4 years the number of high school seniors using marijuana on a daily basis has dropped from 1 in 14 to 1 in 20. The U.S. military has cut the use of illegal drugs among its personnel by 67 percent since 1980. These are a measure of our commitment and emerging signs that we can defeat this enemy. But we still have much to do.

Despite our best efforts, illegal cocaine is coming into our country at alarming levels and 4 to 5 million people regularly use it. Five hundred thousand Americans are hooked on heroin. One in twelve persons smokes marijuana regularly. Regular drug use is even higher among the age group 18 to 25 most likely just entering the workforce. Today there's a new epidemic: smokable cocaine, otherwise known as crack. It is an explosively destructive and often lethal substance which is crushing its users. It is an uncontrolled fire.

And drug abuse is not a so-called victimless crime. Everyone's safety is at stake when drugs and excessive alcohol are used by people on the highways or by those transporting our citizens or operating industrial equipment. Drug abuse costs you and your fellow Americans at least $60 billion a year.

From the early days of our administration, Nancy has been intensely involved in the effort to fight drug abuse. She has since traveled over 100,000 miles to 55 cities in 28 States and 6 foreign countries to fight school-age drug and alcohol abuse. She's given dozens of speeches and scores of interviews and has participated in 24 special radio and TV tapings to create greater awareness of this crisis. Her personal observations and efforts have given her such dramatic insights that I wanted her to share them with you this evening.

NANCY

. . .Drugs steal away so much. They take and take, until finally every time a drug goes into a child, something else is forced out like love and hope and trust and confidence. Drugs take away the dream from every child's heart and replace it with a nightmare, and it's time we in America stand up and replace those dreams. Each of us has to put our principles and consciences on the line, whether in social settings or in the workplace, to set forth solid standards and stick to them. There's no moral middle ground. Indifference is not an option. We want you to help us create an outspoken intolerance for drug use. For the sake of our children, I implore each of you to be unyielding and inflexible in your opposition to drugs.

Our young people are helping us lead the way. Not long ago, in Oakland, California, I was asked by a group of children what to do if they were offered drugs, and I answered, "Just say no." Soon after that, those children in Oakland formed a Just Say No club, and now there are over 10,000 such clubs all over the country. Well, their participation and their courage in saying no needs our encouragement. We can help by using every opportunity to force the issue of not using drugs to the point of making others uncomfortable, even if it means making ourselves unpopular.

Our job is never easy because drug criminals are ingenious. They work everyday to plot a new and better way to steal our children's lives, just as they've done by developing this new drug, crack. For every door that we close, they open a new door to death. They prosper on our unwillingness to act. So, we must be smarter and stronger and tougher than they are. It's up to us to change attitudes and just simply dry up their markets. And finally, to young people watching or listening, I have a very personal message for you: There's a big, wonderful world out there for you. It belongs to you. It's exciting and stimulating and rewarding. Don't cheat yourselves out of this promise. Our country needs you, but it needs you to be clear-eyed and clear-minded. . . .

THE PRESIDENT

. . . First, we seek a drug-free workplace at all levels of government and in the private sector. Second, we'll work toward drug-free schools. Third, we want to ensure that the public is protected and that treatment is available to substance abusers and the chemically dependent. Our fourth goal is to expand international cooperation while treating drug trafficking as a threat to our national security. In October I will be meeting with key U.S. Ambassadors to discuss what can be done to support our friends abroad. Fifth, we must move to strengthen law enforcement activities such as those initiated by Vice President Bush and Attorney General Meese. And finally, we seek to expand public awareness and prevention. . . .

Your government will continue to act aggressively, but nothing would be more effective than for Americans simply to quit using illegal drugs. We seek to create a massive change in national attitudes which ultimately will separate the drugs from the customer, to take the user away from the supply. I believe, quite simply, that we can help them quit. And that's where you come in.

My generation will remember how America swung into action when we were attacked in World War II. The war was not just fought by the fellows flying the planes or driving the tanks. It was fought at home by a mobilized nation, men and women alike building planes and ships, clothing sailors and soldiers, feeding marines and airmen; and it was fought by children planting victory gardens and collecting cans. Well, now we're in another war for our freedom, and it's time for all of us to pull together again. So, for example, if your friend or neighbor or a family member has a drug or alcohol problem, don't turn the other way. Go to his help or to hers. Get others involved with you—clubs, service groups, and community organizations—and provide support and strength. And, of course, many of you've been cured through treatment and self-help. Well, you're the combat veterans, and you have a critical role to play. You can help others by telling your story and providing a willing hand to those in need. Being friends to others is the best way of being friends to ourselves. It's time, as Nancy said, for America to "just say no" to drugs.

Those of you in union halls and workplaces everywhere: Please make this challenge a part of your job every day. Help us preserve the health and dignity of all workers. To businesses large and small: we need the creativity of your enterprise applied directly to this national problem. Help us. And those of you who are educators: Your wisdom and leadership are indispensable to this cause. From the pulpits of this spirit filled land: we would welcome your reassuring message of redemption and forgiveness and of helping one another. On the athletic fields: You men and women are among the most beloved citizens of our country. A child's eyes fill with your heroic achievements. Few of us can give youngsters something as special and strong to look up to as you. Please don't let them down. . . .

In this crusade, let us not forget who we are. Drug abuse is a repudiation of everything America is. The destructiveness and human wreckage mock our heritage. Think for a moment how special it is to be an American. Can we doubt that only a divine providence placed this land, this island of freedom, here as a refuge for all those people on the world who yearn to breathe free? . . .

14

Daniel Patrick Moynihan:
"Defining Deviancy Down" (1993)

The concerns about the decline of morality in America during the 1980s and 1990s were certainly not limited to drug abuse or pornography. A new host of movements emerged, which brought visibility to gay and lesbian rights, single-parent households, and new, unprecedented levels of violent crime that left many people emotionally "numb" to what was transpiring. In the following reading, cultural critic and Senator Daniel Patrick Moynihan explains, in his opinion, the root cause of this desensitization of Americans toward behavior that previously had been determined immoral or deviant.

. . . I proffer the thesis that, over the past generation, since the [1960s], the amount of deviant behavior in American society has increased beyond the levels the community can "afford to recognize" and that, accordingly, we have been re-defining deviancy so as to exempt much conduct previously stigmatized, and also quietly raising the "normal" level in categories where behavior is now abnormal by any earlier standard. This redefining has evoked fierce resistance from defenders of "old" standards, and accounts for much of the present "cultural war" such as proclaimed by many at the 1992 Republican National Convention. . . . .

In 1991 Deborah A. Dawson of the National Institutes of Health, examined the thesis that "the psychological effects of divorce and single parenthood on children were strongly influenced by a sense of shame in being 'different' from the norm." If this were so, the effect should have fallen off in the 1980s, when being from a single-parent home became much more common. It did not. "The problems associated with task overload among single parents are more constant in nature," Dawson wrote, adding that since the adverse effects had not diminished, they were "not based on stigmatization but rather on inherent problems in alternative family structures"—*alternative* here meaning other than two-parent families. We should take note of such candor. Writing in the *Journal of Marriage and the Family* in 1989, Sara McLanahan and Karen Booth noted: "Whereas a decade ago the prevailing view was that single motherhood had no harmful effects on children, recent research is less optimistic." The year 1990 saw more of this lesson. In a paper prepared for the Progressive Policy Institute, Elaine Ciulla Kamarck and William A. Galston wrote that "if the economic effects of family breakdown are clear, the psychological effects are just now coming into focus." . . . We talk about the drug crisis, the education crisis, and the problems of teen pregnancy and juvenile crime. But all these ills trace back predominantly to one source: broken families. . . .

Source: Reprinted from *The American Scholar*, Volume 62, No. 1, Winter 1993. Copyright © 1992 by the author.

In a 1992 essay, "The Expert's Story of Marriage," Barbara Dafoe Whitehead examined "the story of marriage as it is conveyed in today's high school and college textbooks." Nothing amiss in this tale. It goes like this: The life course is full of exciting options. The lifestyle options available to individuals seeking a fulfilling personal relationship include living a heterosexual, homosexual, or bisexual single lifestyle; living in a commune; having a group marriage; being a single parent; or living together. Marriage is yet another lifestyle choice. However, before choosing marriage, individuals should weigh its costs and benefits against other lifestyle options and should consider what they want to get out of their intimate relationships. Even within marriage, different people want different things. For example, some people marry for companionship, some marry in order to have children, some marry for emotional and financial security. Though marriage can offer a rewarding path to personal growth, it is important to remember that it cannot provide a secure or permanent status. Many people will make the decision between marriage and singlehood many times throughout their life. Divorce represents part of the normal family life cycle. It should not be viewed as either deviant or tragic, as it has been in the past. Rather, it establishes a process for "uncoupling" and thereby serves as the foundation for individual renewal and "new beginnings." . . .

From the wild Irish slums of the 19th century Eastern seaboard to the riot-torn suburbs of Los Angeles, there is one unmistakable lesson in American history: a community that allows a large number of young men to grow up in broken families, dominated by women, never acquiring any stable relationship to male authority, never acquiring any set of rational expectations about the future—that community asks for and gets chaos. Crime, violence, unrest, unrestrained lashing out at the whole social structure—that is not only to be expected; it is very near to inevitable. The inevitable, as we now know, has come to pass, but here again our response is curiously passive. Crime is a more or less continuous subject of political pronouncement, and from time to time it will be at or near the top of opinion polls as a matter of public concern. But it never gets much further than that. In the words spoken from the bench, Judge Edwin Torres of the New York State Supreme Court, Twelfth Judicial District, described how "the slaughter of the innocent marches unabated: subway riders, bodega owners, cab drivers, babies; in laundromats, at cash machines, on elevators, in hallways." In personal communication, he writes: "This numbness, this near narcoleptic state can diminish the human condition to the level of combat infantrymen, who, in protracted campaigns, can eat their battlefield rations seated on the bodies of the fallen, friend and foe alike. A society that loses its sense of outrage is doomed to extinction." There is no expectation that this will change, nor any efficacious public insistence that it do so. The crime level has been *normalized*. Consider the St. Valentine's Day Massacre. In 1929 in Chicago during Prohibition, four gangsters killed seven gangsters on February 14. The nation was shocked. The event became legend. It merits not one but two entries in the *World Book Encyclopedia*. I leave it to others to judge, but it would appear that the society in the 1920s was simply not willing to put up with this degree of deviancy. In the end, the

Constitution was amended, and Prohibition, which lay behind so much gang-ster violence, ended. In recent years, again in the context of illegal traffic in controlled substances, this form of murder has returned. But it has done so at a level that induces denial. James Q. Wilson comments that Los Angeles has the equivalent of a St. Valentine's Day Massacre every weekend. Even the most ghastly re-enactments of such human slaughter produce only moderate responses. . . .

Liberals have traditionally been alert for upward redefining that does injus-tice to individuals. Conservatives have been correspondingly sensitive to downward redefining that weakens societal standards. Might it not help if we could all agree that there is a dynamic at work here? It is not revealed truth, nor yet a scientifically derived formula. It is simply a pattern we observe in ourselves. Nor is it rigid. There may once have been an unchanging supply of jail cells which more or less determined the number of prisoners. No longer. We are building new prisons at a prodigious rate. Similarly, the executioner is back. There is something of a competition in Congress to think up new offenses for which the death penalty is seemed the only available deterrent. Possibly also modes of execution, as in "fry the kingpins." Even so, we are get-ting used to a lot of behavior that is not good for us. . . .

DISCUSSION QUESTIONS FOR CHAPTER 2

1. As evidenced by the first several readings, what seems to be the accepted role for women in American society during the late nineteenth and early twentieth centuries? Does Sanger's view toward empowering women sexually indicate a true step forward for women? Why might some argue that steps advocated by Sanger might harm women?

2. What does Roosevelt consider to be the primary duties of American citizenship? How does this correspond to Coolidge's views on individual responsibility? How do the views of both of these leaders reconcile with the founding principle of individual action with simultaneous commu-nity concern?

3. Do you notice any common themes in the Hollywood Motion Picture Code of 1930? Could this have been a reaction to societal developments of the 1920s?

4. How did the affluence of society, as evidenced by the Galbraith read-ing, lead to movements sponsored by groups such as the Students for a Democratic Society (SDS)? What do both readings criticize? What solutions do they offer to remedy the deficiencies they see in American society?

5. Do the stated opinions of Nixon, Carter, and Bush on American character differ, and, if so, what are the main areas of divergence? Do you see common themes in their expectations of American society? Is one observation on American culture more accurate than the others?

6. Although pornography and drug use are sometimes referred to as "victimless" crimes or behaviors, what rationale did the Meese report and President and Nancy Reagan's speech to the American people use to advocate an elimination of such elements in society? According to Moynihan, what has led to the increased prevalence of drug abuse, illegitimacy, and other examples of behavior earlier generations of Americans deemed immoral?

CHAPTER 3

Religion

1

Washington Gladden: *Applied Christianity* (1892)

In the late nineteenth century, most Americans continued to share the founders' belief in the political importance of religion. At this time, however, a new emphasis arose. Although the founders had praised religion as a source of individual moral discipline, the "social gospel" movement, arising after the Civil War, stressed its potential to encourage social reform. In this excerpt, Washington Gladden, one of the social gospel's leading figures, argues that Christian principles require government and society to take steps to improve the situation of the poor and working classes.

[T]he wealth of the country is not equally divided. . . . If anyone will take pains to find out how many millionaires there were in the United States forty years ago, he will get a vivid idea of the increase of wealth. Besides this considerable and constantly growing class of the very rich, there are thousands who have attained to competence, and even to opulence, who are able to live in elegance, without labor, on their accumulations. Then comes a larger class of the well-to-do, who by combining the income from their savings with moderate earnings are able to live in comfort, and even to allow themselves many luxuries. It is impossible to draw a line between the rich and the poor; but as we descend the scale of material possessions, we come next upon a large class of those commonly called poor, who live in a measure of comfort, and who have attained to some degree of independence, who earn a decent livelihood and have a few hundred dollars invested in a dwelling or in the savings-bank or in a life insurance. Below these still, there is another large class of the really poor, of those whose earnings are small, whose life is comfortless, who have nothing laid by, who are often coming to want, many of whom frequently become a charge upon society, either through their failure to fulfill their contracts or through their receipt of public or private charity. This class of the very poor— those who are just on the borders of pauperism or fairly over the borders—is rapidly growing. Wealth is increasing very fast; poverty, even, even pauperism, is increasing still more rapidly. . . .

Plainly there is something out of joint in our machinery of distribution, or this state of things could not be. During the past fourteen years the wealth of this nation has increased much faster than the population, but the people who work for wages are little if any better off than they were fourteen years ago. It is doubtful whether the average yearly wages of the mechanic, the laborer, or the operative will purchase for him more of the necessaries of life now than at that time. . . .

This, then, is the existing state of things. The production of wealth in the country increases enormously year by year; the workingman's share of what is produced . . . increases very slowly. . . .

What has the Christian moralist to say about this state of things? He is bound to say that it is a bad state of things, and must somehow be reformed. He is bound to declare that "the laborer is worthy of his hire"; that, in the words of the apostle Paul, "the husbandman that laboreth must be the first to partake of the fruits." The broad equities of Christ's rule demand that this great increase in wealth be made, somehow, to inure to the benefit, in a far larger degree, of the people by who labor it is produced. He will not deny that the capitalist should have a fair reward for his prudence and his abstinence; he will not refuse to the "undertaker," the *entrepreneur*, the organizer of labor, who stands between capitalist and laborer, enabling them to combine in the production of wealth, that large reward to which his superior intelligence and experience entitle him; but he will still insist that the workman ought to have a greater share than he is getting now of the wealth that grows so rapidly under his hands. And Christianity, by the lips of all its teachers, ought with all its emphasis to say to society: "Your present industrial system, which fosters these enormous inequalities, which permits a few to heap up most of the gains of this advancing civilization, and leaves the many without any substantial share in them, is an inadequate and inequitable system, and needs important changes to make it the instrument of righteousness." . . .

What ought Christians to ask the state to do toward a more equitable distribution of wealth? What should be attempted in this direction by political means? . . .

[I]t is undoubtedly the duty of Christians to do what they can by means of law to secure a better industrial system. But this is not saying that Christians should ask the state to take the property of the rich and distribute it among the poor. . . .

There are, however, one or two things that he will insist upon as the immediate duty of the state. Certain outrageous monopolies exist that the state is bound to crush. It is an outrage on public justice that half a dozen men should be able to control the entire fuel supply of New York and New England, forbidding the miners to work more than two or three days in a week, lest the operatives of the New England mills or the longshoremen of the New York wharves should get their coal at a little smaller price per ton. This forcible suppression of an industry by which one of the necessaries of life is furnished . . . is so contrary to public justice and public policy that some way must be found of making an end of it. The coal barons must not be permitted to enrich themselves by compelling the miners to starve at one end of their lines and the operatives to freeze at the other. . . . All these iniquitous encroachments upon the rights of the people must be arrested; and it is the duty of every Christian, as the servant of a God of justice and righteousness, to say so in terms that cannot be misunderstood. . . .

What does Christianity require individuals to do in their private relations toward securing a juster division of the growing wealth of the nation? . . .

Society results from a combination of egoism and altruism. Self-love and self-sacrifice are both essential; no society can endure if based on either of them to the exclusion of the other. Without the self-regarding virtues it would have no vigor; without the benevolent virtues it would not cohere. But the combination of capitalists and laborers in production is a form of society. Both these elements ought to be combined in this form of society. The proportion of altruism may be less in the factory than in the house or the church, but it is essential to the peace and welfare of all of them. Yet the attempt of the present system is to base this form of society wholly on competition, which is pure egoism. It will not stand securely on this basis. The industrial system as at present organized is a social solecism. It is an attempt to hold society together upon an anti-social foundation. To bring capitalists and laborers together in an association, and set them over against each other, and announce to them the principle of competition as the guide of their conduct, bidding each party to get as much as it can out of the other, and to give as little as it can—for this is precisely what competition means—is simply to declare war—a war in which the strongest will win.

The Christian moralist is, therefore, bound to admonish the Christian employer that the wage-system, when it rests on competition as its sole basis, is anti-social and anti-Christian. "Thou shalt love thy neighbor as thyself" is the Christian law, and he must find some way of incorporating that law into the organization of labor. . . . God has not made men to be associated for any purpose on an egoistic basis; and we must learn God's laws and obey them. It must be possible to shape the organization of our industries in such a way that it shall be the daily habit of the workman to think of the interest of the employer, and of the employer to think of the interest of the workman. . . .

It is not a difficult problem. The solution of it is quite within the power of the Christian employer. All he has to do is to admit his laborers to an industrial partnership with himself by giving them a fixed share in the profits of production, to be divided among them, in proportion to their earnings, at the end of the year. . . .

The sum of all this discussion is that the possession of wealth is justified by the Christian ethics, but that it puts the possessor under heavy obligations to multitudes less fortunate. He could never have become rich without the cooperation of many; he ought not to hold his riches for his own exclusive benefit. The great inequalities arising from the present defective methods of distribution will only be corrected through a deepening sense of the obligations imposed by the possession of wealth. The economic law, like the moral law, can never be fulfilled without love.

2

President Calvin Coolidge: Address Delivered to the Holy Name Society (1924)

In the following speech President Coolidge reaffirms not only the founders' commitment to religious liberty, but also their view that reverence for God is essential to individual morality and the maintenance of free political institutions. He thus concludes that those who promote reverence for God perform both a "pious and a patriotic service."

More than six centuries ago, when in spite of much learning and much piety there was much ignorance, much wickedness and much warfare, when there seemed to be too little light in the world, when the condition of the common people appeared to be sunk in hopelessness, when most of life was rude, harsh and cruel, when the speech of men was too often profane and vulgar, until the earth rang with the tumult of those who took the name of the Lord in vain, the foundation of this day was laid in the formation of the Holy Name Society. It had an inspired purpose. It sought to rededicate the minds of the people to a true conception of the sacredness of the name of the Supreme Being. It was an effort to save all reference to the Deity from curses and blasphemy, and restore the lips of men to reverence and praise. Out of weakness there began to be strength; out of frenzy there began to be self-control; out of confusion there began to be order. This demonstration is a manifestation of the wide extent to which an effort to do the right thing will reach when it is once begun. It is a purpose which makes a universal appeal, an effort in which all may unite.

The importance of the lesson which this Society was formed to teach would be hard to overestimate. Its main purpose is to impress upon the people the necessity for reverence. This is the beginning of a proper conception of ourselves, of our relationship to each other, and our relationship to our Creator. Human nature cannot develop very far without it. The mind does not unfold, the creative faculty does not mature, the spirit does not expand, save under the influence of reverence. It is the chief motive of obedience. It is only by a correct attitude of mind begun early in youth and carried through maturity that these desired results are likely to be secured. It is along the path of reverence and obedience that the race has reached the goal of freedom, of self-government, of a higher morality, and a more abundant spiritual life.

Out of a desire that there may be a progress in these directions, with all that such progress means, this great Society continues its efforts. It recognizes that whoever has an evil tongue cannot have a pure mind. We read that "out of the abundance of the heart the mouth speaketh." This is a truth which is worthy of much thought. He who gives license to his tongue only discloses the contents of his own mind. By the excess of his words he proclaims his lack of discipline. By his very violence he shows his weakness. The youth or man who by disregarding this principle thinks he is displaying his determination and resolution and emphasizing his statements is in reality only revealing an intellectual poverty, a deficiency in self-control and self-respect, a want of accurate thinking and of spiritual insight, which cannot come save from a reverence for the truth. There are no human actions which are unimportant, none to which we can be indifferent. All of them lead either towards destruction and death, or towards construction and life.

To my mind, the great strength of your Society lies in its recognition of the necessity of discipline. We live in an impatient age. We demand results, and demand them at once. We find a long and laborious process very irksome, and are constantly seeking for a short cut. But there is no easy method of securing discipline. It is axiomatic that there is no royal road to learning. The effort for discipline must be intensive, and to a considerable degree it must be lifelong. But it is absolutely necessary, if there is to be any self-direction or any self-control. The worst evil that could be inflicted upon the youth of the land would be to leave them without restraint and completely at the mercy of their own uncontrolled inclinations. Under such conditions education would be impossible, and all orderly development intellectually or morally would be hopeless. I do not need to picture the result. We know too well what weakness and depravity follow when the ordinary processes of discipline are neglected. . . .

Our American government was the result of an effort to establish institutions under which the people as a whole should have the largest possible advantages. Class and privilege were outlawed, freedom and opportunity were guaranteed. They undertook to provide conditions under which service would be adequately rewarded, and where the people would own their own property and control their own government. They had no other motive. They were actuated by no other purpose. If we are to maintain what they established, it is important to understand the foundation on which they built, and the claims by which they justified the sovereign rights and royal estate of every American citizen.

They did not deny the existence of authority. They recognized it and undertook to abide by it, and through obedience to it secure their freedom. They made their appeal and rested their cause not merely upon earthly authority, but in the very first paragraph of the Declaration of Independence asserted that they proposed "to assume, among the powers of the earth, the separate and equal station to which the laws of nature and of nature's God entitle them." And as they closed that noble document in which they submitted their claims to the opinions of mankind they again revealed what they believed to be the ultimate source of authority by stating that they were also "appealing to the Supreme Judge of the world for the rectitude of" their "intentions."

When finally our Constitution was adopted, it contained specific provision that the President and members of the Congress and of state legislatures, and all executive and judicial officials, should be qualified for the discharge of their office by oath or affirmation. By the statute law of the United States, and I doubt not by all States, such oaths are administered by a solemn appeal to

God for help in the keeping of their covenants. I scarcely need to refer to the fact that the houses of the Congress, and so far as I know the state legislatures, open their daily sessions with prayer. The foundation of our independence and our Government rests upon our basic religious convictions. Back of the authority of our laws is the authority of the Supreme Judge of the World, to whom we still appeal for their final justification. . . .

Our conceptions of liberty under the law are not narrow and cramped, but broad and tolerant. Our Constitution guarantees civil, political and religious liberty; fully, completely and adequately; and provides that "no religious test shall ever be required as a qualification to any office or public trust under the United States." This is the essence of freedom and toleration solemnly declared in the fundamental law of the land.

These are some of our American standards. These principles, in the province to which they relate, bestow upon the people all there is to bestow. They recognize in the people all that there is to recognize. They are the ultimates. There is no beyond. They are solely for the benefit and advantage of all the people. If any change is made in these principles it will not be by giving more to the people, but by taking from them something of that which they now have. It cannot be progress. It must be reaction. I do not say that we, as citizens, have always held ourselves to a proper observance of these standards towards each other, but we have nevertheless established them and declared our duty to be obedience to them. This is the American ideal of ordered liberty under the law. It calls for rigid discipline. . . .

Without the protection of the law, and the imposition of its authority, equality cannot be maintained, liberty disappears and property vanishes. This is anarchy. The forces of darkness are traveling in that direction. But the spirit of America turns its face towards the light. That spirit I have faith will prevail. America is not going to abandon its principles or desert its ideals. The foundation on which they are built will remain firm. I believe that the principle which your organization represents is their main support. It seems to me perfectly plain that the authority of law, the right to equality, liberty and property, under American institutions, have for their foundation reverence for God. If we could imagine that to be swept away, these institutions of our American government could not long survive. But that reverence will not fail. It will abide. Unnumbered organizations of which your own is one exist for its promotion. In the inevitable longing of the human soul to do right is the secure guarantee of our American institutions. By maintaining a society to promote reverence for the Holy Name you are performing both a pious and a patriotic service. . . .

3

Justice Robert Jackson: Opinion of the Court in *West Virginia Board of Education* v. *Barnette* (1943)

Although the founders had hoped that religion would prove a source of unity for the nation, religion has sometimes proven a point of conflict, especially as America has grown more religiously diverse. This case involves a conflict between legal standards imposed by the community and the religious beliefs of a minority. Here the Supreme Court first manifested an inclination—followed up in some later cases but rejected in others—to shelter religious minorities from the operation of laws contrary to their beliefs. Interestingly, the Court bases its decision not on the "free exercise" clause of the First Amendment but on its protection for freedom of speech.

Appellees, citizens of the United States and of West Virginia, brought suit in the United States District Court for themselves and others similarly situated asking its injunction to restrain enforcement of these laws and regulations against Jehovah's Witnesses. The Witnesses are an unincorporated body teaching that the obligation imposed by law of God is superior to that of laws enacted by temporal government. Their religious beliefs include a literal version of *Exodus*, Chapter 20, verses 4 and 5, which says: "Thou shalt not make unto thee any graven image, or any likeness of anything that is in heaven above, or that is in the earth beneath, or that is in the water under the earth; thou shalt not bow down thyself to them nor serve them." They consider that the flag is an "image" within this command. For this reason they refuse to salute it. Children of this faith have been expelled from school and are threatened with exclusion for no other cause. Officials threaten to send them to reformatories maintained for criminally inclined juveniles. Parents of such children have been prosecuted and are threatened with prosecutions for causing delinquency. . . .

As the present Chief Justice said in dissent in the *Gobitis* case, the State may "require teaching by instruction and study of all in our history and in the structure and organization of our government, including the guaranties of civil liberty which tend to inspire patriotism and love of country." Here, however, we are dealing with a compulsion of students to declare a belief. They are not merely made acquainted with the flag salute so that they may be informed as to what it is or even what it means. The issue here is whether this slow and easily neglected route to aroused loyalties constitutionally may be short-cut by substituting a compulsory salute and slogan. . . .

There is no doubt that, in connection with the pledges, the flag salute is a form of utterance. Symbolism is a primitive but effective way of communicating ideas. The use of an emblem or flag to symbolize some system, idea, institution, or personality, is a short cut from mind to mind. Causes and nations, political parties, lodges and ecclesiastical groups seek to knit the loyalty of their followings to a flag or banner, a color or design. The State announces rank, function, and authority through crowns and maces, uniforms and black robes; the church speaks through the Cross, the Crucifix, the altar and shrine, and clerical raiment. Symbols of State often convey political ideas just as religious symbols come to convey theological ones. Associated with many of these symbols are appropriate gestures of acceptance or respect: a salute, a bowed or bared head, a bended knee. A person gets from a symbol the meaning he puts into it, and what is one man's comfort and inspiration is another's jest and scorn. . . .

It is also to be noted that the compulsory flag salute and pledge requires affirmation of a belief and an attitude of mind. It is not clear whether the regulation contemplates that pupils forego any contrary convictions of their own and become unwilling converts to the prescribed ceremony or whether it will be acceptable if they simulate assent by words without belief and by a gesture barren of meaning. It is now a commonplace that censorship or suppression of expression of opinion is tolerated by our Constitution only when the expression presents a clear and present danger of action of a kind the State is empowered to prevent and punish. It would seem that involuntary affirmation could be commanded only on even more immediate and urgent grounds than silence. But here the power of compulsion is invoked without any allegation that remaining passive during a flag salute ritual creates a clear and present danger that would justify an effort even to muffle expression. To sustain the compulsory flag salute we are required to say that a Bill of Rights which guards the individual's right to speak his own mind, left it open to public authorities to compel him to utter what is not in his mind. . . .

Nor does the issue as we see it turn on one's possession of particular religious views or the sincerity with which they are held. While religion supplies appellees' motive for enduring the discomforts of making the issue in this case, many citizens who do not share these religious views hold such a compulsory rite to infringe constitutional liberty of the individual. It is not necessary to inquire whether non-conformist beliefs will exempt from the duty to salute unless we first find power to make the salute a legal duty.

4

Justice Felix Frankfurter: Dissenting Opinion in *West Virginia Board of Education* v. *Barnette* (1943)

In this dissenting opinion, Justice Frankfurter argues that to strike down a law because it offends some people's religious scruples effectively subordinates the government to religion, contrary to the intention of the First Amendment.

[O]ne can say with assurance . . . that the history out of which grew constitutional provisions for religious equality and the writings of the great exponents of religious freedom—Jefferson, Madison, John Adams, Benjamin Franklin— are totally wanting in justification for a claim by dissidents of exceptional immunity from civic measures of general applicability, measures not in fact disguised assaults upon such dissident views. The great leaders of the American Revolution were determined to remove political support from every religious establishment. They put on an equality the different religious sects— Episcopalians, Presbyterians, Catholics, Baptists, Methodists, Quakers, Huguenots—which, as dissenters, had been under the heel of the various orthodoxics that prevailed in different colonies. So far as the state was con- cerned, there was to be neither orthodoxy nor heterodoxy. And so Jefferson and those who followed him wrote guaranties of religious freedom into our constitutions. Religious minorities as well as religious majorities were to be equal in the eyes of the political state. But Jefferson and the others also knew that minorities may disrupt society. It never would have occurred to them to write into the Constitution the subordination of the general civil authority of the state to sectarian scruples.

The constitutional protection of religious freedom terminated disabilities, it did not create new privileges. It gave religious equality, not civil immunity. Its essence is freedom from conformity to religious dogma, not freedom from conformity to law because of religious dogma. . . . Otherwise each individual could set up his own censor against obedience to laws conscientiously deemed for the public good by those whose business it is to make laws.

The prohibition against any religious establishment by the government placed denominations on an equal footing—it assured freedom from support by the government to any mode of worship and the freedom of individuals to support any mode of worship. Any person may therefore believe or disbelieve what he pleases. He may practice what he will in his own house of worship or publicly within the limits of public order. But the lawmaking authority is not circumscribed by the variety of religious beliefs, otherwise the constitutional guaranty would be not a protection of the free exercise of religion but a denial of the exercise of legislation.

The essence of the religious freedom guaranteed by our Constitution is therefore this: no religion shall either receive the state's support or incur its hostility. Religion is outside the sphere of political government. This does not mean that all matters on which religious organizations or beliefs may pro- nounce are outside the sphere of government. Were this so, instead of the sep- aration of church and state, there would be the subordination of the state on any matter deemed within the sovereignty of the religious conscience. Much that is the concern of temporal authority affects the spiritual interests of men. But it is not enough to strike down a non-discriminatory law that it may hurt or offend some dissident view. It would be too easy to cite numerous prohibi- tions and injunctions to which laws run counter if the variant interpretations of the Bible were made the tests of obedience to law. The validity of secular laws cannot be measured by their conformity to religious doctrines. It is only in a theocratic state that ecclesiastical doctrines measure legal right or wrong. . . .

5

Justice Hugo Black: Opinion of the Court in *Everson* v. *Board of Education* (1947)

In this case the Supreme Court considered a challenge to a New Jersey law providing for the use of public funds to reimburse the transportation expenses incurred by parents who sent their children to Catholic schools. The case marks the beginning of the modern Court's insistence that the First Amendment's "establishment" clause should be understood in light of Jefferson's thought and that it accordingly requires a "strict separation" of church and state. The Court upheld the New Jersey law, but its reasoning was used in many subsequent cases to strike down aid to religious schools and government-sponsored affirmations of religious belief.

The New Jersey statute is challenged as a "law respecting an establishment of religion." The First Amendment, as made applicable to the states by the Fourteenth, commands that a state "shall make no law respecting an establishment of religion, or prohibiting the free exercise thereof." These words of the First Amendment reflected in the minds of early Americans a vivid mental picture of conditions and practices which they fervently wished to stamp out in order to preserve liberty for themselves and for their posterity. Doubtless their goal has not been entirely reached; but so far has the Nation moved toward it that the expression "law respecting an establishment of religion," probably does not so vividly remind present-day Americans of the evils, fears, and political problems that caused that expression to be written into our Bill of Rights. Whether this New Jersey law is one respecting the "establishment of religion" requires an understanding of the meaning of that language, particularly with respect to the imposition of taxes. Once again, therefore, it is not inappropriate briefly to review the background and environment of the period in which that constitutional language was fashioned and adopted.

A large proportion of the early settlers of this country came here from Europe to escape the bondage of laws which compelled them to support and attend government favored churches. The centuries immediately before and contemporaneous with the colonization of America had been filled with turmoil, civil strife, and persecutions, generated in large part by established sects determined to maintain their absolute political and religious supremacy. With the power of government supporting them, at various times and places, Catholics had persecuted Protestants, Protestants had persecuted Catholics, Protestant sects had persecuted other Protestant sects, Catholics of one shade of belief had persecuted Catholics of another shade of belief, and all of these had from time to time persecuted Jews. . . .

These practices of the old world were transplanted to and began to thrive in the soil of the new America. The very charters granted by the English Crown to the individuals and companies designated to make the laws which would control the destinies of the colonials authorized these individuals and companies to erect religious establishments which all, whether believers or non-believers, would be required to support and attend. An exercise of this authority was accompanied by a repetition of many of the old world practices and persecutions. Catholics found themselves hounded and proscribed because of their faith; Quakers who followed their conscience went to jail; Baptists were peculiarly obnoxious to certain dominant Protestant sects; men and women of varied faiths who happened to be in a minority in a particular locality were persecuted because they steadfastly persisted in worshipping God only as their own consciences dictated. And all of these dissenters were compelled to pay tithes and taxes to support government-sponsored churches whose ministers preached inflammatory sermons designed to strengthen and consolidate the established faith by generating a burning hatred against dissenters. These practices became so commonplace as to shock the freedom-loving colonials into a feeling of abhorrence. The imposition of taxes to pay ministers' salaries and to build and maintain churches and church property aroused their indignation. It was these feelings which found expression in the First Amendment. No one locality and no one group throughout the Colonies can rightly be given entire credit for having aroused the sentiment that culminated in adoption of the Bill of Rights' provisions embracing religious liberty. But Virginia, where the established church had achieved a dominant influence in political affairs and where many excesses attracted wide public attention, provided a great stimulus and able leadership for the movement. The people there, as elsewhere, reached the conviction that individual religious liberty could be achieved best under a government which was stripped of all power to tax, to support, or otherwise to assist any or all religions, or to interfere with the beliefs of any religious individual or group.

The movement toward this end reached its dramatic climax in Virginia in 1785–86 when the Virginia legislative body was about to renew Virginia's tax levy for the support of the established church. Thomas Jefferson and James Madison led the fight against this tax. . . . When the proposal came up for consideration at that session, it not only died in committee, but the Assembly enacted the famous "Virginia Bill for Religious Liberty" originally written by Thomas Jefferson. . . .

[T]he statute . . . enacted "That no man shall be compelled to frequent or support any religious worship, place, or ministry whatsoever, nor shall be enforced, restrained, molested, or burdened, in his body or goods, nor shall otherwise suffer on account of his religious opinions or belief. . . ."

This Court has previously recognized that the provisions of the First Amendment, in the drafting and adoption of which Madison and Jefferson played such leading roles, had the same objective and were intended to provide the same protection against governmental intrusion on religious liberty as the Virginia statute. . . .

The "establishment of religion" clause of the First Amendment means at least this: Neither a state nor the Federal Government can set up a church. Neither can pass laws which aid one religion, aid all religions, or prefer one religion over another. Neither can force nor influence a person to go to or to remain away from church against his will or force him to profess a belief or disbelief in any religion. No person can be punished for entertaining or professing religious beliefs or disbeliefs, for church attendance or non-attendance. No tax in any amount, large or small, can be levied to support any religious activities or institutions, whatever they may be called, or whatever from they may adopt to teach or practice religion. Neither a state nor the Federal Government can, openly or secretly, participate in the affairs of any religious organizations or groups and vice versa. In the words of Jefferson, the clause against establishment of religion by law was intended to erect "a wall of separation between Church and State."

6

President Eisenhower: Statement upon Signing a Bill to Include the Words "Under God" in the Pledge to the Flag (1954)

Even as the Supreme Court was beginning to insist that the government be neutral in regard to religion, the nation's elected leaders wanted to assert the importance of religion to America's political identity. Seeking to distinguish American beliefs from the official atheism of our Cold War rival, the Soviet Union, Congress passed a law amending the Pledge of Allegiance to refer to America as one nation "under God." This language, and its use in public schools, was later challenged in a controversial case that came before the Supreme Court in 2004. See readings 11 and 12 in this chapter.

From this day forward, the millions of our school children will daily proclaim in every city and town, every village and rural school house, the dedication of our nation and our people to the Almighty. To anyone who truly loves America, nothing could be more inspiring than to contemplate this rededication of our youth, on each school morning, to our country's true meaning.

Especially is this meaningful as we regard today's world. Over the globe, mankind has been cruelly torn by violence and brutality and, by the millions, deadened in mind and soul by a materialistic philosophy of life. Man everywhere is appalled by the prospect of atomic war. In this somber setting, this law and its effects today have profound meaning. In this way we are reaffirming the transcendence of religious faith in America's heritage and future; in this way we shall constantly strengthen those spiritual weapons which forever will be our country's most powerful resource, in peace or war.

7

Justice Tom Clark: Opinion of the Court in *School District of Abington Township* v. *Schempp* (1963)

Here the Supreme Court, building on Everson and subsequent cases, holds that the "establishment" clause of the First Amendment requires that government be neutral in regard to religion. It therefore strikes down devotional Bible-reading in public schools, just as it had invalidated organized prayer in public schools a year earlier.

The wholesome "neutrality" of which this Court's cases speak . . . stems from a recognition of the teachings of history that powerful sects or groups might bring about a fusion of governmental and religious functions or a concert or dependency of one upon the other to the end that official support of the State or Federal Government would be placed behind the tenets of one or of all orthodoxies. This the Establishment Clause prohibits. And a further reason for neutrality is found in the Free Exercise Clause, which recognizes the value of religious training, teaching and observance and, more particularly, the right of every person to freely choose his own course with reference thereto, free of any compulsion from the state. This the Free Exercise Clause guarantees. Thus, as we have seen, the two clauses may overlap. As we have indicated, the Establishment Clause has been directly considered by this Court eight times in the past score of years and, with only one Justice dissenting on the point, it has consistently held that the clause withdrew all legislative power respecting religious belief or the expression thereof. The test may be stated as follows: what are the purpose and the primary effect of the enactment? If either is the advancement or inhibition of religion then the enactment exceeds the scope of legislative power as circumscribed by the Constitution. That is to say that to withstand the strictures of the Establishment Clause there must be a secular legislative purpose and a primary effect that neither advances nor inhibits religion. The Free Exercise Clause, likewise considered many times here, withdraws from legislative power, state and federal, the exertion of any restraint on the free exercise of religion. Its purpose is to secure religious liberty in the individual by prohibiting any invasions thereof by civil authority. Hence it is necessary in a free exercise case for one to show the coercive effect of the enactment as it operates against him in the practice of his religion. The distinction between the two clauses is apparent—a violation of the Free Exercise Clause is predicated on coercion while the Establishment Clause violation need not be so attended.

Applying the Establishment Clause principles to the cases at bar we find that the States are requiring the selection and reading at the opening of the school day of verses from the Holy Bible and the recitation of the Lord's Prayer by the students in unison. These exercises are prescribed as part of the curricular activities of students who are required by law to attend school. They are held in the school buildings under the supervision and with the participation of teachers employed in those schools. . . . The trial court . . . has found that such an opening exercise is a religious ceremony and was intended by the State to be so. We agree with the trial court's finding as to the religious character of the exercises. Given that finding, the exercises and the law requiring them are in violation of the Establishment Clause. . . .

The conclusion follows that in both cases the laws require religious exercises and such exercises are being conducted in direct violation of the rights of the appellees and petitioners. Nor are these required exercises mitigated by the fact that individual students may absent themselves upon parental request, for that fact furnishes no defense to a claim of unconstitutionality under the Establishment Clause. Further, it is no defense to urge that the religious practices here may be relatively minor encroachments on the First Amendment. The breach of neutrality that is today a trickling stream may all too soon become a raging torrent and, in the words of Madison, "it is proper to take alarm at the first experiment on our liberties." It is insisted that unless these religious exercises are permitted a "religion of secularism" is established in the schools. We agree of course that the State may not establish a "religion of secularism" in the sense of affirmatively opposing or showing hostility to religion, thus "preferring those who believe in no religion over those who do believe." We do not agree, however, that this decision in any sense has that effect. In addition, it might well be said that one's education is not complete without a study of comparative religion or the history of religion and its relationship to the advancement of civilization. It certainly may be said that the Bible is worthy of study for its literary and historic qualities. Nothing we have said here indicates that such study of the Bible or of religion, when presented objectively as part of a secular program of education, may not be effected consistently with the First Amendment. But the exercises here do not fall into those categories. They are religious exercises, required by the States in violation of the command of the First Amendment that the Government maintain strict neutrality, neither aiding nor opposing religion. . . .

The place of religion in our society is an exalted one, achieved through a long tradition of reliance on the home, the church and the inviolable citadel of the individual heart and mind. We have come to recognize through bitter experience that it is not within the power of government to invade that citadel, whether its purpose or effect be to aid or oppose, to advance or retard. In the relationship between man and religion, the State is firmly committed to a position of neutrality.

8

Justice Potter Stewart: Dissent in *School District of Abington Township* v. *Schempp* (1963)

The Supreme Court's interpretation of the Constitution as requiring a "strict separa-tion" of church and state, and in particular its hostility to religious exercises in public schools, has proven controversial, both on the Court and among Americans generally. Here, in his dissent in the Schempp *case, Justice Stewart contends that the Court's reading of the "establishment" clause may actually impair the free exercise of religion also guaranteed by the First Amendment.*

The First Amendment declares that "Congress shall make no law respecting an establishment of religion, or prohibiting the free exercise thereof. . . ." It is, I think, a fallacious oversimplification to regard these two provisions as estab-lishing a single constitutional standard of "separation of church and state," which can be mechanically applied in every case to delineate the required boundaries between government and religion. We err in the first place if we do not recognize, as a matter of history and as a matter of the imperatives of our free society, that religion and government must necessarily interact in countless ways. Secondly, the fact is that while in many contexts the Establishment Clause and the Free Exercise Clause fully complement each other, there are areas in which a doctrinaire reading of the Establishment Clause leads to irreconcilable conflict with the Free Exercise Clause.

A single obvious example should suffice to make the point. Spending fed-eral funds to employ chaplains for the armed forces might be said to violate the Establishment Clause. Yet a lonely soldier stationed at some faraway out-post could surely complain that a government which did not provide him the opportunity for pastoral guidance was affirmatively prohibiting the free exer-cise of his religion. And such examples could readily be multiplied. The short of the matter is simply that the two relevant clauses of the First Amendment cannot accurately be reflected in a sterile metaphor which by its very nature may distort rather than illumine the problems involved in a particular case. . . .

Unlike other First Amendment guarantees, there is an inherent limitation upon the applicability of the Establishment Clause's ban on state support to religion. That limitation was succinctly put in *Everson* v. *Board of Education*: "State power is no more to be used so as to handicap religions than it is to favor them." And in a later case, this Court recognized that the limitation was one which was itself compelled by the free exercise guarantee. "To hold that a state cannot consistently with the First and Fourteenth Amendments utilize its public school system to aid any or all religious faiths or sects in the dissemina-tion of their doctrines and ideals does not . . . manifest a governmental hostil-ity to religion or religious teachings. A manifestation of such hostility would be at war with our national tradition as embodied in the First Amendment's guaranty of the free exercise of religion." *McCollum* v. *Board of Education*. That the central value embodied in the First Amendment—and, more particularly, in the guarantee of "liberty" contained in the Fourteenth—is the safeguarding of an individual's right to free exercise of his religion has been consistently recognized. . . .

It is this concept of constitutional protection embodied in our decisions which makes the cases before us such difficult ones for me. For there is involved in these cases a substantial free exercise claim on the part of those who affirmatively desire to have their children's school day open with the reading of passages from the Bible.

It has become accepted that the decision in *Pierce* v. *Society of Sisters,* upholding the right of parents to send their children to nonpublic schools, was ultimately based upon the recognition of the validity of the free exercise claim involved in that situation. It might be argued here that parents who wanted their children to be exposed to religious influences in school could, under *Pierce,* send their children to private or parochial schools. But the consideration which renders this contention too facile to be determinative has already been recognized by the Court: "Freedom of speech, freedom of the press, freedom of religion are available to all, not merely to those who can pay their own way." *Murdock* v. *Pennsylvania.*

It might also be argued that parents who want their children exposed to religious influences can adequately fulfill that wish off school property and outside school time. With all its surface persuasiveness, however, this argument seriously misconceives the basic constitutional justification for permitting the exercises at issue in these cases. For a compulsory state educational system so structures a child's life that if religious exercises are held to be an impermissible activity in schools, religion is placed at an artificial and state-created disadvantage. Viewed in this light, permission of such exercises for those who want them is necessary if the schools are truly to be neutral in the matter of religion. And a refusal to permit religious exercises thus is seen, not as the realization of state neutrality, but rather as the establishment of a religion of secularism, or at the least, as government support of the beliefs of those who think that religious exercises should be conducted only in private. . . .

The governmental neutrality which the First and Fourteenth Amendments require in the cases before us, in other words, is the extension of evenhanded treatment to all who believe, doubt, or disbelieve—a refusal on the part of the State to weight the scales of private choice. In these cases, therefore, what is involved is not state action based on impermissible categories, but rather an attempt by the State to accommodate those differences which the existence in our society of a variety of religious beliefs makes inevitable. The Constitution requires that such efforts be struck down only if they are proven to entail the use of the secular authority of government to coerce a preference among such beliefs. . . .

What our Constitution indispensably protects is the freedom of each of us, be he Jew or Agnostic, Christian or Atheist, Buddhist or Freethinker, to believe or disbelieve, to worship or not worship, to pray or keep silent, according to his own conscience, uncoerced and unrestrained by government. It is conceivable that these school boards, or even all school boards, might eventually find it impossible to administer a system of religious exercises during school hours in such a way as to meet this constitutional standard—in such a way as completely to free from any kind of official coercion those who do not affirmatively want to participate. But I think we must not assume that school boards so lack the qualities of inventiveness and good will as to make impossible the achievement of that goal.

9

President Ronald Reagan: Remarks at an Ecumenical Prayer Breakfast in Dallas, Texas (1984)

Here President Reagan criticizes not only the Supreme Court's expulsion of religion from public schools, but also what he perceives as a growing intolerance of religion in America's public life. Like his predecessor Calvin Coolidge, President Reagan affirms both the importance of religious liberty as well as the need to encourage religion as the moral support necessary for a decent political order.

I believe that faith and religion play a critical role in the political life of our nation—and always has—and that the church—and by that I mean all churches, all denominations—has had a strong influence on the state. And this has worked to our benefit as a nation.

Those who created our country—the Founding Fathers and Mothers—understood that there is a divine order which transcends the human order. They saw the state, in fact, as a form of moral order and felt that the bedrock of moral order is religion.

The *Mayflower Compact* began with the words, "In the name of God, amen." The *Declaration of Independence* appeals to "Nature's God" and the "Creator" and "the Supreme Judge of the world." Congress was given a chaplain, and the oaths of office are oaths before God.

James Madison in the *Federalist Papers* admitted that in the creation of our Republic he perceived the hand of the Almighty. John Jay, the first Chief Justice of the Supreme Court, warned that we must never forget the God from whom our blessings flowed.

George Washington referred to religion's profound and unsurpassed place in the heart of our nation quite directly in his Farewell Address in 1796. . . .

I believe that George Washington knew the City of Man cannot survive without the City of God, that the Visible City will perish without the Invisible City.

Religion played not only a strong role in our national life; it played a positive role. The abolitionist movement was at heart a moral and religious movement; so was the modern civil rights struggle. And throughout this time, the state was tolerant of religious belief, expression, and practice. Society, too, was tolerant.

But in the 1960's this began to change. We began to make great steps toward secularizing our nation and removing religion from its honored place.

In 1962 the Supreme Court in the New York prayer case banned the compulsory saying of prayers. In 1963 the Court banned the reading of the Bible in our public schools. From that point on, the courts pushed the meaning of the ruling ever outward, so that now our children are not allowed voluntary prayer. We even had to pass a law ... in the Congress just a few weeks ago to allow student prayer groups the same access to schoolrooms after classes that a young Marxist society, for example, would already enjoy with no opposition.

The 1962 decision opened the way to a flood of similar suits. Once religion had been made vulnerable, a series of assaults were made in one court after another, on one issue after another. Cases were started to argue against tax-exempt status for churches. Suits were brought to abolish the words "under God" from the Pledge of Allegiance and to remove "In God We Trust" from public documents and from our currency.

Today there are those who are fighting to make sure voluntary prayer is not returned to the classrooms. And the frustrating thing for the great majority of Americans who support and understand the special importance of religion in the national life—the frustrating thing is that those who are attacking religion claim they are doing it in the name of tolerance, freedom, and open-mindedness. Question: Isn't the real truth that they are intolerant of religion? They refuse to tolerate its importance in our lives.

If all the children of our country studied together all of the many religions in our country, wouldn't they learn greater tolerance of each other's beliefs? If children prayed together, would they not understand what they have in common, and would this not, indeed, bring them closer, and is this not to be desired? So, I submit to you that those who claim to be fighting for tolerance on this issue may not be tolerant at all.

When John Kennedy was running for President in 1960, he said that his church would not dictate his Presidency any more than he would speak for his church. Just so, and proper. But John Kennedy was speaking in an America in which the role of religion—and by that I mean the role of all churches—was secure. Abortion was not a political issue. Prayer was not a political issue. The right of church schools to operate was not a political issue. And it was broadly acknowledged that religious leaders had a right and a duty to speak out on the issues of the day. They held a place of respect, and a politician who spoke to or of them with a lack of respect would not long survive in the political arena.

It was acknowledged then that religion held a special place, occupied a special territory in the hearts of the citizenry. The climate has changed greatly since then. And since it has, it logically follows that religion needs defenders against those who care only for the interests of the state.

There are, these days, many questions on which religious leaders are obliged to offer their moral and theological guidance, and such guidance is a good and necessary thing. To know how a church and its members feel on a public issue expands the parameters of debate. It does not narrow the debate; it expands it.

The truth is, politics and morality are inseparable. And as morality's foundation is religion, religion and politics are necessarily related. We need religion as a guide. We need it because we are imperfect, and our government needs the church, because only those humble enough to admit they're sinners can bring to democracy the tolerance it requires in order to survive.

A state is nothing more than a reflection of its citizens; the more decent the citizens, the more decent the state. If you practice a religion, whether you're Catholic, Protestant, Jewish, or guided by some other faith, then your private life will be influenced by a sense of moral obligation, and so, too, will your public life. One affects the other. The churches of America do not exist by the grace of the state; the churches of America are not mere citizens of the state. The churches of America exist apart; they have their own vantage point, their own authority. Religion is its own realm; it makes its own claims.

We establish no religion in this country, nor will we ever. We command no worship. We mandate no belief. But we poison our society when we remove its theological underpinnings. We court corruption when we leave it bereft of belief. All are free to believe or not believe; all are free to practice a faith or not. But those who believe must be free to speak of and act on their belief, to apply moral teaching to public questions.

I submit to you that the tolerant society is open to and encouraging of all religions. And this does not weaken us; it strengthens us, it makes us strong. You know, if we look back through history to all those great civilizations, those great nations that rose up to even world dominance and then deteriorated, declined, and fell, we find they all had one thing in common. One of the significant forerunners of their fall was their turning away from their God or gods.

Without God, there is no virtue, because there's no prompting of the conscience. Without God, we're mired in the material, that flat world that tells us only what the senses perceive. Without God, there is a coarsening of the society. And without God, democracy will not and cannot long endure. If we ever forget that we're one nation under God, then we will be a nation gone under.

10

Justice William Rehnquist: Dissenting Opinion in *Wallace* v. *Jaffree* (1985)

In this case the Supreme Court struck down an Alabama law providing for observance of a moment of silence in public schools. The Court held that the law was intended to allow for prayer and therefore had, in violation of the "establishment" clause, a religious purpose. In the following dissent, Justice Rehnquist, who was appointed Chief Justice the following year by President Reagan, contends that the framers of the First Amendment never intended it to erect a "wall of separation" between church and state and that it allows for some government support for religion.

Thirty-eight years ago this Court, in *Everson v. Board of Education* (1947), summarized its exegesis of Establishment Clause doctrine thus:"In the words of Jefferson, the clause against establishment of religion by law was intended to erect 'a wall of separation between church and State.'" . . .

It is impossible to build sound constitutional doctrine upon a mistaken understanding of constitutional history, but unfortunately the Establishment Clause has been expressly freighted with Jefferson's misleading metaphor for nearly forty years. Thomas Jefferson was of course in France at the time the constitutional Amendments known as the Bill of Rights were passed by Congress and ratified by the States. His letter to the Danbury Baptist Association was a short note of courtesy, written 14 years after the Amendments were passed by Congress. He would seem to any detached observer as a less than ideal source of contemporary history as to the meaning of the Religion Clauses of the First Amendment.

Jefferson's fellow Virginian, James Madison, with whom he was joined in the battle for the enactment of the Virginia Statute of Religious Liberty of 1786, did play as large a part as anyone in the drafting of the Bill of Rights. He had two advantages over Jefferson in this regard: he was present in the United States, and he was a leading Member of the First Congress. But when we turn to the record of the proceedings in the First Congress leading up to the adoption of the Establishment Clause of the Constitution, including Madison's significant contributions thereto, we see a far different picture of its purpose than the highly simplified "wall of separation between church and State." . . .

On the basis of the record of these proceedings in the House of Representatives, James Madison was undoubtedly the most important architect among the Members of the House of the Amendments which became the Bill of Rights, but it was James Madison speaking as an advocate of sensible legislative compromise, not as an advocate of incorporating the Virginia Statute of Religious Liberty into the United States Constitution. During the ratification debate in the Virginia Convention, Madison had actually opposed the idea of any Bill of Rights. His sponsorship of the Amendments in the House was obviously not that of a zealous believer in the necessity of the Religion Clauses, but of one who felt it might do some good, could do no harm, and would satisfy those who had ratified the Constitution on the condition that Congress propose a Bill of Rights. His original language "nor shall any national religion be established" obviously does not conform to the "wall of separation" between church and State idea which latter-day commentators have ascribed to him. His explanation on the floor of the meaning of his language—"that Congress should not establish a religion, and enforce the legal observation of it by law"— is of the same ilk. When he replied to Huntington in the debate over the proposal which came from the Select Committee of the House, he urged that the language "no religion shall be established by law" should be amended by inserting the word "national" in front of the word "religion."

It seems indisputable from these glimpses of Madison's thinking, as reflected by actions on the floor of the House in 1789, that he saw the Amendment as designed to prohibit the establishment of a national religion, and perhaps to prevent discrimination among sects. He did not see it as requiring neutrality on the part of government between religion and irreligion. Thus the Court's opinion in *Everson*—while correct in bracketing Madison and Jefferson together in their exertions in their home State leading to the enactment of the Virginia Statute of Religious Liberty—is totally incorrect in suggesting that Madison carried these views onto the floor of the United States House of Representatives when he proposed the language which would ultimately become the Bill of Rights. . . .

None of the other Members of Congress who spoke during the August 15th debate expressed the slightest indication that they thought the language before them from the Select Committee, or the evil to be aimed at, would require that the Government be absolutely neutral as between religion and irreligion. The evil to be aimed at, so far as those who spoke were concerned, appears to have been the establishment of a national church, and perhaps the preference of one religious sect over another; but it was definitely not concerned about whether the Government might aid all religions evenhandedly. . . .

The actions of the First Congress, which reenacted the Northwest Ordinance for the governance of the Northwest Territory in 1789, confirm the view that Congress did not mean that the Government should be neutral between religion and irreligion. The House of Representatives took up the Northwest Ordinance on the same day as Madison introduced his proposed amendments which became the Bill of Rights; while at that time the Federal Government was of course not bound by draft amendments to the Constitution which had not yet been proposed by Congress, to say nothing of ratified by the States, it seems highly unlikely that the House of Representatives would simultaneously consider proposed amendments to the Constitution and enact an important piece of territorial legislation which conflicted with the intent of those proposals. The Northwest Ordinance . . . provided that "[r]eligion, morality, and knowledge, being necessary to good government and the happiness of mankind, schools and the means of education shall forever be encouraged." Land grants for schools in the Northwest Territory were not limited to public schools. It was not until 1845 that Congress limited land grants in the new States and Territories to nonsectarian schools.

On the day after the House of Representatives voted to adopt the form of the First Amendment Religion Clauses which was ultimately proposed and ratified, Representative Elias Boudinot proposed a resolution asking President George Washington to issue a Thanksgiving Day Proclamation. Boudinot said he "could not think of letting the session pass over without offering an opportunity to all the citizens of the United States of joining with one voice, in returning to Almighty God their sincere thanks for the many blessings he had poured down upon them." . . .

Boudinot's resolution was carried in the affirmative on September 25, 1789. . . .

As the United States moved from the 18th into the 19th century, Congress appropriated time and again public moneys in support of sectarian Indian education carried on by religious organizations. Typical of these was Jefferson's treaty with the Kaskaskia Indians, which provided annual cash support for the Tribe's Roman Catholic priest and church. It was not until 1897, when aid to sectarian education for Indians had reached $500,000 annually, that Congress decided thereafter to cease appropriating money for education in sectarian schools. This history shows the fallacy of the notion found in *Everson* that "no tax in any amount" may be levied for religious activities in any form. . . .

It would seem from this evidence that the Establishment Clause of the First Amendment had acquired a well-accepted meaning: it forbade establishment of a national religion, and forbade preference among religious sects or denominations. . . . The Establishment Clause did not require government neutrality between religion and irreligion nor did it prohibit the Federal Government from providing nondiscriminatory aid to religion. There is simply no historical foundation for the proposition that the Framers intended to build the "wall of separation" that was constitutionalized in *Everson*.

11

Judge Alfred Goodwin: Opinion for the United States Court of Appeals for the Ninth Circuit in *Newdow* v. *United States Congress* (2002)

In this case a federal appeals court ruled that Congress had violated the Constitution by adding the words "under God" to the Pledge of Allegiance. It further held that a California school district's policy of having a daily recitation of the Pledge coerced students into accepting the Pledge's monotheistic message, even though students were free not to take part in the Pledge. The case caused considerable public controversy and eventually came before the Supreme Court under a slightly different name. See reading 12 in this chapter.

The Establishment Clause of the First Amendment states that "Congress shall make no law respecting an establishment of religion," a provision that "the Fourteenth Amendment makes applicable with full force to the States and their school districts." *Lee v. Weisman* (1992). . . .

The Court formulated the "coercion test" when it held unconstitutional the practice of including invocations and benedictions in the form of "nonsectarian" prayers at public school graduation ceremonies. . . . "[T]he Court in *Lee* . . . relied on the principle that "at a minimum, the Constitution guarantees that government may not coerce anyone to support or participate in religion or its exercise, or otherwise to act in a way which establishes a state religion or religious faith, or tends to do so." The Court first examined the degree of school involvement in the prayer, and found that "the graduation prayers bore the imprint of the State and thus put school-age children who objected in an untenable position." The next issue the Court considered was "the position of the students, both those who desired the prayer and she who did not." Noting that "there are heightened concerns with protecting freedom of conscience from subtle coercive pressure in the elementary and secondary public schools," the Court held that the school district's supervision and control of the graduation ceremony put impermissible pressure on students to participate in, or at least show respect during, the prayer. The Court concluded that primary and secondary school children may not be placed in the dilemma of either participating in a religious ceremony or protesting. . . .

In the context of the Pledge, the statement that the United States is a nation "under God" is an endorsement of religion. It is a profession of a religious belief, namely, a belief in monotheism. The recitation that ours is a nation "under God" is not a mere acknowledgment that many Americans believe in a deity. Nor is it merely descriptive of the undeniable historical significance of religion in the founding of the Republic. Rather, the phrase "one nation under God" in the context of the Pledge is normative. To recite the Pledge is not to describe the United States; instead, it is to swear allegiance to the values for which the flag stands: unity, indivisibility, liberty, justice, and— since 1954—monotheism. The text of the official Pledge, codified in federal law, impermissibly takes a position with respect to the purely religious question of the existence and identity of God. A profession that we are a nation "under God" is identical, for Establishment Clause purposes, to a profession that we are a nation "under Jesus," a nation "under Vishnu," a nation "under Zeus," or a nation "under no god," because none of these professions can be neutral with respect to religion. . . . Furthermore, the school district's practice of teacher-led recitation of the Pledge aims to inculcate in students a respect for the ideals set forth in the Pledge, and thus amounts to state endorsement of these ideals. Although students cannot be forced to participate in recitation of the Pledge, the school district is nonetheless conveying a message of state endorsement of a religious belief when it requires public school teachers to recite, and lead the recitation of, the current form of the Pledge. . . .

Just as in *Lee*, the policy and the Act place students in the untenable position of choosing between participating in an exercise with religious content or protesting. As the Court observed with respect to the graduation prayer in that case: "What to most believers may seem nothing more than a reasonable request that the nonbeliever respect their religious practices, in a school context may appear to the nonbeliever or dissenter to be an attempt to employ the machinery of the State to enforce a religious orthodoxy." Although the defendants argue that the religious content of "one nation under God" is minimal, to an atheist or a believer in certain non-Judeo-Christian religions or philosophies, it may reasonably appear to be an attempt to enforce a "religious orthodoxy" of monotheism, and is therefore impermissible. The coercive effect of this policy is particularly pronounced in the school setting given the age and impressionability of schoolchildren, and their understanding that they are required to adhere to the norms set by their school, their teacher and their fellow students. Furthermore, under *Lee*, the fact that students are not required to participate [does not make the practice noncoercive] . . . because, even without a recitation requirement for each child, the mere fact that a pupil is required to listen every day to the statement "one nation under God" has a coercive effect. The coercive effect of the Act is apparent from its context and legislative history, which indicate that the Act was designed to result in the daily recitation of the words "under God" in school classrooms. President Eisenhower, during the Act's signing ceremony, stated: "From this day forward, the millions of our school children will daily proclaim in every city and town, every village and rural schoolhouse, the dedication of our Nation and our people to the Almighty." Therefore, the policy and the Act fail the coercion test. . . .

The Court has unambiguously concluded that the individual freedom of conscience protected by the First Amendment embraces the right to select any religious faith or none at all. This conclusion derives support not only from the interest in respecting the individual's freedom of conscience, but also from the conviction that religious beliefs worthy of respect are the product of a free and voluntary choice by the faithful, and from recognition of the fact that the political interest in forestalling intolerance extends beyond intolerance among Christian sects—or even intolerance among "religions"—to encompass intolerance of the disbeliever and the uncertain.

12

Chief Justice William Rehnquist: Concurring Opinion in *Elk Grove Unified School District* v. *Newdow* (2004)

The Supreme Court agreed to hear the Newdow case, but in the end it refused to decide on the merits of the constitutional question. Instead, the Court ruled that Newdow lacked standing to sue on behalf of his daughter, who attended the public school in which the Pledge was recited, because her mother, from whom Newdow was divorced, had primary custody. Chief Justice Rehnquist's concurring opinion is included here because it provides a rejoinder to Judge Goodwin's opinion for the Ninth Circuit Court of Appeals (see previous reading). The Chief Justice contends that the Pledge is not a violation of the "establishment" clause but part of a long tradition of ceremonial recognitions of the role of religion in America's history.

The phrase "under God" in the Pledge seems, as a historical matter, to sum up the attitude of the Nation's leaders, and to manifest itself in many of our public observances. Examples of patriotic invocations of God and official acknowledgments of religion's role in our Nation's history abound. . . .

[A]fter encouragement from Congress, Washington issued his first Thanksgiving proclamation, which began: "Whereas it is the duty of all Nations to acknowledge the providence of Almighty God, to obey His will, to be grateful for his benefits, and humbly to implore his protection and favor—and whereas both Houses of Congress have by their joint Committee requested me 'to recommend to the People of the United States a day of public thanksgiving and prayer to be observed by acknowledging with grateful hearts the many signal favors of Almighty God especially by affording them an opportunity peaceably to establish a form of government for their safety and happiness.'"

Almost all succeeding Presidents have issued similar Thanksgiving proclamations.

Later Presidents, at critical times in the Nation's history, have likewise invoked the name of God. Abraham Lincoln, concluding his masterful Gettysburg Address in 1863, used the very phrase "under God." . . .

Woodrow Wilson appeared before Congress in April 1917, to request a declaration of war against Germany. He finished with these words: "But the right is more precious than peace, and we shall fight for the things which we have always carried nearest our hearts—for democracy, for the right of those who submit to authority to have a voice in their own Governments, for the rights and liberties of small nations, for a universal dominion of right for such a concert of free peoples as shall bring peace and safety to all nations and make the world itself at last free. To such a task we can dedicate our lives and our fortunes, everything that we are and everything that we have, with the pride of those who know that the day has come when America is privileged to spend her blood and her might for the principles that gave her birth and happiness and the peace which she has treasured. God helping her, she can do no other."

President Franklin Delano Roosevelt, taking the office of the Presidency in the depths of the Great Depression, concluded his first inaugural address with these words: "In this dedication of a nation, we humbly ask the blessing of God. May He protect each and every one of us! May He guide me in the days to come!" . . .

The motto "In God We Trust" first appeared on the country's coins during the Civil War. Secretary of the Treasury Salmon P. Chase, acting under the authority of an Act of Congress passed in 1864, prescribed that the motto should appear on the two cent coin. The motto was placed on more and more denominations, and since 1938 all United States coins bear the motto. Paper currency followed suit at a slower pace; Federal Reserve notes were so inscribed during the decade of the 1960's. Meanwhile, in 1956, Congress declared that the motto of the United States would be "In God We Trust."

Our Court Marshal's opening proclamation concludes with the words "God save the United States and this honorable Court." The language goes back at least as far as 1827.

All of these events strongly suggest that our national culture allows public recognition of our Nation's religious history and character. In the words of the House Report that accompanied the insertion of the phrase "under God" in the Pledge: "From the time of our earliest history our peoples and our institutions have reflected the traditional concept that our Nation was founded on a fundamental belief in God." . . .

As pointed out by the Court, California law requires public elementary schools to "conduc[t] . . . appropriate patriotic exercises" at the beginning of the schooldays, and notes that the "giving of the Pledge of Allegiance to the Flag of the United States of America shall satisfy the requirements of this section." The School District complies with this requirement by instructing that "[e]ach elementary school class recite the pledge of allegiance to the flag once each day." Students who object on religious (or other) grounds may abstain from the recitation.

Notwithstanding the voluntary nature of the School District policy, the Court of Appeals, by a divided vote, held that the policy violates the Establishment Clause of the First Amendment because it "impermissibly coerces a religious act." To reach this result, the court relied primarily on our decision in *Lee v. Weisman* (1992). That case arose out of a graduation ceremony for a public high school in Providence, Rhode Island. The ceremony was begun with an invocation, and ended with a benediction, given by a local rabbi. The Court held that even though attendance at the ceremony was voluntary, students who objected to the prayers would nonetheless feel coerced to attend and to stand during each prayer. But the Court throughout its opinion referred to the prayer as "an explicit religious exercise," and "a formal religious exercise."

As the Court notes in its opinion, "the Pledge of Allegiance evolved as a common public acknowledgement of the ideals that our flag symbolizes. Its recitation is a patriotic exercise designed to foster national unity and pride in those principles."

I do not believe that the phrase "under God" in the Pledge converts its recital into a "religious exercise" of the sort described in *Lee*. Instead, it is a declaration of belief in allegiance and loyalty to the United States flag and the Republic that it represents. The phrase "under God" is in no sense a prayer, nor an endorsement of any religion, but a simple recognition of the fact noted in H. R. Rep. No. 1693, at 2: "From the time of our earliest history our peoples and our institutions have reflected the traditional concept that our Nation was founded on a fundamental belief in God." Reciting the Pledge, or listening to others recite it, is a patriotic exercise, not a religious one; participants promise fidelity to our flag and our Nation, not to any particular God, faith, or church.

There is no doubt that respondent is sincere in his atheism and rejection of a belief in God. But the mere fact that he disagrees with this part of the Pledge does not give him a veto power over the decision of the public schools that willing participants should pledge allegiance to the flag in the manner prescribed by Congress. There may be others who disagree, not with the phrase "under God," but with the phrase "with liberty and justice for all." But surely that would not give such objectors the right to veto the holding of such a ceremony by those willing to participate. Only if it can be said that the phrase "under God" somehow tends to the establishment of a religion in violation of the First Amendment can respondent's claim succeed, where one based on objections to "with liberty and justice for all" fails. Our cases have broadly interpreted this phrase, but none have gone anywhere near as far as the decision of the Court of Appeals in this case. The recital, in a patriotic ceremony pledging allegiance to the flag and to the Nation, of the descriptive phrase "under God" cannot possibly lead to the establishment of a religion, or anything like it.

When courts extend constitutional prohibitions beyond their previously recognized limit, they may restrict democratic choices made by public bodies. Here, Congress prescribed a Pledge of Allegiance, the State of California required patriotic observances in its schools, and the School District chose to comply by requiring teacher-led recital of the Pledge of Allegiance by willing students. Thus, we have three levels of popular government—the national, the state, and the local—collaborating to produce the Elk Grove ceremony. The Constitution only requires that schoolchildren be entitled to abstain from the ceremony if they chose to do so. To give the parent of such a child a sort of "heckler's veto" over a patriotic ceremony willingly participated in by other students, simply because the Pledge of Allegiance contains the descriptive phrase "under God," is an unwarranted extension of the Establishment Clause, an extension which would have the unfortunate effect of prohibiting a commendable patriotic observance.

DISCUSSION QUESTIONS FOR CHAPTER 3

1. Compare the understandings of Washington Gladden and President Coolidge. Is religious belief a useful support for social reform? Does it encourage an individual moral discipline that makes political freedom possible?

2. Contrast the positions of Justices Jackson and Frankfurter in *West Virginia Board of Education v. Barnette.* Should the government make special exceptions to accommodate the beliefs of religious minorities, or would that render the government subordinate to religion, contrary to the aims of the Constitution?

3. What are the differences between the position of Justices Black and Clark, on the one hand, and, on the other, that of President Reagan and Justices Stewart and Rehnquist (in reading 10)? Does the Constitution require a strict separation of church and state, or does the striving for such a separation violate the founders' intentions and unfairly marginalize religious believers?

4. Contrast the views of Judge Goodwin and Chief Justice Rehnquist (in reading 12) on the question of the inclusion of the words "under God" in the Pledge of Allegiance. Do these words wrongly impose religious beliefs on students in schools where the Pledge is recited, or do they merely represent a reasonable ceremonial recognition of the role of religion in American history?

CHAPTER 4

$$\approx\!\!\!\!\times\!\!\!\!\approx$$

Education

1

Booker T. Washington: "The Awakening of the Negro" (1896)

Following the Civil War the emergence of Jim Crow in the South and continued discrimination in many areas of the North caused difficulties for African Americans on a variety of levels. Most importantly, African Americans faced significant hurdles in obtaining quality education to improve their economic conditions. The following two readings highlight the divergent opinions of the two most important African American leaders of the early twentieth century, Booker T. Washington and W. E. B. Du Bois, on the topic of education. Note the significant differences between the two regarding the immediate and long-term needs of the African American community.

When a mere boy, I saw a young colored man, who had spent several years in school, sitting in a common cabin in the South, studying a French grammar. I noted the poverty, the untidiness, the want of system and thrift, that existed about the cabin, notwithstanding his knowledge of French and other academic subjects. Another time, when riding on the outer edges of a town in the South, I heard the sound of a piano coming from a cabin of the same kind. Contriving some excuse, I entered, and began a conversation with the young colored woman who was playing, and who had recently returned from a boarding-school, where she had been studying instrumental music among other things. Despite the fact that her parents were living in a rented cabin, eating poorly cooked food, surrounded with poverty, and having almost none of the conveniences of life, she had persuaded them to rent a piano for four or five dollars per month. Many such instances as these, in connection with my own struggles, impressed upon me the importance of making a study of our needs as a race, and applying the remedy accordingly. Some one may be tempted to ask, Has not the negro boy or girl as good a right to study a French grammar and instrumental music as the white youth? I answer, Yes, but in the present condition of the negro race in this country there is need of something more. . . .

From the outset, in connection with religious and academic training, [Tuskegee] has emphasized industrial or hand training as a means of finding the way out of present conditions. First, we have found the industrial teaching useful in giving the student a chance to work out a portion of his expenses while in school. Second, the school furnishes labor that has an economic value, and at the same time gives the student a chance to acquire knowledge and skill while performing the labor. Most of all, we find the industrial system valuable in teaching economy, thrift, and the dignity of labor, and in giving moral backbone to students. The fact that a student goes out into the world conscious of his power to build a house or a wagon, or to make a harness, gives him a certain confidence and moral independence that he would not possess without such training. . . .

One of the objections sometimes urged against industrial education for the negro is that it aims merely to teach him to work on the same plan that he was made to follow when in slavery. This is far from being the object at Tuskegee. At the head of each of the twenty-five industrial departments we have an intelligent and competent instructor, just as we have in our history classes, so that the student is taught not only practical brick-masonry, for example, but also the underlying principles of that industry, the mathematics and the mechanical and architectural drawing. Or he is taught how to become master of the forces of nature so that, instead of cultivating corn in the old way, he can use a corn cultivator, that lays off the furrows, drops the corn into them, and covers it, and in this way he can do more work than three men by the old process of corn-planting; at the same time much of the toil is eliminated and labor is dignified. In a word, the constant aim is to show the student how to put brains into every process of labor; how to bring his knowledge of mathematics and the sciences into farming, carpentry, forging, foundry work; how to dispense as soon as possible with the old form of ante-bellum labor. . . .

Nothing else so soon brings about right relations between the two races in the South as the industrial progress of the negro. Friction between the races will pass away in proportion as the black man, by reason of his skill, intelligence, and character, can produce something that the white man wants or respects in the commercial world. This is another reason why at Tuskegee we push the industrial training. We find that as every year we put into a Southern community colored men who can start a brick-yard, a sawmill, a tin-shop, or a printing-office,—men who produce something that makes the white man partly dependent upon the negro, instead of all the dependence being on the other side,—a change takes place in the relations of the races. Let us go on for a few more years knitting our business and industrial relations into those of the white man, till a black man gets a mortgage on a white man's house that he can foreclose at will. The white man on whose house the mortgage rests will not try to prevent that negro from voting when he goes to the polls. It is through the dairy farm, the truck garden, the trades, and commercial life, largely, that the negro is to find his way to the enjoyment of all his rights. Whether he will or not, a white man respects a negro who owns a two-story brick house. . . .

Immediately after the war, there was a large class of Southern people who feared that the opening of the free schools to the freedmen and the poor whites—the education of the head alone—would result merely in increasing the class who sought to escape labor, and that the South would soon be overrun by the idle and vicious. But as the results of industrial combined with academic training begin to show themselves in hundreds of communities that have been lifted up through the medium of the Tuskegee system, these former prejudices against education are being removed. Many of those who a few years ago opposed general education are now among its warmest advocates. This industrial training, emphasizing as it does the idea of economic production, is gradually bringing the South to the point where it is feeding itself. Before the war, and long after it, the South made what little profit was received from the cotton crop, and sent its earnings out of the South to purchase food supplies,—meat, bread, canned vegetables, and the like; but the improved methods of agriculture are fast changing this habit. With the newer methods of labor, which teach promptness and system, and emphasize the worth of the beautiful,—the moral value of the well-painted house, and the fence with every paling and nail in its place,—we are bringing to bear upon the South an influence that is making it a new country in industry, education, and religion.

2

W. E. B. Du Bois: "Of the Training of Black Men" (1902)

. . .[W]e daily hear that an education that encourages aspiration, that sets the loftiest of ideals and seeks as an end culture and character rather than breadwinning, is the privilege of white men and the danger and delusion of black.

. . . This development has been sharply ridiculed as a logical anomaly and flat reversal of nature. Soothly we have been told that first industrial and manual training should have taught the Negro to work, then simple schools should have taught him to read and write, and finally, after years, high and normal schools could have completed the system, as intelligence and wealth demanded. . . .

Fifty years ago the ability of Negro students in any appreciable numbers to master a modern college course would have been difficult to prove. To-day it is proved by the fact that four hundred Negroes, many of whom have been reported as brilliant students, have received the bachelor's degree from Harvard, Yale, Oberlin, and seventy other leading colleges. Here we have, then nearly twenty-five hundred Negro graduates, of whom the crucial query must be made, How far did their training fit them for life? It is of course extremely difficult to collect satisfactory data on such a point,—difficult to reach the men, to get trustworthy testimony, and to gauge that testimony by any generally acceptable criterion of success. In 1900, the Conference at Atlanta University undertook to study these graduates, and published the results. First they sought to know what these graduates were doing, and succeeded in getting answers from nearly two thirds of the living. The direct testimony was in almost all cases corroborated by the reports of the colleges where they graduated, so that in the main the reports were worthy of credence. Fifty-three per cent of these graduates were teachers,—presidents of institutions, heads of normal schools, principals of city school systems, and the like. Seventeen per cent were clergymen; another seventeen per cent were in the professions, chiefly as physicians. Over six per cent were merchants, farmers, and artisans, and four per cent were in the government civil service. Granting even that a considerable proportion of the third unheard from are unsuccessful, this is a record of usefulness. Personally I know many hundreds of these graduates, and have corresponded with more than a thousand; through others I have followed carefully the life-work of scores; I have taught some of them and some of the pupils whom they have taught, lived in homes which they have builded, and looked at life through their eyes. Comparing them as a class with my fellow students in New England and in Europe, I cannot hesitate in saying that nowhere have I met men and women with a broader spirit of helpfulness, with deeper devotion to their life-work, or with more consecrated determination to succeed in the face of bitter difficulties than among Negro college-bred men. They have, to be sure, their proportion of ne'er-do-weels, their pedants and lettered fools, but they have a surprisingly small proportion of them; they have not that culture of manner which we instinctively associate with university men, forgetting that in reality it is the heritage from cultured homes, and that no people a generation removed from slavery can escape a certain unpleasant rawness and gaucherie, despite the best of training. . . . If white people need colleges to furnish teachers, ministers, lawyers, and doctors, do black people need nothing of the sort? . . .

What place in the future development of the South ought the Negro college and college-bred man to occupy? That the present social separation and acute race sensitiveness must eventually yield to the influences of culture as the South grows civilized is clear. But such transformation calls for singular wisdom and patience. If, while the healing of this vast sore is progressing, the races are to live for many years side by side, united in economic effort, obeying a common government, sensitive to mutual thought and feeling, yet subtly and silently separate in many matters of deeper human intimacy—if this unusual and dangerous development is to progress amid peace and order, mutual respect and growing intelligence, it will call for social surgery at once the delicatest and nicest in modern history. It will demand broad-minded, upright men both white and black, and in its final accomplishment American civilization will triumph. So far as white men are concerned, this fact is to-day being recognized in the South, and a happy renaissance of university education seems imminent. But the very voices that cry Hail! to this good work are, strange to relate, largely silent or antagonistic to the higher education of the Negro. . . .

If you deplore their presence here, they ask, Who brought us? When you shriek, Deliver us from the vision of intermarriage, they answer, that legal marriage is infinitely better than systematic concubinage and prostitution. And if in just fury you accuse their vagabonds of violating women, they also in fury quite as just may wail: the rape which your gentlemen have done against help-less black women in defiance of your own laws is written on the foreheads of two millions of mulattoes, and written in in-effaceable blood. And finally, when you fasten crime upon this race as its peculiar train, they answer that slavery was the arch-crime, and lynching and lawlessness its twin abortion; that color and race are not crimes, and yet they it is which in this land receive most unceasing condemnation, North, East, South, and West.

I will not say such arguments are wholly justified—I will not insist that there is no other side to the shield; but I do say that of the nine millions of Negroes in this nation, there is scarcely one out of the cradle to whom these arguments do not daily present themselves in the guise of terrible truth. I insist that the question of the future is how best to keep these millions from brood-ing over the wrongs of the past and the difficulties of the present, so that all their energies may be bent toward a cheerful striving and cooperation with their white neighbors toward a larger, juster, and fuller future. That one wise method of doing this lies in the closer knitting of the Negro to the great indus-trial possibilities of the South is a great truth. And this the common schools and the manual training and trade schools are working to accomplish. But these alone are not enough. The foundations of knowledge in this race, as in others, must be sunk deep in the college and university if we would build a solid, permanent structure. Internal problems of social advance must inevitably come,—problems of work and wages, of families and homes, of morals and the true valuing of the things of life; and all these and other inevitable problems of civilization the Negro must meet and solve largely for himself, by reason of his isolation; and can there be any possible solution other than by study and thought and an appeal to the rich experience of the past? Is there not, with such a group and in such a crisis, infinitely more danger to be apprehended from half-trained minds and shallow thinking than from over-education and over-refinement? Surely we have wit enough to found a Negro college so manned and equipped as to steer successfully between the dilettante and the fool. We shall hardly induce black men to believe that if their bellies be full it matters little about their brains. They already dimly perceive that the paths of peace winding between honest toil and dignified manhood call for the guid-ance of skilled thinkers, the loving, reverent comradeship between the black lowly and black men emancipated by training and culture.

The function of the Negro college then is clear: it must maintain the stan-dards of popular education, it must seek the social regeneration of the Negro, and it must help in the solution of problems of race contact and cooperation. And finally, beyond all this, it must develop men. Above our modern social-ism, and out of the worship of the mass, must persist and evolve that higher individualism which the centres of culture protect; there must come a loftier respect for the sovereign human souls that seeks to know itself and the world about it; that seeks a freedom for expansion and self-development; that will love and hate and labor in its own way, untrammeled alike by old and new.

Such souls aforetime have inspired and guided worlds, and if we be not wholly bewitched by our Rhine-gold, they shall again. Herein the longing of black men must have respect: the rich and bitter depth of their experience, the unknown treasures of their inner life, the strange rendings of nature they have seen, may give the world new points of view and make their loving, living, and doing precious to all human hearts. And to themselves in these the days that try their souls the chance to soar in the dim blue air above the smoke is to their finer spirits boon and guerdon for what they lose on earth by being black. . . .

3

William James:
The Social Value of the College-Bred (1907)

By the turn of the twentieth century the demographics of colleges and universities were changing. Along with increasing numbers of coeducational institutions, larger numbers of middle class and even working class students were beginning to seek postsecondary degrees to improve their occupational prospects. In the following reading, the famous American philosopher, psychologist, and pragmatist William James expounds on the importance of a college education and attempts to answer critics who argue that postsecondary training is of little practical value.

OF WHAT USE is a college training? We who have had it seldom hear the question raised—we might be a little nonplussed to answer it offhand. A certain amount of meditation has brought me to this as the pithiest reply which I myself can give: The best claim that a college education can possibly make on your respect, the best thing it can aspire to accomplish for you, is this: that it should *help you to know a good man when you see him.* . . .

What talk do we commonly hear about the contrast between college education and the education which business or technical or professional schools confer? The college education is called higher because it is supposed to be so general and so disinterested. At the "schools" you get a relatively narrow practical skill, you are told, whereas the "colleges" give you the more liberal culture, the broader outlook, the historical perspective, the philosophic atmosphere, or something which phrases of that sort try to express. . . .

It is certain, to begin with, that the narrowest trade or professional training does something more for a man than to make a skilful practical tool of him—it makes him also a judge of other men's skill. Whether his trade be pleading at the bar or surgery or plastering or plumbing, it develops a critical sense in him for that sort of occupation. He understands the difference between second-rate and first-rate work in his whole branch of industry; he gets to know a good job in his own line as soon as he sees it; and getting to know this in his own line, he gets a faint sense of what good work may mean anyhow, that may, if circumstances favor, spread into his judgments elsewhere. Sound work, clean work, finished work; feeble work, slack work, sham work—these words express an identical contrast in many different departments of activity. In so far forth, then, even the humblest manual trade may beget in one a certain small degree of power to judge of good work generally.

Now, what is supposed to be the line of us who have the higher college training? Is there any broader line—since our education claims primarily not to be "narrow"—in which we also are made good judges between what is first-rate and what is second-rate only? What is especially taught in the colleges has long been known by the name of the "humanities," and these are often identified with Greek and Latin. But it is only as literatures, not as languages, that Greek and Latin have any general humanity-value; so that in a broad sense the humanities mean literature primarily, and in a still broader sense the study of masterpieces in almost any field of human endeavor. . . .

The sifting of human creations!—nothing less than this is what we ought to mean by the humanities. Essentially this means biography; what our colleges should teach is, therefore, biographical history, that not of politics merely, but of anything and everything so far as human efforts and conquests are factors that have played their part. Studying in this way, we learn what types of activity have stood the test of time; we acquire standards of the excellent and durable. All our arts and sciences and institutions are but so many quests of perfection on the part of men; and when we see how diverse the types of excellence may be, how various the tests, how flexible the adaptations, we gain a richer sense of what the terms "better" and "worse" may signify in general. Our critical sensibilities grow both more acute and less fanatical. We sympathize with men's mistakes even in the act of penetrating them; we feel the pathos of lost causes and misguided epochs even while we applaud what overcame them. . . .

In our essential function of indicating the better men, we now have formidable competitors outside. McClure's Magazine, the American Magazine, Collier's Weekly, and, in its fashion, the World's Work, constitute together a real popular university along this very line. It would be a pity if any future historian were to have to write words like these: "By the middle of the twentieth century the higher institutions of learning had lost all influence over public opinion in the United States. But the mission of raising the tone of democracy, which they had proved themselves so lamentably unfitted to exert, was assumed with rare enthusiasm and prosecuted with extraordinary skill and success by a new educational power; and for the clarification of their human sympathies and elevation of their human preferences, the people at large acquired the habit of resorting exclusively to the guidance of certain private literary adventures, commonly designated in the market by the affectionate name of ten-cent magazines."

Must not we of the colleges see to it that no historian shall ever say anything like this? Vague as the phrase of knowing a good man when you see him may be, diffuse and indefinite as one must leave its application, is there any other formula that describes so well the result at which our institutions *ought* to aim? If they do that, they do the best thing conceivable. If they fail to do it, they fail in very deed. It surely is a fine synthetic formula. If our faculty and graduates could once collectively come to realize it as the great underlying purpose toward which they have always been more or less obscurely groping, a great clearness would be shed over many of their problems; and, as for their influence in the midst of our social system, it would embark upon a new career of strength.

4

John Dewey: *Democracy and Education* (1916)

The foremost educational theorist of the early twentieth century, John Dewey was an advocate of experiential learning. Most importantly, he was also a great believer in the ability of education, if properly structured, to mold proper citizens. In the following excerpt of his famous work Democracy and Education, *Dewey echoes the sentiments of the Founding Fathers, such as Thomas Jefferson, and maintains that in a democratic, socially fluid culture, education is a necessity for maximizing society's potential.*

. . . Lack of the free and equitable intercourse which springs from a variety of shared interests makes intellectual stimulation unbalanced. Diversity of stimulation means novelty, and novelty means challenge to thought. The more activity is restricted to a few definite lines—as it is when there are rigid class lines preventing adequate interplay of experiences—the more action tends to become routine on the part of the class at a disadvantage, and capricious, aimless, and explosive on the part of the class having the materially fortunate position. Plato defined a slave as one who accepts from another the purposes which control his conduct. This condition obtains even where there is no slavery in the legal sense. It is found wherever men are engaged in activity which is socially serviceable, but whose service they do not understand and have no personal interest in. Much is said about scientific management of work. It is a narrow view which restricts the science which secures efficiency of operation to movements of the muscles. The chief opportunity for science is the discovery of the relations of a man to his work—including his relations to others who take part—which will enlist his intelligent interest in what he is doing. Efficiency in production often demands division of labor. But it is reduced to a mechanical routine unless workers see the technical, intellectual, and social relationships involved in what they do, and engage in their work because of the motivation furnished by such perceptions. The tendency to reduce such things as efficiency of activity and scientific management to purely technical externals is evidence of the one-sided stimulation of thought given to those in control of industry—those who supply its aims. Because of their lack of all-round and well-balanced social interest, there is not sufficient stimulus for attention to the human factors and relationships in industry. Intelligence is narrowed to the factors concerned with technical production and marketing of goods. No doubt, a very acute and intense intelligence in these narrow lines can be developed, but the failure to take into account the significant social factors means none the less an absence of mind, and a corresponding distortion of emotional life. . . .

The devotion of democracy to education is a familiar fact. The superficial explanation is that a government resting upon popular suffrage cannot be successful unless those who elect and who obey their governors are educated. Since a democratic society repudiates the principle of external authority, it must find a substitute in voluntary disposition and interest; these can be created only by education. But there is a deeper explanation. A democracy is more than a form of government; it is primarily a mode of associated living, of conjoint communicated experience. The extension in space of the number of individuals who participate in an interest so that each has to refer his own action to that of others, and to consider the action of others to give point and direction to his own, is equivalent to the breaking down of those barriers of class, race, and national territory which kept men from perceiving the full import of their activity. These more numerous and more varied points of contact denote a greater diversity of stimuli to which an individual has to respond; they consequently put a premium on variation in his action. They secure a liberation of powers which remain suppressed as long as the incitations to action are partial, as they must be in a group which in its exclusiveness shuts out many interests. . . .

Obviously a society to which stratification into separate classes would be fatal, must see to it that intellectual opportunities are accessible to all on equable and easy terms. A society marked off into classes need be specially attentive only to the education of its ruling elements. A society which is mobile, which is full of channels for the distribution of a change occurring anywhere, must see to it that its members are educated to personal initiative and adaptability. Otherwise, they will be overwhelmed by the changes in which they are caught and whose significance or connections they do not perceive. The result will be a confusion in which a few will appropriate to themselves the results of the blind and externally directed activities of others.

5

Justice James Clark McReynolds: Opinion of the Court in *Pierce* v. *Society of Sisters* (1925)

By the 1920s every state in the union had made efforts to enact compulsory education laws to ensure the proper education of children. Although most of these laws and regulations were altruistically motivated, not everyone embraced the centralization and standardization of education. Numerous private, religious schools were especially distraught that such government mandates in the realm of education did not allow parents to maintain influence over the direction of their children's scholastic training. In response to such criticism the Supreme Court struck down, in Pierce v. Society of Sisters, *an Oregon law that essentially deemed private schools as legal and equal entities with their publicly funded counterparts.*

Syllabus

1. The fundamental theory of liberty upon which all governments of this Union rest excludes any general power of the State to standardize its children by forcing them to accept instruction from public teachers only.

2. The Oregon Compulsory Education Act which, with certain exemptions, requires every parent, guardian or other person having control of a child between the ages of eight and sixteen years to send him to the public school in the district where he resides, for the period during which the school is held for the current year, is an unreasonable interference with the liberty of the parents and guardians to direct the upbringing of the children, and in that respect violates the Fourteenth Amendment.

3. In a proper sense, it is true that corporations cannot claim for themselves the liberty guaranteed by the Fourteenth Amendment, and, in general, no person in any business has such an interest in possible customers as to enable him to restrain exercise of proper power by the State upon the ground that he will be deprived of patronage.

4. But where corporations owning and conducting schools are threatened with destruction of their business and property through the improper and unconstitutional compulsion exercised by this statute upon parents and guardians, their interest is direct and immediate, and entitles them to protection by injunction.

From the Majority opinion:

. . . No question is raised concerning the power of the State reasonably to regulate all schools, to inspect, supervise and examine them, their teachers and pupils; to require that all children of proper age attend some school, that teachers shall be of good moral character and patriotic disposition, that certain studies plainly essential to good citizenship must be taught, and that nothing be taught which is manifestly inimical to the public welfare.

The inevitable practical result of enforcing the Act under consideration would be destruction of appellees' primary schools, and perhaps all other private primary schools for normal children within the State of Oregon. These parties are engaged in a kind of undertaking not inherently harmful, but long regarded as useful and meritorious. Certainly there is nothing in the present records to indicate that they have failed to discharge their obligations to patrons, students or the State. And there are no peculiar circumstances or present emergencies which demand extraordinary measures relative to primary education.

. . . [W]e think it entirely plain that the Act of 1922 unreasonably interferes with the liberty of parents and guardians to direct the upbringing and education of children under their control: as often heretofore pointed out, rights guaranteed by the Constitution may not be abridged by legislation which has no reasonable relation to some purpose within the competency of the State. The fundamental theory of liberty upon which all governments in this Union repose excludes any general power of the State to standardize its children by forcing them to accept instruction from public teachers only. The child is not the mere creature of the State; those who nurture him and direct his destiny have the right, coupled with the high duty, to recognize and prepare him for additional obligations.

6

President Franklin Roosevelt: Message to Congress on the Education of War Veterans (1943)

By 1943, millions of American men had or would soon enter the armed forces to serve during World War II. Recognizing the need to properly educate the soldiers and sailors who either had their scholastic pursuits interrupted or who did not have the opportunity to begin them, President Franklin Roosevelt issued the following address to Congress, which eventually manifested itself as the G.I. Bill. Utilized by veterans even today, the G.I. Bill became one of the most democratizing forces in the history of American education.

To the Congress:

On November 13, 1942, on signing the bill calling for the induction by Selective Service of young men eighteen and nineteen years old, I appointed a committee of educators, under the auspices of the War and Navy Departments, to study the problem of education of our service men and women after the war. The objective was to enable those young people, whose education had been interrupted, to resume their schooling, and to provide an opportunity for the education and technical training of other young men and women of ability, after their discharge from the armed services.

This committee has sent me a preliminary report which I am herewith transmitting to the Congress for its consideration, and, I hope, for its early action.

We, at home, owe a special and continuing obligation to these men and women in the armed services. During the war we have seen to it that they have received the best training and equipment, the best food, shelter, and medical attention, the best protection and care which planning, ingenuity, physical resources, and money could furnish in time of war. But after the war shall have been won, the best way that we can repay a portion of that debt is to see to it, by planning and by action now, that those men and women are demobilized into an economy which is sound and prosperous, with a minimum of unemployment and dislocation; and that, with the assistance of Government, they are given the opportunity to find a job for which they are fitted and trained, in a field which offers some reasonable assurance of well-being and continuous employment.

For many, what they desire most in the way of employment will require special training and further education. As a part of a general program for the benefit of the members of our armed services, I believe that the Nation is morally obligated to provide this training and education and the necessary financial assistance by which they can be secured. It is an obligation which should be recognized now; and legislation to that end should be enacted as soon as possible.

This is a good time not merely to be thinking about the subject, but actually to do something about it. Nothing will be more conducive to the maintenance of high morale in our troops than the knowledge that steps are being taken now to give them education and technical training when the fighting is over. Every day that the war continues interrupts the schooling and training of more men and women, and deprives them of the education and skills which they would otherwise acquire for use in later life. Not only the individual welfare of our troops, but the welfare of the Nation itself, requires that we reverse this trend just as quickly as possible after the war.

Vocational and educational opportunities for veterans should be of the widest range. There will be those of limited education who now appreciate, perhaps for the first time, the importance of general education, and who would welcome a year in school or college. There will be those who desire to learn a remunerative trade or to fit themselves more adequately for specialized work in agriculture or commerce. There will be others who want professional courses to prepare them for their life's work.

Lack of money should not prevent any veteran of this war from equipping himself for the most useful employment for which his aptitudes and willingness qualify him. The money invested in this training and schooling program will reap rich dividends in higher productivity, more intelligent leadership, and greater human happiness.

We must replenish our supply of persons qualified to discharge the heavy responsibilities of the postwar world. We have taught our youth how to wage war; we must also teach them how to live useful and happy lives in freedom, justice, and decency.

Specifically, I agree with the recommendations made by the committee in this regard as follows:

1. The Federal Government should make it financially feasible for every man and woman who has served honorably for a minimum period in the armed forces since September 16, 1940, to spend a period up to one calendar year in a school, a college, a technical institution, or in actual training in industry, so that he can further his education, learn a trade, or acquire the necessary knowledge and skill for farming, commerce, manufacturing, or other pursuits.

2. In addition, the Federal Government should make it financially possible for a limited number of ex-service men and women selected for their special aptitudes, to carry on their general, technical, or professional education for a further period of one, two, or three years.

This assistance from Government should include not only cost of instruction but a certain amount of money for maintenance. One incidental benefit of permitting discharged veterans to put in a year or more of schooling or training would be to simplify and cushion the return to civilian employment of service personnel. And I might call to your attention the fact that it costs less per year to keep a man at school or college or training on the job, than to maintain him on active military duty for a year.

While the Federal Government should provide the necessary funds and should have the responsibility of seeing that they are spent providently and under generally accepted standards, the control of the educational processes and the certification of trainees and students should reside in the States and localities.

I am sure that the Congress will agree with me that the report of this committee constitutes a helpful and constructive point of departure in the working out of a practical program for the meeting of this situation. Various recommendations are contained in the report concerning the administration of the plan. While there may be differences as to some of the details, I am confident that the Congress will find merit in the general objectives.

So far as disabled soldiers are concerned, the Congress is aware that, pursuant to existing statutes, the Veterans Administration is prepared to conduct a program of rehabilitation for veterans with service-connected disability. The program is designed to provide for the special needs of war-disabled veterans, and to furnish educational and training opportunities to help them take their places in civilian life. The program has already been initiated, and will be expanded as the war proceeds.

The new program of the Federal Security Agency will make provisions for veterans whose disabilities are not service-connected.

The Army and the Navy require a large number of workers skilled and experienced in various occupations and professions. Men who are filling these posts are acquiring valuable training and experience. A man who has become a mechanical draftsman, a cartographer, a meteorologist, a cook, or a baker may succeed in finding a similar post in civilian life. In a great many other occupations, such as those dealing with tank or tractor maintenance and repair, or with radio operation and maintenance, men are acquiring basic skill and experience which will provide a solid foundation for learning a related civilian occupation.

In addition, the United States Armed Forces Institute, which is a joint operation of the Army and Navy, offers men and women in the armed services a chance to enroll in courses usually offered by colleges, high schools, technical and occupational schools, in which they can study in their off-duty time. The Institute prepares self-teaching textbooks which enable them to learn a subject entirely on their own initiative; or, if they prefer, they may join any one of hundreds of classes which have been or are being established in Army camps and posts and in Navy installations, and in Army and Navy hospitals, here in the United States and in places all over the world. Or if they wish, they can study by the correspondence method with the Institute or with one of its overseas branches the same as any student in a correspondence school.

Opportunities for vocational training and for systematic schooling within the armed services will be expanded and reoriented during periods of demobilization and up to the moment of discharge.

Therefore, if the Congress adopts the general objective outlined herein, our men and women in the armed forces will be afforded opportunities for continuance of their education and vocational training—first, during the war; second, during the demobilization period; and third, for a year or more after their separation from the service.

While the successful conclusion of this great war is by no means within our sight, yet it may well be said that the time to prepare for peace is at the height of war.

7

President's Commission on Higher Education: *Higher Education for American Democracy* (1947)

With the emergence of the Cold War following World War II and the global ideological battle that ensued, the United States sought to establish a coherent and collective national identity that could serve as a model for international movements. To promote this collective identify, many American leaders advocated education as a tool for promoting a unique American identity. By the late 1940s, the intensification of the Cold War and concerns over the spread of communism increased interest in the direction of American education. The first reading that follows contains the findings of a presidential commission, which notes its interpretation of proper educational training and the stresses the importance of such to the collective embrace of core American values. The second reading includes a resolution passed by the University of California declaring that Communist Party affiliation by employees at the university is unacceptable and will be grounds for termination.

Today's college graduate may have gained technical or professional training in one field of work or another, but is only incidentally, if at all, made ready for performing his duties as a man, a parent, and a citizen. Too often he is "educated" in that he has acquired competence in some particular occupation, yet falls short of that human wholeness and civic conscience which the cooperative activities of citizenship require.

The failure to provide any core of unity in the essential diversity of higher education is a cause for grave concern. A society whose members lack a body of common experience and common knowledge is a society without a fundamental culture; it tends to disintegrate into a mere aggregation of individuals. Some community of values, ideas, and attitudes is essential as a cohesive force in this age of minute division of labor and intense conflict of separate interests.

The crucial task of higher education today, therefore, is to provide a unified general education for American youth. Colleges must find the right relationship between specialized training on the one hand, aiming at a thousand different careers, and the transmission of a common cultural heritage toward a common citizenship on the other.

There have already been many efforts to define this relationship. Attempts to reach conclusions about the ends and means of general education have been a major part of debate and experimentation in higher education for at least two decades.

"General education" is the term that has come to be accepted for those phases of nonspecialized and nonvocational learning which should be the common experience of all educated men and women. General education should give to the student the values, attitudes, knowledge, and skills that will equip him to live rightly and well in a free society. It should enable him to identify, interpret, select, and build into his own life those components of his cultural heritage that would contribute richly to understanding and appreciation of the world in which he lives. It should therefore embrace ethical values, scientific generalizations, and aesthetic conceptions, as well as an understanding of the purposes and character of the political, economic, and social institutions that men have devised.

But the knowledge and understanding which general education aims to secure whether drawn from the past or from a living present, are not to be regarded as ends in themselves. They are means to a more abundant personal life and a stronger, freer, social order.

Thus conceived, general education is not sharply distinguished from liberal education; the two differ mainly in degree, not in kind. General education undertakes to refine liberal education in terms of life's problems as men face them, to give it human orientation and social direction, to invest it with content that is directly relevant to the demands of contemporary society. General education aids liberal education with its matter and method shifted from its original aristocratic intent to the service of democracy. General education seeks to extend to all men the benefits of an education that liberates.

This purpose calls for a unity in the program of studies that a uniform system of courses cannot supply. The unity must come, instead, from a consistency of aim that will infuse and harmonize all teaching and all campus activities.

Objectives of General Education

1. To develop for the regulation of one's personal and civic life a code of behavior based on ethical principles consistent with democratic ideals. . . .

2. To participate actively as an informed and responsible citizen in solving the social, economic, and political problems of one's community State, and Nation. . . .

3. To recognize the interdependence of the different peoples of the world and one's personal responsibility for fostering international understanding and peace. . . .

4. To understand the common phenomena in one's physical environment, to apply habits of scientific thought to both personal and civic problems, and to appreciate the implications of scientific discoveries for human welfare. . . .

5. To understand the ideas of others and to express one's own effectively.

6. To attain a satisfactory emotional and social adjustment. . . .

7. To maintain and improve his own health and to cooperate actively and intelligently in solving community health problems. . . .

8. To understand and enjoy literature, art, music, and other cultural activities, as expressions of personal and social experience, and to participate to some extent in some form of creative activity. . . .

9. To acquire the knowledge and attitudes basic to a satisfying family life. . . .

10. To choose a socially useful and personally satisfying vocation that will permit one to use to the full his particular interests and abilities. . . .

11. To acquire and use the skills and habits involved in critical and constructive thinking.

8

Resolution Adopted by the Regents of the University of California (1950)

The Regents of the University of California confirm and emphasize their policy designed to bar members of the Communist Party from employment by the University as members of the faculty or otherwise, as embodied in various statements and resolutions including those of October 11, 1940 and June 24, 1949, which policy is hereby reaffirmed. The Regents are gratified that the Academic Senate, both Northern and Southern sections, has concurred in this policy by an overwhelming vote, reported on March 22, 1950.

The Regents have given further consideration to the most effective methods for the implementation of this established policy, and it is their view that the objectives previously defined and announced can best be achieved in the following manner:

After July 1, 1950, which will mark the beginning of a new academic year, conditions precedent to employment or renewal of employment of American citizens in the University shall be (1) execution of the constitutional oath of office required of public officials of the State of California and (2) acceptance of appointment by a letter which shall include the following provision:

> Having taken the constitutional oath of office required of public officials of the State of California, I hereby formally acknowledge my acceptance of the position and salary named, and also state that I am not a member of the Communist Party or any other organization which advocates the overthrow of the Government by force or violence, and that I have no commitments in conflict with my responsibilities with respect to impartial scholarship and free pursuit of truth. I understand that the foregoing statement is a condition of my employment and a consideration of payment of my salary.

Inasmuch as aliens are not lawfully subject to an oath of allegiance to the United States or the State of California, their letters of acceptance shall be drawn without reference to such oath but shall otherwise in all respects be identical with those of American citizens.

In any case of failure to sign the constitutional oath and the prescribed form of letter of acceptance the right of petition and review (referred to below) will be fully observed.

The foregoing is intended to govern employment and reemployment after June 30, 1950. For the balance of the current academic year, to wit, until July 1, 1950, account must be taken both of the large majority of faculty and employees who have subscribed to the loyalty oath of June 24, 1949, and of the minority who have not. The Regents have on various occasions indicated that an alternative affirmation would be accepted from the latter group if in form approved by the Regents. It is hereby provided that execution of the constitutional oath of office required of public officials of the State of California, and acceptance of appointment in the form herein stated, will be acceptable affirmation in lieu of the oath of June 24, 1949.

The Secretary of the Regents shall promptly mail to all faculty members and employees of the University new letters of acceptance of appointment for the academic year 1949–50, containing the text of the provision set forth above, and accompanied by the text of the constitutional oath of office of the State of California. Acceptance in the form prescribed shall be obligatory for all who have not filed with the Secretary the loyalty oath previously required by the Regents. Those who have already taken the latter oath need not follow the described procedure for the current academic year but may do so if they wish. In such case the oaths to which they have subscribed may be withdrawn.

In the event that a member of the faculty fails to comply with any foregoing requirement applicable to him he shall have the right to petition the President of the University for a review of his case by the Committee on Privilege and Tenure of the Academic Senate, including an investigation of and full hearing on the reasons for his failure so to do. Final action shall not be taken by the Board of Regents until the Committee on Privilege and Tenure, after such investigation and hearing, shall have had an opportunity to submit to the Board, through the President of the University, its findings and recommendations. It is recognized that final determination in each case is the prerogative of the Regents.

In order to provide a reasonable time for completion of the foregoing procedures, the Regents hereby fix May 15, 1950 as the date on or before which the constitutional oath and contract form shall be signed, and June 15, 1950 as the date on or before which all proceedings before the President and the Committee on Privilege and Tenure shall be completed and their findings and recommendations submitted to the Regents.

The regulations and procedures herein enacted, as applied and enforced by the administrative authorities of the University, will henceforth govern and control over all previous actions of the Regents to the extent they may be inconsistent with such previous actions to the end that the policy of the Regents and the Academic Senate barring members of the Communist Party from employment in the University may be fairly and effectively implemented.

9

President John F. Kennedy: Address to Congress on Education (1963)

The Cold War provided the impetus for allocation of resources in areas such as defense, intelligence, and education that strengthened the likelihood of ultimate victory for the United States over the Soviet Union. In the following address to Congress, President Kennedy emphasizes the importance of education in maintaining the global supremacy of the United States over "totalitarian discipline." Note especially the fact that Kennedy does not focus on the moral or ideological roles of education, but instead argues from a pragmatic perspective that the United States needs to train more Ph.D.s to remedy deficiencies in the training of individuals for vital industries.

In the new age of science and space, improved education is essential to give new meaning to our national purpose and power. In the last 20 years, mankind has acquired more scientific information than in all of previous history. Ninety percent of all the scientists that ever lived are alive and working today. Vast stretches of the unknown are being explored every day for military, medical, commercial and other reasons. And finally, the twisting course of the Cold War requires a citizenry that understands our principles and problems. It requires skilled manpower and brainpower to match the power of totalitarian discipline. It requires a scientific effort which demonstrates the superiority of freedom. And it requires an electorate in every state with sufficiently broad horizons and sufficient maturity of judgment to guide this nation safely through whatever lies ahead.

In short, from every point of view, education is of paramount concern to the national interest as well as to each individual. Today we need a new standard of excellence in education, matched by the fullest possible access to educational opportunities, enabling each citizen to develop his talents to the maximum possible extent.

Our concern as a nation for the future of our children—and the growing demands of modern education which Federal financing is better able to assist—make it necessary to expand Federal aid to education beyond the existing limited number of special programs. We can no longer afford the luxury of endless debate over all the complicated and sensitive questions raised by each new proposal on Federal participation in education. To be sure, these are all hard problems—but this Nation has not come to its present position of leadership by avoiding hard problems. We are at a point in history when we must face and resolve these problems.

State and local governments and private institutions, responsive to individual and local circumstances, have admirably served larger national purposes as well. They have written a remarkable record of freedom of thought and independence of judgment; and they have, in recent years, devoted sharply increased resources to education. Total national outlays for education nearly trebled during the 1940's and more than doubled during the 1950's, reaching a level of nearly $25 billion in 1960. As a proportion of national income, this represented a rise from little more than 4 percent in 1940 to nearly 6 percent in 1960, an increase of over 40 percent in total effort.

But this has not been enough. And the Federal Government—despite increasing recognition of education as a nationwide challenge, and despite the increased financial difficulties encountered by states, communities and private institutions in carrying this burden—has clearly not met its responsibilities in education. It has not offered sufficient help to our present educational system to meet its inadequacies and overcome its obstacles. . . .

A serious barrier to increased graduate study is the lack of adequate financial aid for graduate students. Only 1500 fellowships are permitted annually under the National Defense Education Act program, upon which we are dependent for urgently needed increases in the number of college teachers and the number of graduate students pursuing other courses essential to the Nation's advancement and security. The National Science Foundation has broad authority for fellowships and training grants, but its program, too, has been restricted by limited appropriations. The President's Science Advisory Committee has predicted that the dramatically increasing demand for engineers, mathematicians, and physical scientists, will require that the output of Ph.D.'s in these fields alone be increased 2½ times, to a total of 7500 annually by 1970, and that the number of Master degrees awarded annually be substantially increased. In all fields the need exceeds the supply of doctoral recipients. The shortage is particularly acute in college teaching, where at present rates the Nation will lack 90,000 doctoral degree holders by 1970. It is clearly contrary to the national interest to have the number of graduate students limited by the financial ability of those able and interested in pursuing advanced degrees. Fellowship programs can ease much of the financial burden and, most importantly, encourage and stimulate a fuller realization and utilization of our human resources.

The welfare and security of the Nation require that we increase our investment in financial assistance for college students both at undergraduate and graduate levels. In keeping with present needs and our traditions of maximum self-help, I recommend that the Congress enact legislation to:

1. Extend the National Defense Education Act student loan program, liberalize the repayment forgiveness for teachers, raise the ceiling on total appropriations and eliminate the limitation on amounts available to individual institutions.

2. Authorize a supplementary new program of Federal insurance for commercial loans made by banks and other institutions to college students for educational purposes.

3. Establish a new work-study program for needy college students unable to carry too heavy a loan burden, providing up to half the pay for students employed by the colleges in work of an educational character—as, for example, laboratory, library, or research assistants.

4. Increase the number of National Defense Education Act fellowships to be awarded by the Office of Education from 1,500 to 12,000, including summer session awards.

5. Authorize a thorough survey and evaluation of the need for scholarships or additional financial assistance to undergraduate students so that any further action needed in this area can be considered by the next Congress.

6. In addition, as part of this program to increase financial assistance to students, the 1964 budget recommendations for the National Science Foundation, which are already before Congress, include a proposed increase of $35 million to expand the number of fellowships and new teaching grants for graduate study from 2800 in 1963 to 8700 in fiscal 1964.

10

Students for a Democratic Society: The Port Huron Statement (1962)

The 1960s were a time of enormous change and upheaval at colleges and universities across the country. As the baby boom generation descended on college campuses throughout the 1960s, they brought with them new ideas about the role of America in the international community as well as expectations about the obligations of institutions of higher education to precipitate social change. The following reading became the manifesto for student activism in combating racism, economic inequality, and the war in Vietnam during the 1960s and early 1970s.

UNIVERSITY AS LOCUS OF POWER

We believe that the universities are an overlooked seat of influence. First, the university is located in a permanent position of social influence. Its educational function makes it indispensable and automatically makes it a crucial institution in the formation of social attitudes. Second, in an unbelievably complicated world, it is the central institution for organizing, evaluating and transmitting knowledge. Third, the extent to which academic resources presently are used to buttress immoral social practice is revealed, first, by the extent to which defense contracts make the universities engineers of the arms race. Too, the use of modern social science as a manipulative tool reveals itself in the "human relations" consultants to the modern corporations, who introduce trivial sops to give laborers feelings of "participation" or "belonging," while actually deluding them in order to further exploit their labor. And, of course, the use of motivational research is already infamous as a manipulative aspect of American politics. But these social uses of the universities' resources also demonstrate the unchangeable reliance by men of power on the men and storehouses of knowledge: this makes the university functionally tied to society in new ways, revealing new potentialities, new levers for change. Fourth, the university is the only mainstream institution that is open to participation by individuals of nearly any viewpoint.

UNIVERSITY AS LOCUS OF CHANGE

These, at least, are facts, no matter how dull the teaching, how paternalistic the rules, how irrelevant the research that goes on. Social relevance, the accessibility to knowledge, and internal openness—these together make the university a potential base and agency in a movement of social change.

1. Any new left in America must be, in large measure, a left with real intellectual skills, committed to deliberativeness, honesty, reflection as working tools. The university permits the political life to be an adjunct to the academic one, and action to be informed by reason.

2. A new left must be distributed in significant social roles throughout the country. The universities are distributed in such a manner.

3. A new left must consist of younger people who matured in the postwar world, and partially be directed to the recruitment of younger people. The university is an obvious beginning point.

4. A new left must include liberals and socialists, the former for their relevance, the latter for their sense of thoroughgoing reforms in the system. The university is a more sensible place than a political party for these two traditions to begin to discuss their differences and look for political synthesis.

5. A new left must start controversy across the land, if national policies and national apathy are to be reversed. The ideal university is a community of controversy, within itself and in its effects on communities beyond.

6. A new left must transform modern complexity into issues that can be understood and felt close up by every human being. It must give form to the feelings of helplessness and indifference, so that people may see the political, social, and economic sources of their private troubles, and organize to change society.

In a time of supposed prosperity, moral complacency, and political manipulation, a new left cannot rely on only aching stomachs to be the engine force of social reform. The case for change, for alternatives that will involve uncomfortable personal efforts, must be argued as never before. The university is a relevant place for all of these activities. But we need not indulge in illusions: the university system cannot complete a movement of ordinary people making demands for a better life. From its schools and colleges across the nation, a militant left might awaken its allies, and by beginning the process towards peace, civil rights, and labor struggles, reinsert theory and idealism where too often reign confusion and political barter.

The power of students and faculty united is not only potential; it has shown its actuality in the South, and in the reform movements of the North. The bridge to political power, though, will be built through genuine cooperation, locally, nationally, and internationally, between a new left of young people and an awakening community of allies. In each community we must look within the university and act with confidence that we can be powerful, but we must look outwards to the less exotic but more lasting struggles for justice.

To turn these mythic possibilities into realities will involve national efforts at university reform by an alliance of students and faculty. They must wrest control of the educational process from the administrative bureaucracy. They must make fraternal and functional contact with allies in labor, civil rights, and other liberal forces outside the campus. They must import major public issues into the curriculum—research and teaching on problems of war and peace is an outstanding example. They must make debate and controversy, not dull pedantic cant, the common style for educational life. They must consciously build a base for their assault upon the loci of power.

As students for a democratic society, we are committed to stimulating this kind of social movement, this kind of vision and program in campus and community across the country. If we appear to seek the unattainable, as it has been said, then let it be known that we do so to avoid the unimaginable.

11

James Coleman:
Equality of Educational Opportunity (1966)

By the middle of the 1960s it was clear that, despite legal barriers being removed and President Johnson's "war on poverty," the meritocracy that the Founding Fathers envisioned for the United States was not a realistic scenario for many minority groups. Continuing economic and educational discrimination caused substantial socioeconomic gaps between racial groups. In the following federal report, sociologist James Coleman examines some of the reasons behind the achievement disparities between white children and those of other races.

If 100 students within a school take a certain test, there is likely to be great variation in their scores. One student may score 97 percent, another 13; several may score 78 percent. This represents variability in achievement within the particular school.

It is possible, however, to compute the average of the scores made by the students within that school and to compare it with the average score, or achievement, of pupils within another school, or many other schools. These comparisons then represent variations between the schools.

When one sees that the average score on a verbal achievement test in school X is 55 and in school Y is 72, the natural question to ask is: what accounts for the difference?

There are many factors that may be associated with the difference. This analysis concentrates on one cluster of those factors. It attempts to describe what relationship the school's characteristics themselves (libraries, for example, and teachers and laboratories, and so on) seem to have to the achievement of majority and minority groups (separately for each group on a nationwide basis, and also for Negro and white pupils in the North and South).

The first finding is that the schools are remarkably similar in the way they relate to the achievement of their pupils when the socioeconomic background of the students is taken into account. It is known that socioeconomic factors bear a strong relation to academic achievement. When these factors are statistically controlled, however, it appears that differences between schools account for only a small fraction of the difference in pupil achievement.

The schools do differ, however, in their relation to the various racial and ethnic groups. The average white student's achievement seems to be less affected by the strength or weakness of his school's facilities, curriculums, and teachers than is the average minority pupil's. To put it another way, the achievement of minority pupils depends more on the schools they attend than does the achievement of majority pupils. Thus, 20 percent of the achievement of Negroes in the South is associated with the particular schools they go to, whereas only 10 percent of the achievement of whites in the South is. Except for Oriental Americans, this general result is found for all minorities.

The inference might then be made that improving the school of a minority pupil may increase his achievement more than would improving the school of a white child increase his. Similarly, the average minority pupil's achievement may suffer more in a school of low quality than might the average white pupil's. In short, whites, and to a lesser extent, Oriental Americans, are less affected one way or the other by the quality of their schools than are minority pupils. This indicates that it is for the most disadvantaged children that improvements in school quality will make the most difference in achievement.

All of these results suggest the next question: What are the school characteristics that are most related to achievement? In other words, what factors in the school seem to be most important in affecting achievement?

It appears that variations in the facilities and curriculums of the schools account for relatively little variation in pupil achievement insofar as this is measured by standard tests. Again, it is for majority whites that the variations make the least difference; for minorities, they make somewhat more difference. Among the facilities that show some relationship to achievement are several for which minority pupils' schools are less well equipped relative to whites. For example, the existence of science laboratories showed a small but consistent relationship to achievement, and . . . minorities, especially Negroes, are in schools with fewer of these laboratories.

The quality of teachers shows a stronger relationship to pupil achievement. Furthermore, it is progressively greater at higher grades, indicating a cumulative impact of the qualities of teaching in a school on the pupil's achievements. Again, teacher quality seems more important to minority achievement than that of the majority. . . .

Finally, it appears that a pupil's achievement is strongly related to the educational backgrounds and aspirations of the other students in the school. Only crude measures of these variables were used (principally the proportion of pupils with encyclopedias in the home and the proportion planning to go to college). Analysis indicates, however, that children from a given family background, when put in schools of different social composition, will achieve at quite different levels. This effect is again less for white pupils than for any minority group other than Orientals. Thus if a white pupil from a home that is strongly and effectively supportive of education is put in a school where most pupils do not come from such homes, his achievement will be little different than if he were in a school composed of others like himself. But if a minority pupil from a home without much educational strength is put with schoolmates with strong educational backgrounds, his achievement will be likely to increase.

This general result, taken together with the earlier examinations of school differences, has important implications for equality of educational opportunity. . . . The principal way in which the school environments of Negroes and whites differ is in the composition of their student bodies, and it turns out that the composition of the student bodies has a strong relationship to the achievement of Negro and other minority pupils.

12

National Commission on Excellence in Education: *A Nation at Risk* (1983)

The 1970s and early 1980s was a period of economic recession and stagnation in the United States. An energy crisis as well as high rates of inflation and unemployment caused many Americans to seek answers for the downward spiral of the national economy, which threatened the international supremacy of the United States. Published by the U.S. Department of Education, the following report identifies the deterioration of the American educational system as one of the root causes for that downward spiral.

Our Nation is at risk. Our once unchallenged preeminence in commerce, industry, science, and technological innovation is being overtaken by competitors throughout the world. This report is concerned with only one of the many causes and dimensions of the problem, but it is the one that undergirds American prosperity, security, and civility. We report to the American people that while we can take justifiable pride in what our schools and colleges have historically accomplished and contributed to the United States and the well-being of its people, the educational foundations of our society are presently being eroded by a rising tide of mediocrity that threatens our very future as a Nation and a people. What was unimaginable a generation ago has begun to occur—others are matching and surpassing our educational attainments. If an unfriendly foreign power had attempted to impose on America the mediocre educational performance that exists today, we might well have viewed it as an act of war. As it stands, we have allowed this to happen to ourselves. We have even squandered the gains in student achievement made in the wake of the Sputnik challenge. Moreover, we have dismantled essential support systems which helped make those gains possible. We have, in effect, been committing an act of unthinking, unilateral educational disarmament. . . .

History is not kind to idlers. The time is long past when American's destiny was assured simply by an abundance of natural resources and inexhaustible human enthusiasm, and by our relative isolation from the malignant problems of older civilizations. The world is indeed one global village. We live among determined, well-educated, and strongly motivated competitors. We compete with them for international standing and markets, not only with products but also with the ideas of our laboratories and neighborhood workshops. America's position in the world may once have been reasonably secure with only a few exceptionally well-trained men and women. It is no longer.

The risk is not only that the Japanese make automobiles more efficiently than Americans and have government subsidies for development and export. It is not just that the South Koreans recently built the world's most efficient steel mill, or that American machine tools, once the pride of the world, are being displaced by German products. It is also that these developments signify a redistribution of trained capability throughout the globe. Knowledge, learning, information, and skilled intelligence are the new raw materials of international commerce and are today spreading throughout the world as vigorously as miracle drugs, synthetic fertilizers, and blue jeans did earlier. If only to keep and improve on the slim competitive edge we still retain in world markets, we must dedicate ourselves to the reform of our educational system for the benefit of all—old and young alike, affluent and poor, majority and minority. Learning is the indispensable investment required for success in the "information age" we are entering.

Our concern, however, goes well beyond matters such as industry and commerce. It also includes the intellectual, moral, and spiritual strengths of our people which knit together the very fabric of our society. The people of the United States need to know that individuals in our society who do not possess the levels of skill, literacy, and training essential to this new era will be effectively disenfranchised, not simply from the material rewards that accompany competent performance, but also from the chance to participate fully in our national life. A high level of shared education is essential to a free, democratic society and to the fostering of a common culture, especially in a country that prides itself on pluralism and individual freedom. . . .

Part of what is at risk is the promise first made on this continent: All, regardless of race or class or economic status, are entitled to a fair chance and to the tools for developing their individual powers of mind and spirit to the utmost. This promise means that all children by virtue of their own efforts, competently guided, can hope to attain the mature and informed judgment needed to secure gainful employment, and to manage their own lives, thereby serving not only their own interests but also the progress of society itself. . . .

On the personal level the student, the parent, and the caring teacher all perceive that a basic promise is not being kept. More and more young people emerge from high school ready neither for college nor for work. This predicament becomes more acute as the knowledge base continues its rapid expansion, the number of traditional jobs shrinks, and new jobs demand greater sophistication and preparation.

On a broader scale, we sense that this undertone of frustration has significant political implications, for it cuts across ages, generations, races, and political and economic groups. We have come to understand that the public will demand that educational and political leaders act forcefully and effectively on these issues. Indeed, such demands have already appeared and could well become a unifying national preoccupation. This unity, however, can be achieved only if we avoid the unproductive tendency of some to search for scapegoats among the victims, such as the beleaguered teachers. . . .

In a world of ever-accelerating competition and change in the conditions of the workplace, of ever-greater danger, and of ever-larger opportunities for those prepared to meet them, educational reform should focus on the goal of creating a Learning Society. At the heart of such a society is the commitment to a set of values and to a system of education that affords all members the opportunity to stretch their minds to full capacity, from early childhood through adulthood, learning more as the world itself changes. Such a society has as a basic foundation the idea that education is important not only because of what it contributes to one's career goals but also because of the value it adds to the general quality of one's life. Also at the heart of the Learning Society are educational opportunities extending far beyond the traditional institutions of learning, our schools and colleges. They extend into homes and workplaces; into libraries, art galleries, museums, and science centers; indeed, into every place where the individual can develop and mature in work and life. In our view, formal schooling in youth is the essential foundation for learning throughout one's life. But without life-long learning, one's skills will become rapidly dated.

In contrast to the ideal of the Learning Society, however, we find that for too many people education means doing the minimum work necessary for the moment, then coasting through life on what may have been learned in its first quarter. But this should not surprise us because we tend to express our educational standards and expectations largely in terms of "minimum requirements." And where there should be a coherent continuum of learning, we have none, but instead an often incoherent, outdated patchwork quilt. Many individual, sometimes heroic, examples of schools and colleges of great merit do exist. Our findings and testimony confirm the vitality of a number of notable schools and programs, but their very distinction stands out against a vast mass shaped by tensions and pressures that inhibit systematic academic and vocational achievement for the majority of students. In some metropolitan areas basic literacy has become the goal rather than the starting point. In some colleges maintaining enrollments is of greater day-to-day concern than maintaining rigorous academic standards. And the ideal of academic excellence as the primary goal of schooling seems to be fading across the board in American education. . . .

The most recent (1982) Gallup Poll of the *Public's Attitudes Toward the Public Schools* strongly supported a theme heard during our hearings: People are steadfast in their belief that education is the major foundation for the future strength of this country. They even considered education more important than developing the best industrial system or the strongest military force, perhaps because they understood education as the cornerstone of both. They also held that education is "extremely important" to one's future success, and that public education should be the top priority for additional Federal funds. Education occupied first place among 12 funding categories considered in the survey— above health care, welfare, and military defense, with 55 percent selecting public education as one of their first three choices. Very clearly, the public understands the primary importance of education as the foundation for a satisfying life, an enlightened and civil society, a strong economy, and a secure Nation. . . .

And perhaps most important, citizens know and believe that the meaning of America to the rest of the world must be something better than it seems to many today. Americans like to think of this Nation as the preeminent country for generating the great ideas and material benefits for all mankind. The citizen is dismayed at a steady 15-year decline in industrial productivity, as one great American industry after another falls to world competition. The citizen wants the country to act on the belief, expressed in our hearings and by the large majority in the Gallup Poll, that education should be at the top of the Nation's agenda.

13

Diane Ravitch: "Left Back: A Century of Failed School Reforms" (2000)

Beginning primarily in the 1970s, some American educational reformers had begun to target for restructuring the manner in which students were educated in primary and secondary schools. Self-esteem training, "ebonics," and differentiation all were movements intended to maximize the learning environment and adapt to the learning capabilities of each individual child. However, serious concerns with this perceived dilution of school curricula led to a substantial reaction against the "dumbing down" of American students. The following two readings—the first by education professor and author Diane Ravitch, and the second an excerpt from President George W. Bush's No Child Left Behind Act—are both indicative of this traditionalist reaction that stressed hard work by students and accountability by teachers as the best recipe for educational success.

. . . [A]t the beginning the 20th century, there was a clearly established democratic ideal. The ideal was referred to at the time by the simile of the educational ladder, that every child for as long as he or she stayed in school should have access to a high-quality education, one which included history and literature, math and science, and certainly a foreign language. And as it happened, most parents, for some reason, wanted their children to study Latin. The reason they wanted them to study Latin was that Latin was considered the language of culture and high literacy and immigrant parents and poor parents and black parents wanted their children to study Latin. So, at the beginning of the century, that small minority of kids who actually made it to high school, most of them would study Latin. A few studied Greek. But every child studied a foreign language.

And then the movement grew—it was modernism, and it was a revolt against tradition. It was part of being the avant-garde, which was very trendy and exciting. But the movement grew amongst educational leaders to say this is not socially efficient. Schools should serve society and the ways they should serve society is to create job preparation programs, vocational education,

Source: Excerpts from "Left Back: A Century of Failed School Reforms," speech made by Diane Ravitch. Used by permission of Diane Ravitch.

industrial education. Begin as early as possible, preferably around the age of 12 directing young children for their job preparation. And so it became the thing to do.

And the story I tell is of one school district after another adopting what they called a "differentiated curriculum." What used to be called a "common curriculum" was then re-labeled the college preparatory curriculum. And instead of having all children rising up the educational ladder as far as they could go, the ladder went in different directions with a very small number going towards the college prep curriculum even though they probably weren't going to go to college, and most kids pushed forward into vocational or industrial education.

Now, I come back to Cleveland to say that the superintendent of schools there insisted that the differentiation should begin as early as elementary school and the earlier tradition, the 19th century tradition was that the first eight grades were a common curriculum. After that, you went your own way. And so the superintendent of Cleveland said that the elementary curriculum had to be reorganized because he said the social order needs lawyers, doctors, preachers, teachers, men of science, et cetera, but they will only be 4 percent of the bread-winners and another 1 percent would be needed—or they will be only 1 percent and another 4 percent would do all the professional work of society. The 95 percent must be trained for industry and commerce and the program of the public schools should reflect their occupations.

Now, the question arises—and this I find again and again and again and documented extensively—how would the schools know which children were likely to go to college as early as fourth or fifth grade and which would work in industry? And so the superintendent of Cleveland writes, "It is obvious that the educational needs of the child in a district where the streets are well-paved and clean, where the homes are spacious and surrounded by lawns and trees, where the language of the child's playfellows is pure, and where life in general in permeated with the spirit and ideals of America, it is obvious that the educational needs of such a child are radically different from those of the child who lives in a foreign and tenement section." That is how you determine who would get into the college-bound track and who were the other 95 percent of the kids.

So, this story repeats itself in city after city. And the movements come very thick and fast after this. And this is the story of my book, is all of these movements. And the movements are—and I won't even list them, I have like at least 20 different movements—it is the industrial education movement, the social efficiency movement, the junior high school movement. The reason that junior high schools were created was to start the tracking not in ninth grade but in six or seventh grade. The IQ testing movement becomes very powerful when added to this initial impulse because the IQ test, which was developed for group use during World War I, then becomes the mechanism that allows educators en mass to track kids and to predict as early as first or second or third grade, these are the children that we should give the good stuff to and these are the children who are going to go into the professions—or not into the professions, into the occupations, into industry. And so the sorting becomes very early and it is the IQ testing, which spreads like wild fire, that makes this kind of differentiation possible and also makes it seem to be the essence of science. Every school district has to use IQ testing because it is scientific.

And we even get something called the school survey movement where all the experts from the universities come to local communities and they say, "The trouble with this community is you are not using enough IQ testing. You are not dividing the kids up early enough. You are not sending them off for industrial education at a young enough age." And you get this kind of report going on in city after city.

And then comes other movements, the child-centered movement. And the child-centered movement essentially says it is not about the traditional— education is not about the traditional curriculum. That is very old-fashioned, and we don't want to do anything old-fashioned. We want children to be interested and have fun and so having fun becomes very important. Well, that had more of an impact in the private schools than in the public schools, but I document story after story where this becomes very important and the differentiation that most of us grew up with.

Now, as it happens, most of us were placed on the college track. I was in the college track. I went to public schools in Texas, so I thought everything was fine. Most educated people were in the college track, so we didn't notice that most of the kids that we were going to school with were not in the college track.

And I conclude, after going through some 18, 19 or 20 or more movements, my conclusion is that educational movements should be avoided like the plague. That it is this very idea that education needs a movement to re-order all of its priorities every few years that is itself a problem. We need to focus on teaching and learning. And, again, as Donna said, my point was not to say ignore all of the other social needs of children. Of course, you shouldn't ignore them. But at the heart of schools is the teacher and child and the focus on the teaching and learning.

I have often asked myself, "Why would I want to go to a doctor who was always using the latest, most experimental method?" I don't. I want to go to a doctor who knows what to do when I come in and says, "This has been tested on thousands of other people. We know that it will work in 99 percent of the cases." And if he wants to use an experimental method, he sure better get my permission before he does it. But we are constantly introducing innovation after innovation and somehow the hallmark of education in this country—at least for the last 50 or more years—has been, is it innovative? Well, why don't we think about does it work, is it effective, do children learn because you are doing this? . . .

[T]here has been this constant search for the magic feather, what magic thing can we do so that it won't be hard to teach and learn? And we never found the easy way. I remember when I was a kid, there used to be ads in the magazines about sleep-learning and you could put the record on and go to sleep and during the night, the information would somehow get into your brain while you were sleeping. That didn't work. Easy ways don't work. Teaching and learning is difficult, as every good teacher will tell you. And it does require effort.

And I think that one of the lessons of this history is the point that Harold Stevenson at the University of Michigan made in his book, *The Learning Gap,* and that is that we have been too inclined in our country to think that what counts is not effort but ability. And I think this goes back to our many decades of reliance on IQ testing, this notion that either you have got it or you don't. And I don't have it for math, so therefore I am not going to study math. But I have heard many a parent tell me, "You know, my daughter really isn't good at math but she had to take the tests and she learned it and she passed the tests. And she found out she is good at math." And this was something new. So, I don't think—you know, everyone is not going to be good at everything, but if you work hard, you can learn it. And there is nothing that schools are doing now in the way of the curriculum that is beyond the reach of virtually any child. . . .

14

The No Child Left Behind Act (2001)

. . . The purpose of this title is to ensure that all children have a fair, equal, and significant opportunity to obtain a high-quality education and reach, at a minimum, proficiency on challenging State academic achievement standards and state academic assessments. This purpose can be accomplished by—

(1) ensuring that high-quality academic assessments, accountability systems, teacher preparation and training, curriculum, and instructional materials are aligned with challenging State academic standards so that students, teachers, parents, and administrators can measure progress against common expectations for student academic achievement;

(2) meeting the educational needs of low-achieving children in our Nation's highest-poverty schools, limited English proficient children, migratory children, children with disabilities, Indian children, neglected or delinquent children, and young children in need of reading assistance;

(3) closing the achievement gap between high- and low-performing children, especially the achievement gaps between minority and nonminority students, and between disadvantaged children and their more advantaged peers;

(4) holding schools, local educational agencies, and States accountable for improving the academic achievement of all students, and identifying and turning around low-performing schools that have failed to provide a high-quality education to their students, while providing alternatives to students in such schools to enable the students to receive a high-quality education;

(5) distributing and targeting resources sufficiently to make a difference to local educational agencies and schools where needs are greatest;

(6) improving and strengthening accountability, teaching, and learning by using State assessment systems designed to ensure that students are meeting challenging State academic achievement and content standards and increasing achievement overall, but especially for the disadvantaged;

(7) providing greater decisionmaking authority and flexibility to schools and teachers in exchange for greater responsibility for student performance;

(8) providing children an enriched and accelerated educational program, including the use of schoolwide programs or additional services that increase the amount and quality of instructional time;

(9) promoting schoolwide reform and ensuring the access of children to effective, scientifically based instructional strategies and challenging academic content;

(10) significantly elevating the quality of instruction by providing staff in participating schools with substantial opportunities for professional development;

(11) coordinating services under all parts of this title with each other, with other educational services, and, to the extent feasible, with other agencies providing services to youth, children, and families; and

(12) affording parents substantial and meaningful opportunities to participate in the education of their children. . . .

DISCUSSION QUESTIONS FOR CHAPTER 4

1. What are the main objectives in educating African Americans for Washington and Du Bois? Why are their opinions so radically different? Who makes a stronger argument in outlining the proper path for the ultimate success of African Americans?

2. How do James and Dewey suggest that education will improve society? Are schools the proper venues for molding the character of individuals? How does the *Pierce* decision relate to molding the character of students?

3. Why was the expansion of education such a concern following the Second World War? Is it possible to "educate for democracy"? Why were the California Regents, as well as other community leaders around the country, so adamant about restricting the employment of communists as educators?

4. According to the Coleman Report (*Equality of Educational Opportunity*), why were educational opportunities for minorities still lagging far behind those of whites by the 1960s? Can you identify any other reasons for lack of educational opportunities for African Americans? How does the Port Huron Statement address inequalities, both within and outside education?

5. Why has there been such an increased concern within the last twenty years about Americans being "at risk" in the field of education? Does Ravitch construct a sound argument about why the American school system is failing? Is the No Child Left Behind Act part of the problem or part of the solution for improving schools?

CHAPTER 5

Republican Government

1

Susan B. Anthony:
Speech in Favor of Women's Suffrage (1872)

Many women who were active in the movement to abolish slavery were, like Anthony, also keen to see the right to vote extended to women. Disappointed that the Fifteenth Amendment prohibited only denial of the right to vote because of color, they turned their efforts late in the nineteenth century to the struggle for women's suffrage. In the following speech Anthony argues that respect for America's fundamental principles requires that women be allowed to vote.

Friends and Fellow-citizens: I stand before you to-night, under indictment for the alleged crime of having voted at the last Presidential election, without having a lawful right to vote. It shall be my work this evening to prove to you that in thus voting, I not only committed no crime, but, instead, simply exercised my citizen's right, guaranteed to me and all United States citizens by the National Constitution, beyond the power of any State to deny.

Our democratic-republican government is based on the idea of the natural right of every individual member thereof to a voice and a vote in making and executing the laws. We assert the province of government to be to secure the people in the enjoyment of their unalienable rights. We throw to the winds the old dogma that governments can give rights. Before governments were organized, no one denies that each individual possessed the right to protect his own life, liberty and property. And when 100 or 1,000,000 people enter into a free government, they do not barter away their natural rights; they simply pledge themselves to protect each other in the enjoyment of them, through prescribed judicial and legislative tribunals. They agree to abandon the methods of brute force in the adjustment of their differences, and adopt those of civilization.

Nor can you find a word in any of the grand documents left us by the fathers that assumes for government the power to create or to confer rights.

The Declaration of Independence, the United States Constitution, the constitutions of the several states and the organic laws of the territories, all alike propose to protect the people in the exercise of their God-given rights. Not one of them pretends to bestow rights. "All men are created equal, and endowed by their Creator with certain unalienable rights. Among these are life, liberty and the pursuit of happiness. That to secure these, governments are instituted among men, deriving their just powers from the consent of the governed."

Here is no shadow of government authority over rights, nor exclusion of any from their full and equal enjoyment. Here is pronounced the right of all men, and "consequently," as the Quaker preacher said, "of all women," to a voice in the government. And here, in this very first paragraph of the declaration, is the assertion of the natural right of all to the ballot; for, how can "the consent of the governed" be given, if the right to vote be denied. Again:

"That whenever any form of government becomes destructive of these ends, it is the right of the people to alter or abolish it, and to institute a new government, laying its foundations on such principles, and organizing its powers in such forms as to them shall seem most likely to effect their safety and happiness."

Surely, the right of the whole people to vote is here clearly implied. For however destructive of their happiness this government might become, a disfranchised class could neither alter nor abolish it, nor institute a new one, except by the old brute force method of insurrection and rebellion. One-half of the people of this nation today are utterly powerless to blot from the statute books an unjust law, or to write there a new and a just one. The women, dissatisfied as they are with this form of government, that enforces taxation without representation, that compels them to obey laws to which they have never given their consent, that imprisons and hangs them without a trial by a jury of their peers, that robs them, in marriage, of the custody of their own persons, wages and children, are this half of the people left wholly at the mercy of the other half, in direct violation of the spirit and letter of the declarations of the framers of this government, every one of which was based on the immutable principle of equal rights to all. By those declarations, kings, priests, popes, aristocrats, were all alike dethroned, and placed on a common level politically, with the lowliest born subject or serf. By them, too, men, as such, were deprived of their divine right to rule, and placed on a political level with women. By the practice of those declarations all class and caste distinction will be abolished; and slave, serf, plebeian, wife, woman, all alike, bound from their subject position to the proud platform of equality.

The preamble of the federal constitution says:

"We, the people of the United States, in order to form a more perfect union, establish justice, insure domestic tranquility, provide for the common defense, promote the general welfare and secure the blessings of liberty to ourselves and our posterity, do ordain and established this constitution for the United States of America."

It was we, the people, not we, the white male citizens, nor yet we, the male citizens; but we, the whole people, who formed this Union. And we formed it, not to give the blessings or liberty, but to secure them; not to the half of ourselves and the half of our posterity, but to the whole people—women as well as men. And it is downright mockery to talk to women of their enjoyment of the blessings of liberty while they are denied the use of the only means of securing them provided by this democratic-republican government—the ballot. . . .

But is urged, the use of the masculine pronouns he, his and him, in all the constitutions and laws, is proof that only men were meant to be included in their provisions. If you insist on this version of the letter of the law, we shall insist that you be consistent, and accept the other horn of the dilemma, which would compel you to exempt women from taxation for the support of the government, and from penalties for the violation of laws. . . .

There is no she, or her, or hers, in the tax laws.

The statute of New York reads:

"Every person shall be assessed in the town or ward where he resides when the assessment is made, or the lands owned by him." "Every collector shall call at least once on the person taxed, or at his usual place of residence, and shall demand payment of the taxes charged on him. If any one shall refuse to pay the tax imposed on him, the collector shall levy the same by distress and sale of his property."

The same is true of all the criminal laws: "No person shall be compelled to be a witness against himself." . . .

Though the words persons, people, inhabitants, electors, citizens, are all used indiscriminately in the national and state constitutions, there was always a conflict of opinion, prior to the war, as to whether they were synonymous terms, as for instance:

"No person shall be a representative who shall not have been seven years a citizen, and who shall not, when elected, be an inhabitant of that state in which he is chosen. No person shall be a senator who shall not have been a citizen of the United States, and an inhabitant of that state in which he is chosen." But, whatever there was for a doubt, under the old regime, the adoption of the fourteenth amendment settled that question forever, in its first sentence: "All persons born or naturalized in the United States and subject to the jurisdiction thereof, are citizens of the United States and of the state wherein they reside."

And the second settles the equal status of all persons—all citizens:

"No states shall make or enforce any law which shall abridge the privileges or immunities of citizens; nor shall any state deprive any person of life, liberty or property, without due process of law, nor deny to any person within its jurisdiction the equal protection of the laws."

The only question left to be settled, now, is: Are women persons? And I hardly believe any of our opponents will have the hardihood to say they are not. Being persons, then, women are citizens, and no state has a right to make any new law, or to enforce any old law, that shall abridge their privileges or immunities. Hence, every discrimination against women in the constitutions and laws of the several states, is today null and void, precisely as is every one against negroes.

Is the right to vote one of the privileges or immunities of citizens? I think the disfranchised ex-rebels, and the ex-state prisoners will agree with me, that it is not only one of them, but the one without which all the others are nothing. Seek first the kingdom of the ballot, and all things else shall be given thee, is the political injunction. . . .

2

Catharine Beecher: Excerpts from *Woman's Profession as Mother and Educator, with Views in Opposition to Woman Suffrage* (1872)

Catharine Beecher was the daughter of a prominent Presbyterian clergyman and the sister of Harriet Beecher Stowe, the author of Uncle Tom's Cabin. *Catharine was also a lifelong advocate of education for women with a view to their domestic duties, and author of a popular book,* A Treatise on Domestic Economy. *In the following speech, published in 1872 but first delivered in 1870, she argues against extending the right to vote to women on the grounds that political activity would distract them from their distinctive and more important role as educators of children and managers of the home. The nation ultimately extended the franchise to women with the Nineteenth Amendment, ratified in 1920.*

I appear this evening to present the views of that large portion of my sex who are opposed to such a change of our laws and customs as would place the responsibility of civil government on women.

This may be done without impugning the motives, or the character, or the measures of that respectable party who hold the contrary position. As in the physical universe the nicely-balanced *centripetal* and *centrifugal* forces hold in steady curve every brilliant orbit, so, too, in the moral world, the radical element, which would forsake the beaten path of ages, is held in safe and steady course by the conservative; while that, also, is preserved from dangerous torpor by the antagonistic power.

And so, while claiming to represent the conservative element, I meet with respect and kindness for my centrifugal friend. . . .

My object, in this address, is not to discuss the question of woman's natural and abstract right to the ballot, nor to point out the evils that might follow the exercise of this power, nor to controvert the opinions of those advocating woman's suffrage in any particular point.

Instead of this, I propose . . . to present reasons for assuming that it must be a very long time before woman suffrage can be gained. . . .

The first reason for believing that the gift of the ballot must be long delayed is, that it is contrary to the customs of Christian people, by which the cares of civil life, and the outdoor and heavy labor which take a man from home, are given to the stronger sex, and the lighter labor and care of the family state, to woman.

The more society has advanced in civilization and in Christian culture, the more perfectly have these *distinctive* divisions of responsibility for the two sexes been maintained; and in no age of country more strictly than in our own.

Those of us who oppose woman suffrage concede that there are occasions in which general laws and customs should yield to temporary emergencies; as when, in the stress of family sickness, the husband becomes nurse and cook; or, in the extremities of war, the women plow, sow, and reap; and it were well if every boy and girl were so trained that they could well meet such emergencies.

But while this is conceded, the main question is still open, namely, Is there any such emergency in our national history as demands so great a change in our laws and customs as would be involved in placing the responsibility of civil government on our whole sex? For, with the gift of the ballot, comes the connected responsibility of framing wise laws to regulate finance, war, agriculture, commerce, mining, manufactures, and all the many fields of man's outdoor labor. And the charge of these outdoor responsibilities would be assigned by the ballot; and not alone to that class of women who are demanding woman suffrage, but *to our whole sex*.

For, whenever the time comes that a single vote of one woman may decide the most delicate, the most profound, and the most perilous measures of the state and nation, it will be the duty of every woman, not only to go to the polls, but to vote intelligently and conscientiously.

It is in view of such considerations that, at the present time, a large majority of American women would regard the gift of the ballot, not as a privilege conferred, but as an act of oppression, forcing them to assume responsibilities belonging to man, for which they are not and can not be qualified; and, consequently, withdrawing attention and interest from the distinctive and more important duties of their sex. For the question is not whether a class of women, who have no family responsibilities, shall take charge of civil government; but it is whether this duty shall be imposed on the whole of our sex. With the chivalrous tenderness toward women so prevalent in our nation, this would never be done till at least a majority of women ask for it; and the time must be afar off ere such a majority will be found.

I wish to verify this statement by an extract from one of the many letters of sympathy and approbation received since it became known that I am publicly to present my views on Woman Suffrage:

My Dear Madam: Though personally a stranger, I feel impelled to write and thank you for coming before the public in opposition to the advocates of woman suffrage.

I have no doubt that an exceedingly large majority of the educated and thoughtful women of the country feel a strong personal repugnance to becoming voters, as well as a conviction that this proposed innovation, far from working a beneficial change in the condition of the country, would actually lower the present standard of political morality. But they form a class but little accustomed to make their voices heard outside of their own social circle, and therefore in danger of being overlooked by those reformers who, with a thankworthy zeal for "woman's rights," are, I think, striving to perpetrate a great woman's *wrong*.

It is sometimes said that all women ought at least to have a chance to vote, if they wish it; but none are obliged to do so unless they like. And when compliant men have said this, they consider themselves magnanimous and chivalrous, and think the whole question happily settled. It might be so if we had no *conscience*. But wider privileges mean wider duties. From the bottom of my soul I hate the idea of meeting women at the polls; and yet, if woman suffrage ever becomes a fact, I can not stay away. For my fraction of power inevitably makes me thus much responsible for the civil government of my country. If I *may* vote, I *must* vote. I have no right, by withholding my vote, to throw its weight into the wrong scale. And yet, held back as I am, and must be, from the life of the caucus, and the primary political meetings, and not more for my incapacity for man's work than by his incapacity for mine—living chiefly at home, because my work is home work—what can I know of the fitness of candidates for local offices, or of the machinery of political parties?"

This perspicuous statement expresses the present views of probably nine tenths of the most intelligent and conscientious women of our country.

3

Representative John Alfred Adair: Speech on the Seventeenth Amendment (1911)

The original Constitution provided for the indirect election of United States senators. The founders wanted one branch of the legislature to be somewhat insulated from the influence of public opinion, so they provided that senators should be elected by the state legislatures. However, the late nineteenth century saw an increasing demand for more purely democratic institutions by which the people could directly influence the government. At the same time, there was a growing impression that the Senate was a "millionaire's club," that wealthy interests were able to control the membership of the Senate by the influence they wielded over the state legislatures. These factors combined to discredit the notion of an indirectly elected Senate in the minds of many Americans, and political pressure grew for a change. In the following speech, Representative Adair, an Indiana Democrat, defends the proposed constitutional amendment providing for direct election of senators.

Mr. Speaker, I introduced a joint resolution in the Sixtieth Congress, reintroduced it in the Sixty-First Congress, and again introduced it on the first day of this session proposing an amendment to the Constitution providing for the election of Senators of the United States by a direct vote of the people. . . .

I am one of those who believe the people can be trusted, and the closer the relationship between the Government and the people the better it will be for all concerned. In my judgment the nearer a governmental agency is to the source of power the greater will be its value, probity, and efficiency. Direct responsibility results in honesty, and good faith sustains the wavering, lends encouragement to the timid, and exposes and defeats the unworthy, incompetent, and corrupt. The tendency of government the world over is toward the people. The movement is gradual, but continuous and persistent; there has been no backward step; no retrogression or recession. Without haste or thought of retracing our steps we have moved forward in the direction of liberty and the closer relationship between the people and the Government.

Mr. Speaker, the resolution before the House is one of great importance. It is a long step in the right direction, and when enacted into law the will of the people will be supreme in the United States Senate. Wealth, plutocracy, and subserviency to the interests will no longer be the qualifications necessary for a Senator, but rugged honesty, recognized ability, admitted capacity, and wide experience will be required of those who occupy a seat in the highest lawmaking body of the land. I know, Mr. Speaker, there are some who style themselves as "watch dogs" of the Constitution, who come forward with a storm of condemnation whenever it is proposed to amend that document. I am happy to confess that in my humble judgment no instrument in the history of the world compares with the Constitution of the United States, but Article V of the Constitution gives Congress the power of amendment, and this right has been exercised time and again as the exigencies demanded.

Both time and experience have shown that as a whole the Constitution is good and wise and the people have given it their heartiest approval; but devotion to the instrument itself should prompt us to make such changes as will ensure to the people the greatest degree of liberty. When those who formed this Government looked over the world they saw nothing but arbitrary governments; a monarchical government prevailed everywhere. Their experiment was great and grand, yet it was hazardous. They were determined, however, to form a government of the people. Some of them, realizing the splendid ability and the vast capacity of the American people for self-government, were willing to lay aside all of the shackles and forms of arbitrary government, but there were others who had less faith in the people for self-government and insisted on retaining some of the influences and agencies peculiar to a monarchical form of government. I believe experience has taught us that such agencies can safely be dispensed with and that we can with perfect safety bring the Government closer to the people by allowing them to vote direct for United States Senators.

Mr. Speaker, the present method of electing Senators has made the United States Senate the home of many men of great wealth, whose hearts do not beat in sympathy with the interests of the plain people and who never would have occupied a seat in that body if their election had been left to a direct vote of the people. We have reached a time in the history of the country when the Senate is no longer looked upon as the safe, conservative body, the so-called balance wheel, but is looked upon with dread and apprehension by the average American citizen, while the House, with all its faults and uncertainties, is regarded as the representative body of the American people, where can be heard the voice of the average citizen and where his rights will be protected and enforced. This condition is due to the fact that legislatures are frequently invaded by men of great wealth, shrewdness, and audacity, and the rights of the people give way to the exactions of corporate power; and he who can serve the corporations by controlling a legislature, through intrigue or persuasion, is regarded as fully equipped for service as a Senator, in which position he can guard and protect the interests of the corporation he serves. In this way the standard for the exalted position of United States Senator is debased by corporate influence. The wire-puller and schemer are frequently preferred to the statesman and the patriot, and the proud title of United States Senator has lost much of its power in the suspicions which rest in the public mind as to the manner and conditions of their selection.

Mr. Speaker, when Senators are elected by the people there will be no legislative deadlocks, which in the past have not only resulted in scandal, but have frequently deprived certain States of an equal representation in this body. The Constitution provides that each State shall be entitled to two Senators, but during the past 20 years there has scarcely been a time when one or more States were not tied up in a deadlock over the election of a Senator, and therefore were deprived of their fair and equal representation. This was an injustice to the State and unfair to the whole country.

The present system has had an evil effect on the election of members of the legislatures. The two seats in the United States Senate for each State are highly coveted prizes in American public life, and as long as the legislatures choose our Senators, those who covet these prizes will make it their business to choose members of the legislatures, and in this way much corruption and fraud will creep into our public life. . . .

Mr. Speaker, I believe the only way to remedy these evils is to so change the Constitution that the people may vote direct for Senators the same as they now vote for Members of the House. Every Member of Congress who believes in a republican form of government, a government by the people and for the people, and who is in favor of preserving the sovereignty in the hands of the citizens will vote for this resolution.

4

Senator Francis Warren:
Speech on the Seventeenth Amendment (1911)

Though the notion of direct election of senators was politically popular in the country as a whole, a number of members of Congress, particularly in the Senate, continued to defend the old mode of election. Here Senator Warren, a Wyoming Republican, sketches the case for retaining the work of the founders, despite his voting to pass the amendment so that the people would have a chance to decide the question. In the end, Congress passed the amendment, which was ratified by a sufficient number of states in 1913.

I voted against the measure on a former occasion because I believed it would not bring about a better condition of affairs. I believe that now; but I am convinced that a large majority of the people in a large number of the States desire the opportunity to vote upon this amendment; and realizing that the people must and should rule in the end I propose to vote for this measure and give the people an opportunity to vote upon the proposed constitutional amendment in the usual way, through their legislative bodies.

For myself, I am not convinced that the change in the Constitution of the United States proposed by this resolution would benefit the people of this country or their institutions. . . .

The method of electing Members of the United States Senate was not hastily determined upon. On the contrary, it was adopted after long deliberation and debate and after considering also the plan which is proposed by the pending resolution.

Very briefly I refer to this historical phase of the question. After long discussion the plans for electing Senators narrowed down to four: First, they were to be selected by the House of Representatives; second, by the President of the United States; third, by a direct vote of the people; fourth, by the State legislatures. It was contended that the first plan would make the Senate a dependency; the second would be a step in the direction of a monarchy; the third would lead to confusion and to clashes between the farming and manufacturing or commercial interests; the fourth method was unanimously supported by the members of the convention and was finally adopted when the question of the number of Senators to represent each State was settled.

This settlement was effected by the States of larger populations surrendering what they considered their right of proportional representation in the Senate and giving all the States equal representation.

Here, I might ask, if Senators are to represent the people directly, and not the sovereign States, how long will the populous Eastern States like New York, Pennsylvania, or Ohio, be content to exercise no more power in the Senate than the sparsely settled Western States like Nevada, Wyoming, Utah, and others, notwithstanding the original compact.

If there were time, countless quotations of approval from recognized great masters of political economy could be given for the plan of State legislative selection of United States Senators. I mention but a few of the many: . . .

Alexander Hamilton, in the *Federalist*, wrote:

> Through the medium of the State legislatures, which are to appoint the members of the National Senate, there is reason to expect that this branch will be generally composed with peculiar care and judgment; that these circumstances promise greater knowledge and more extensive information in the national councils, and that they will be less apt to be tainted by the spirit of faction and more out of reach of those occasional ill humors or temporary prejudices and propensities which in smaller societies frequently contaminate the public councils, beget injustice and oppression of a part of the community, and engender schemes which, though they gratify a momentary inclination or desire, terminate in general distress, dissatisfaction, and disgust.

The late Senator Hoar, in one of his great arguments on the question, said: "Our fathers were profound students of history. They found that no republic, although there had been many examples, ever lasted long without a Senate. The term Senate implied to their minds, as to ours, a body of men of mature age and of a tenure of office which was removed from all temptation of being affected by temporary currents of public sentiment. The word Senate is a misnomer when applied to any legislative body of whom these things are not true."

The plan proposed by the pending resolution proposes, in effect, to deprive the Republic of a Senate.

Senator Hoar also said: "I am convinced that the provision of the Constitution framed by the makers of that great instrument by which the popular will was to be expressed through the representatives of the people in the legislature has been eminently successful in its results, has preserved the rights of the States as such, and has protected their equality and their integrity as well as their powers of local self-government, which are so essential to the maintenance of government by and for the people."

Mr. President, the testimony of the great students and thinkers has endorsed the plan of the creation of the Senate framed by the makers of our Federal Constitution, and in my belief an impartial analysis of its results shows no necessity for a change.

5

Theodore Roosevelt: Address Before the Ohio Constitutional Convention (1912)

Many members of the progressive movement hoped to speed the pace of social reform by giving the people much more direct power over government policy. America's commitment to republican government, or rule by the people, they contended, required such steps. Here, Theodore Roosevelt, who had occupied the presidency as a Republican and was now planning to run for it as a Progressive, argues for state constitutional measures that would give the people the ability to discipline and overrule state judges who stood in the way of the popular will.

I am emphatically a believer in constitutionalism, and because of this fact I no less emphatically protest against any theory that would make of the constitution a means of thwarting instead of securing the absolute right of the people to rule themselves and to provide for their social and industrial well-being. . . .

I therefore very earnestly ask you clearly to provide in this constitution means which will enable the people readily to amend it if at any point it works injustice, and also means which will permit the people themselves by popular vote, after due deliberation and discussion, but finally and without appeal, to settle what the proper construction of any constitutional point is. . . .

The only safe course to follow in this great American democracy is to provide for making the popular judgment really effective.

When this is done, then it is our duty to see that the people, having the full power, realize their heavy responsibility for exercising that power aright.

But it is a false constitutionalism, a false statesmanship, to endeavor by the exercise of a perverted ingenuity to seem to give the people full power and at the same time to trick them out of it. Yet this is precisely what is done in every case where the State permits its representatives, whether on the bench or in the legislature or in executive office, to declare that it has not the power to right grave social wrongs, or that any of the officers created by the people, and rightfully the servants of the people, can set themselves up to be the masters of the people. Constitution-makers should make it clear beyond a shadow of doubt that the people in their legislative capacity have the power to enact into law any measure they deem necessary for the betterment of social and industrial conditions. The wisdom of framing any particular law of this kind is a proper subject of debate; but the power of the people to enact the law should not be subject to debate. To hold the contrary view is to be false to the cause of the people, to the cause of American democracy. . . .

An independent and upright judiciary which fearlessly stands for the right, even against popular clamor, but which also understands and sympathizes with popular needs, is a great asset of popular government. . . .

There is no public servant and no private man whom I place above a judge of the best type, and very few whom I rank beside him. I believe in the cumulative value of the law and in its value as an impersonal, disinterested basis of control. I believe in the necessity for the courts' interpretation of the law as law without the power to change the law or to substitute some other thing than law for it. But I agree with every great jurist, from Marshall downward, when I say that every judge is bound to consider two separate elements in his decision of a case, one the terms of the law; and the other the conditions of actual life to which the law is to be applied. Only by taking both of these elements into account is it possible to apply the law as its spirit and intent demand that it be applied. . . . Moreover, never forget that the judge is just as much the servant of the people as any other official. Of course he must act conscientiously. So must every other official. He must not do anything wrong because there is popular clamor for it, any more than under similar circumstances a governor or a legislator or a public-utilities commissioner should do wrong. Each must follow his conscience, even though to do so costs him his place. But in their turn the people must follow their conscience, and when they have definitely decided on a given policy they must have public servants who will carry out that policy.

Keep clearly in mind the distinction between the end and the means to attain that end. Our aim is to get the type of judge that I have described, to keep him on the bench as long as possible, and to keep off the bench and, if necessary, take off the bench, the wrong type of judge. In some communities one method may work well which in other communities does not work well, and each community should adopt and preserve or reject a given method according to its practical working. . . .

I do not believe in adopting the recall save as a last resort, when it has become clearly evident that no other course will achieve the desired result.

But either the recall will have to be adopted or else it will have to be made much easier than it now is to get rid, not merely of a bad judge, but of a judge who, however virtuous, has grown so out of touch with social needs and facts that he is unfit longer to render good service on the bench.

It is nonsense to say that impeachment meets the difficulty. In actual practice we have found that impeachment does not work, that unfit judges stay on the bench in spite of it, and indeed because of the fact that impeachment is the only remedy that can be used against them. Where such is the actual fact it is idle to discuss the theory of the case. Impeachment as a remedy for the ills of which the people justly complain is a complete failure. A quicker, a more summary, remedy is needed. . . . And whenever it be found in actual practice that such remedy does not give the needed results, I would unhesitatingly adopt the recall.

But there is one kind of recall in which I very earnestly believe, and the immediate adoption of which I urge.

There are sound reasons for being cautious about the recall of a good judge who has rendered an unwise and improper decision. Every public servant, no matter how valuable—and not omitting Washington or Lincoln or Marshall—at times makes mistakes. Therefore we should be cautious about recalling the judge, and we should be cautious about interfering in any way with the judge in decisions which he makes in the ordinary course as between individuals. But when a judge decides a constitutional question, when he decides what the people as a whole can or cannot do, the people should have the right to recall that decision if they think it wrong. We should hold the judiciary in all respect; but it is both absurd and degrading to make a fetish a judge or of any one else. . . .

Again and again in the past justice has been scandalously obstructed by State courts declaring State laws in conflict with the Federal Constitution, although the Supreme Court of the nation had never so decided or had even decided in a contrary sense.

When the supreme court of the State declares a given statute unconstitutional, because in conflict with the State or the National Constitution, its opinion should be subject to revision by the people themselves. Such an opinion ought always to be treated with great respect by the people, and unquestionably in the majority of cases would be accepted and followed by them. But actual experience has shown the vital need of the people reserving to themselves the right to pass upon such opinion. If any considerable number of the people feel that the decision is in defiance of justice, they should be given the right by petition to bring before the voters at some subsequent election, special or otherwise, as might be decided, and after the fullest opportunity for deliberation and debate, the question whether or not the judges' interpretation of the Constitution is to be sustained. If it is sustained, well and good. If not, then the popular verdict is to be accepted as final, the decision is to be treated as reversed, and the construction of the Constitution definitely decided— subject only to action by the Supreme Court of the United States. . . .

The true view is that legislators and judges alike are the servants of the people, who have been created by the people just as the people have created the Constitution; and they hold only such power as the people have for the time being delegated to them. If these two sets of public servants disagree as to the amounts of power respectively delegated to them by the people under the Constitution, and if the case is of sufficient importance, then, as a matter of course, it should be the right of the people themselves to decide between them.

I do not say that the people are infallible. But I do say that our whole history shows that the American people are more often sound in their decisions than is the case with any of the governmental bodies to whom, for their convenience, they have delegated portions of their power.

If this is not so, then there is no justification for the existence of our government; and if it is so, then there is no justification for refusing to give the people the real, and not merely the nominal, ultimate decision on questions of constitutional law.

6

President William Howard Taft: Veto Message (1912)

In 1912 Congress passed an enabling act providing for Arizona's admission to the Union. However, President Taft vetoed the law because of provisions in the proposed Arizona constitution similar to those called for by Theodore Roosevelt in the previous reading. Taft argues that a judicial recall would imperil the independence of courts and therefore the rights of individuals and minorities. He thus defends a position closer to that of the founders, who believed that republican government required institutions designed to moderate majority rule.

Under the Arizona constitution all elective officers, and this includes county and State judges, six months after their election are subject to the recall. . . .

This provision of the Arizona constitution, in its application to county and State judges, seems to me so pernicious in its effect, so likely to subject the rights of the individual to the possible tyranny of a popular majority, and, therefore, to be so injurious to the cause of free government, that I must disapprove a constitution containing it. . . .

[A]s the government is for all the people, and is not solely for a majority of them, the majority in exercising control either directly or through its agents is bound to exercise the power for the benefit of the minority as well as the majority. But all have recognized that the majority of a people, unrestrained by law, when aroused and without the sobering effect of deliberation and discussion, may do injustice to the minority or the individual when the selfish interest of the majority prompts. Hence arises the necessity for a constitution by which the will of the majority shall be permitted to guide the course of the government only under controlling checks that experience has shown to be necessary to secure for the minority its share of the benefit to the whole people that a popular government is established to bestow. A popular government is not a government of a majority, by a majority, for a majority of the people. It is a government of the whole people, by a majority of the whole people under such rules and checks as will secure a wise, just, and beneficent government for all the people. It is said you can always trust the people to do justice. If that means all the people and they all agree, you can. But ordinarily they do not all agree, and the maxim is interpreted to mean that you can always trust a majority of the people. This is not invariably true; and every limitation imposed by the people upon the power of the majority in their constitutions is an admission that it is not always true. No honest, clear-headed man, however great a lover of popular government, can deny that the unbridled expression of the majority of a community converted hastily into law or action would sometimes make a government tyrannical and cruel. Constitutions are checks upon the hasty action of the majority. They are the self-imposed restraints of a whole people upon a majority of them to secure sober action

and a respect for the rights of the minority, and of the individual in his relation to other individuals, and in his relation to the whole people in their character as a state or government. . . .

By the recall in the Arizona constitution it is proposed to give to the
majority power to remove arbitrarily, and without delay, any judge who may
have the courage to render an unpopular decision. By the recall it is proposed
to enable a minority of 25 percent of the voters of the district or State, for no
prescribed cause, after the judge has been in office six months, to submit the
question of his retention in office to the electorate. The petitioning minority
must say on the ballot what they can against him in 200 words, and he must
defend as best he can in the same space. Other candidates are permitted to
present themselves and have their names printed on the ballot, so that the recall
is not based solely on the record or the acts of the judge, but also on the question whether some other and more popular candidate has been found to unseat
him. Could there be a system more ingeniously devised to subject judges to
momentary gusts of popular passion than this? We can not be blind to the fact
that often an intelligent and respectable electorate may be so roused upon an
issue that it will visit with condemnation the decision of a just judge, though
exactly in accord with the law governing the case, merely because it affects
unfavorably their contest. . . .

No period of delay is interposed for the abatement of popular feeling. The
recall is devised to encourage quick action, and to lead the people to strike
while the iron is hot. . . . On the instant of an unpopular ruling, while the spirit
of protest has not had time to cool and even while an appeal may be pending
from his ruling in which he may be sustained, he is to be haled before the
electorate as a tribunal, with no judicial hearing, evidence, or defense, and
thrown out of office, and disgraced because he has failed, in a single decision,
it may be, to satisfy the popular demand. Think of the opportunity such a system would give to unscrupulous political bosses in control, as they have been
in control not only of conventions but elections! Think of the enormous
power for evil given to the sensational, muckraking portion of the press in
rousing prejudice against a just judge by false charges and insinuations, the
effect of which in the short period of the election it would be impossible for
him to meet and offset! Supporters of such a system seem to think that it will
work only in the interest of the poor, the humble, the weak, and the oppressed;
that it will strike down only the judge who is supposed to favor corporations
and to be affected by the corrupting influence of the rich. Nothing could be
further from the ultimate result. The motive it would offer to unscrupulous
combinations to seek to control politics in order to control judges is clear.
Those would profit by the recall who have the best opportunity of rousing the
majority of the people to action on a sudden impulse. Are they likely to be
the wisest or the best people in a community? Do they not include those who
have money enough to employ the firebrands and slanderers in a community
and the stirrers up of social hate? Would not self-respecting men well hesitate
to accept judicial office with such a sword of Damocles hanging over them?

What kind of judgments might those on the unpopular side expect from courts whose judges must make their decisions under such legalized terrorism? The character of the judges would deteriorate to that of trimmers and time-servers, and independent judicial action would be a thing of the past.

7

President Lyndon Johnson: "We Shall Overcome" Speech (1965)

Although the Fifteenth Amendment to the Constitution, which was ratified in 1870, prohibited denying anyone the right to vote because of race (see reading in Chapter 5 of Volume I), many states continued to bar African Americans from exercising the franchise. They did so by making use of means, such as literacy tests and poll taxes, that were in principle race-neutral but in practice were applied in a discriminatory manner so as to disenfranchise blacks. Thus the right to vote was only effectively extended to African Americans by the Voting Rights Act of 1965, which was the final version of the legislation here proposed by President Johnson.

This was the first nation in the history of the world to be founded with a purpose. The great phrases of that purpose still sound in every American heart, North and South: "All men are created equal," "government by consent of the governed," "give me liberty or give me death." Well, those are not just clever words, or those are not just empty theories. In their name Americans have fought and died for two centuries, and tonight around the world they stand there as guardians of our liberty, risking their lives. Those words are a promise to every citizen that he shall share in the dignity of man. This dignity cannot be found in a man's possessions; it cannot be found in his power, or in his position. It really rests on his right to be treated as a man equal in opportunity to all others. It says that he shall share in freedom, he shall choose his leaders, educate his children, provide for his family according to his ability and his merits as a human being. To apply any other test—to deny a man his hopes because of his color, or race, or his religion, or the place of his birth is not only to do injustice, it is to deny America and to dishonor the dead who gave their lives for American freedom.

Our fathers believed that if this noble view of the rights of man was to flourish, it must be rooted in democracy. The most basic right of all was the right to choose your own leaders. The history of this country, in large measure, is the history of the expansion of that right to all of our people. Many of the issues of civil rights are very complex and most difficult. But about this there can and should be no argument.

Every American citizen must have an equal right to vote.

There is no reason which can excuse the denial of that right. There is no duty which weighs more heavily on us than the duty we have to ensure that right.

Yet the harsh fact is that in many places in this country men and women are kept from voting simply because they are Negroes. Every device of which human ingenuity is capable has been used to deny this right. The Negro citizen may go to register only to be told that the day is wrong, or the hour is late, or the official in charge is absent. And if he persists, and if he manages to present himself to the registrar, he may be disqualified because he did not spell out his middle name or because he abbreviated a word on the application. And if he manages to fill out an application, he is given a test. The registrar is the sole judge of whether he passes this test. He may be asked to recite the entire Constitution, or explain the most complex provisions of State law. And even a college degree cannot be used to prove that he can read and write. For the fact is that the only way to pass these barriers is to show a white skin. Experience has clearly shown that the existing process of law cannot overcome systematic and ingenious discrimination. No law that we now have on the books—and I have helped to put three of them there—can ensure the right to vote when local officials are determined to deny it. In such a case our duty must be clear to all of us. The Constitution says that no person shall be kept from voting because of his race or his color. We have all sworn an oath before God to support and to defend that Constitution. We must now act in obedience to that oath.

Wednesday, I will send to Congress a law designed to eliminate illegal barriers to the right to vote.

The broad principles of that bill will be in the hands of the Democratic and Republican leaders tomorrow. After they have reviewed it, it will come here formally as a bill. I am grateful for this opportunity to come here tonight at the invitation of the leadership to reason with my friends, to give them my views, and to visit with my former colleagues. I've had prepared a more comprehensive analysis of the legislation which I had intended to transmit to the clerk tomorrow, but which I will submit to the clerks tonight. But I want to really discuss with you now, briefly, the main proposals of this legislation.

This bill will strike down restrictions to voting in all elections—Federal, State, and local—which have been used to deny Negroes the right to vote. This bill will establish a simple, uniform standard which cannot be used, however ingenious the effort, to flout our Constitution. It will provide for citizens to be registered by officials of the United States Government, if the State officials refuse to register them. It will eliminate tedious, unnecessary lawsuits which delay the right to vote. Finally, this legislation will ensure that properly registered individuals are not prohibited from voting.

I will welcome the suggestions from all of the Members of Congress—I have no doubt that I will get some—on ways and means to strengthen this law and to make it effective. But experience has plainly shown that this is the only path to carry out the command of the Constitution.

To those who seek to avoid action by their National Government in their own communities, who want to and who seek to maintain purely local control over elections, the answer is simple: open your polling places to all your people.

Allow men and women to register and vote whatever the color of their skin. Extend the rights of citizenship to every citizen of this land.

There is no constitutional issue here. The command of the Constitution is plain. There is no moral issue. It is wrong—deadly wrong—to deny any of your fellow Americans the right to vote in this country. There is no issue of States' rights or national rights. There is only the struggle for human rights. I have not the slightest doubt what will be your answer.

But the last time a President sent a civil rights bill to the Congress, it contained a provision to protect voting rights in Federal elections. That civil rights bill was passed after eight long months of debate. And when that bill came to my desk from the Congress for my signature, the heart of the voting provision had been eliminated. This time, on this issue, there must be no delay, or no hesitation, or no compromise with our purpose.

We cannot, we must not, refuse to protect the right of every American to vote in every election that he may desire to participate in. And we ought not, and we cannot, and we must not wait another eight months before we get a bill. We have already waited a hundred years and more, and the time for waiting is gone.

So I ask you to join me in working long hours—nights and weekends, if necessary—to pass this bill. And I don't make that request lightly. For from the window where I sit with the problems of our country, I recognize that from outside this chamber is the outraged conscience of a nation, the grave concern of many nations, and the harsh judgment of history on our acts.

8

Justice William O. Douglas: Opinion of the Court in *Harper* v. *Virginia State Board of Elections* (1966)

The development of America's understanding of republican government was accomplished not only by amendments and laws approved by legislative bodies, but also by the Supreme Court's interpretation of the Constitution. In the 1960s, the Court issued a number of important rulings invalidating formerly approved restrictions on the franchise and requiring legislative districts to be drawn in such a way as to render each citizen's vote of roughly equal value. In the following case, the Court declared it unconstitutional for states to deny citizens the right to vote because of failure to pay a poll tax.

While the right to vote in federal elections is conferred by Art. I, 2, of the Constitution, the right to vote in state elections is nowhere expressly mentioned. It is argued that the right to vote in state elections is implicit, particularly by reason of the First Amendment and that it may not constitutionally be conditioned upon the payment of a tax or fee. We do not stop to canvass the relation between voting and political expression. For it is enough to say that once the franchise is granted to the electorate, lines may not be drawn which are inconsistent with the Equal Protection Clause of the Fourteenth Amendment. That is to say, the right of suffrage "is subject to the imposition of state standards which are not discriminatory and which do not contravene any restriction that Congress, acting pursuant to its constitutional powers, has imposed." *Lassiter* v. *Northampton Election Board*. We were speaking there of a state literacy test which we sustained, warning that the result would be different if a literacy test, fair on its face, were used to discriminate against a class. But the *Lassiter* case does not govern the result here, because, unlike a poll tax, the "ability to read and write . . . has some relation to standards designed to promote intelligent use of the ballot." Id., at 51.

We conclude that a State violates the Equal Protection Clause of the Fourteenth Amendment whenever it makes the affluence of the voter or payment of any fee an electoral standard. Voter qualifications have no relation to wealth nor to paying or not paying this or any other tax. Our cases demonstrate that the Equal Protection Clause of the Fourteenth Amendment restrains the States from fixing voter qualifications which invidiously discriminate. Thus without questioning the power of a State to impose reasonable residence restrictions on the availability of the ballot, we held in *Carrington* v. *Rash*, that a State may not deny the opportunity to vote to a bona fide resident merely because he is a member of the armed services. "By forbidding a soldier ever to controvert the presumption of non-residence, the Texas Constitution imposes an invidious discrimination in violation of the Fourteenth Amendment." Previously we had said that neither homesite nor occupation "affords a permissible basis for distinguishing between qualified voters within the State." We think the same must be true of requirements of wealth or affluence or payment of a fee.

Long ago in *Yick Wo* v. *Hopkins*, the Court referred to "the political franchise of voting" as a "fundamental political right, because preservative of all rights." Recently in *Reynolds* v. *Sims*, we said, "Undoubtedly, the right of suffrage is a fundamental matter in a free and democratic society. Especially since the right to exercise the franchise in a free and unimpaired manner is preservative of other basic civil and political rights, any alleged infringement of the right of citizens to vote must be carefully and meticulously scrutinized." There we were considering charges that voters in one part of the State had greater representation per person in the State Legislature than voters in another part of the State. We concluded: "A citizen, a qualified voter, is no more nor no less so because he lives in the city or on the farm. This is the clear and strong command of our Constitution's Equal Protection Clause. This is an essential part of the concept of a government of laws and not men. This is at the heart of Lincoln's vision of 'government of the people, by the people, [and] for the people.' The Equal Protection Clause demands no less than substantially equal state legislative representation for all citizens, of all places as well as of all races."

We say the same whether the citizen, otherwise qualified to vote, has $1.50 in his pocket or nothing at all, pays the fee or fails to pay it. The principle that denies the State the right to dilute a citizen's vote on account of his economic status or other such factors by analogy bars a system which excludes those unable to pay a fee to vote or who fail to pay.

It is argued that a State may exact fees from citizens for many different kinds of licenses; that if it can demand from all an equal fee for a driver's license, it can demand from all an equal poll tax for voting. But we must remember that the interest of the State, when it comes to voting, is limited to the power to fix qualifications. Wealth, like race, creed, or color, is not germane to one's ability to participate intelligently in the electoral process. Lines drawn on the basis of wealth or property, like those of race, are traditionally disfavored. To introduce wealth or payment of a fee as a measure of a voter's qualifications is to introduce a capricious or irrelevant factor. The degree of the discrimination is irrelevant. In this context—that is, as a condition of obtaining a ballot—the requirement of fee paying causes an "invidious" discrimination that runs afoul of the Equal Protection Clause. . . .

We agree, of course, with Mr. Justice Holmes that the Due Process Clause of the Fourteenth Amendment "does not enact Mr. Herbert Spencer's Social Statistics" (*Lochner* v. *New York*). Likewise, the Equal Protection Clause is not shackled to the political theory of a particular era. In determining what lines are unconstitutionally discriminatory, we have never been confined to historic notions of equality, any more than we have restricted due process to a fixed catalogue of what was at a given time deemed to be the limits of fundamental rights. Notions of what constitutes equal treatment for purposes of the Equal Protection Clause do change. This Court in 1896 held that laws providing for separate public facilities for white and Negro citizens did not deprive the latter of the equal protection and treatment that the Fourteenth Amendment commands. *Plessy* v. *Ferguson*. Seven of the eight Justices then sitting subscribed to the Court's opinion, thus joining in expressions of what constituted unequal and discriminatory treatment that sound strange to a contemporary ear. When, in 1954—more than a half-century later—we repudiated the "separate-but-equal" doctrine of *Plessy* as respects public education we stated: "In approaching this problem, we cannot turn the clock back to 1868 when the Amendment was adopted, or even to 1896 when *Plessy* v. *Ferguson* was written." *Brown* v. *Board of Education*.

In a recent searching re-examination of the Equal Protection Clause, we held, as already noted, that "the opportunity for equal participation by all voters in the election of state legislators" is required. *Reynolds* v. *Sims*. We decline to qualify that principle by sustaining this poll tax. Our conclusion, like that in *Reynolds* v. *Sims*, is founded not on what we think governmental policy should be, but on what the Equal Protection Clause requires.

9

Justice John M. Harlan: Dissenting Opinion in *Harper* v. *Virginia State Board of Elections* (1966)

Justice M. Harlan was the grandson of the Justice John Marshall Harlan who wrote the famous dissenting opinion in Plessy v. Ferguson. *In his dissenting opinion he contends that the Court, in striking down the poll tax, is imposing on the states contemporary, egalitarian notions of democracy that are not in fact required by the Constitution.*

The final demise of state poll taxes, already totally proscribed by the Twenty-Fourth Amendment with respect to federal elections and abolished by the States themselves in all but four States with respect to state elections, is perhaps in itself not of great moment. But the fact that the coup de grace has been administered by this Court instead of being left to the affected States or to the federal political process should be a matter of continuing concern to all interested in maintaining the proper role of this tribunal under our scheme of government.

I do not propose to retread ground covered in my dissents in *Reynolds* v. *Sims* and *Carrington* v. *Rash*, and will proceed on the premise that the Equal Protection Clause of the Fourteenth Amendment now reaches both state apportionment (*Reynolds*) and voter-qualification (*Carrington*) cases. My disagreement with the present decision is that in holding the Virginia poll tax violative of the Equal Protection Clause the Court has departed from long-established standards governing the application of that clause.

The Equal Protection Clause prevents States from arbitrarily treating people differently under their laws. Whether any such differing treatment is to be deemed arbitrary depends on whether or not it reflects an appropriate differentiating classification among those affected, the clause has never been thought to require equal treatment of all persons despite differing circumstances. The test evolved by this Court for determining whether an asserted justifying classification exists is whether such a classification can be deemed to be founded on some rational and otherwise constitutionally permissible state policy. This standard reduces to a minimum the likelihood that the federal judiciary will judge state policies in terms of the individual notions and predilections of its own members, and until recently it has been followed in all kinds of "equal protection" cases.

Reynolds v. *Sims*, among its other breaks with the past, also marked a departure from these traditional and wise principles. Unless its "one man, one vote" thesis of state legislative apportionment is to be attributed to the unsupportable proposition that "Equal Protection" simply means indiscriminate equality, it seems inescapable that what *Reynolds* really reflected was but this Court's own views of how modern American representative government should be run. For it can hardly be thought that no other method of apportionment may be considered rational.

Following *Reynolds* the Court, in *Carrington* v. *Rash*, applied the traditional equal protection standard in striking down a Texas statute disqualifying as voters in state elections certain members of the Armed Forces of the United States. But today in holding unconstitutional state poll taxes and property qualifications for voting . . . the Court reverts to the highly subjective judicial approach manifested by *Reynolds*. In substance the Court's analysis of the equal protection issue goes no further than to say that the electoral franchise is "precious" and "fundamental," and to conclude that "[t]o introduce wealth or payment of a fee as a measure of a voter's qualifications is to introduce a capricious or irrelevant factor." These are of course captivating phrases, but they are wholly inadequate to satisfy the standard governing adjudication of the equal protection issue: Is there a rational basis for Virginia's poll tax as a voting qualification? I think the answer to that question is undoubtedly "yes."

Property qualifications and poll taxes have been a traditional part of our political structure. In the Colonies the franchise was generally a restricted one. Over the years these and other restrictions were gradually lifted, primarily because popular theories of political representation had changed. Often restrictions were lifted only after wide public debate. The issue of woman suffrage, for example, raised questions of family relationships, of participation in public affairs, of the very nature of the type of society in which Americans wished to live; eventually a consensus was reached, which culminated in the Nineteenth Amendment no more than 45 years ago.

Similarly with property qualifications, it is only by fiat that it can be said, especially in the context of American history, that there can be no rational debate as to their advisability. Most of the early Colonies had them; many of the States have had them during much of their histories; and, whether one agrees or not, arguments have been and still can be made in favor of them. For example, it is certainly a rational argument that payment of some minimal poll tax promotes civic responsibility, weeding out those who do not care enough about public affairs to pay $1.50 or thereabouts a year for the exercise of the franchise. It is also arguable, indeed it was probably accepted as sound political theory by a large percentage of Americans through most of our history, that people with some property have a deeper stake in community affairs, and are consequently more responsible, more educated, more knowledgeable, more worthy of confidence, than those without means, and that the community and Nation would be better managed if the franchise were restricted to such citizens. . . .

These viewpoints, to be sure, ring hollow on most contemporary ears. Their lack of acceptance today is evidenced by the fact that nearly all of the States, left to their own devices, have eliminated property or poll-tax qualifications; by the cognate fact that Congress and three-quarters of the States quickly ratified the Twenty-Fourth Amendment; and by the fact that rules such as the "pauper exclusion" in Virginia law have never been enforced.

Property and poll-tax qualifications, very simply, are not in accord with current egalitarian notions of how a modern democracy should be organized. It is of course entirely fitting that legislatures should modify the law to reflect such changes in popular attitudes. However, it is all wrong, in my view, for the

Court to adopt the political doctrines popularly accepted at a particular moment of our history and to declare all others to be irrational and invidious, barring them from the range of choice by reasonably minded people acting through the political process. It was not too long ago that Mr. Justice Holmes felt impelled to remind the Court that the Due Process Clause of the Fourteenth Amendment does not enact the laissez-faire theory of society. *Lochner* v. *New York.* The times have changed, and perhaps it is appropriate to observe that neither does the Equal Protection Clause of that Amendment rigidly impose upon America an ideology of unrestrained egalitarianism.

10

Senator Charles Percy: Speech on the Twenty-sixth Amendment (1971)

In 1970 Congress altered the Voting Rights Act to require that those eighteen and older be allowed to vote in all state and federal elections. The Supreme Court, however, struck down the former requirement, arguing that the principle of Federalism did not allow the federal government to set the voting qualifications for state elections. This partial invalidation of the law posed a serious practical problem: the possibility of an election in 1972 in which some citizens would be qualified to vote for some offices but not for others. Congress accordingly acted quickly to propose a constitutional amendment creating a uniform minimum voting age for both the states and the federal government. Here Senator Percy, an Illinois Republican, argues for passage of the amendment.

[T]he principal reason for my support of the constitutional amendment giving the right to vote to 18–year–olds in State and local elections goes far beyond the serious mechanical problems posed by dual elections.

It also goes far beyond the often cited issue of the "voteless soldier." The argument that an individual who is old enough to fight and die for his country should also be old enough to vote is certainly very persuasive, but there are others that are equally impressive. Eighteen–year–olds are regarded as adults by the penal codes, by the insurance companies, by the state agencies that issue automobile operator's licenses. They can enter the Federal Civil Service; they can be taxed; they are legally entitled to marry in any State.

In brief, Americans who are 18, 19, and 20 are adults in virtually every legal sense. There is no justifiable reason for withholding from them the most basic of their civil rights—the right to vote, in any and all elections. . . .

The contention that young people are too ill–informed about public affairs to exercise wisely the right to vote can have little credence. Perhaps this argument had some validity at the turn of the century, when only 6 percent of the Americans who had reached 18 were high school graduates, or in 1940, when only about half had completed high school.

But in the year 1971, when 81 percent of all Americans have graduated from high school by the age of 18 and when nearly half of the 18-, 19-, and 20-year-olds are college students, young Americans have the education and the maturity to participate fully in our political process. Anyone who watches television or reads a newspaper understands that they already are deeply involved in questions of public policy. Their commitment is likely to become even deeper if we give them a peaceful means to achieve the ends they seek. . . .

Mr. President, the argument that the vote should be denied to young people because a small minority of them hold views that are unacceptable to many adults would not be worth discussing were it not so prevalent. To do so would be comparable to taking the franchise away from any group whose views are not held by a majority of Americans—whether they be prohibitionists, Presbyterians or—for that matter—Republicans. Diversity of belief is one of this country's most important assets. It must be encouraged—not merely tolerated—if we wish to avoid the intellectual stagnation that is characteristic of nations in which ideas are imposed upon the people. . . .

The Census Bureau's projections indicate that approximately 11.5 million Americans between 18 and 20 years old will be eligible to vote in the 1972 elections. We will determine today whether or not they will be fully or partially enfranchised citizens, eligible to vote in all elections or simply in presidential and congressional contests. . . .

The basic question we are examining today . . . can be summarized in one word—justice. We must give 18- to 20-year-olds the vote because it is right. Mr. President, I strongly urge the adoption by the Senate of this constitutional amendment.

I would like to close by stating that young people in this country have had a tremendous impact on public affairs. It was young people who went South to register voters, and had their skulls cracked open sometimes, but that resulted in the Voting Rights Act of 1964 and a whole new policy. It was young people who started the trend to get out of Vietnam rather than deeper into it. Young people saw that this was getting no place fast, and we had to have a policy of getting out and a clear-cut policy enunciated to the South Vietnamese, rather than getting into it deeper. They were right. Everyone agrees with that. Young people brought about the environmental control we face today.

11

Representative Barry Goldwater, Jr.: Remarks Against the Twenty-sixth Amendment (1971)

Although the possible mechanical difficulties mentioned by Senator Percy led most members of Congress to support the amendment, some members who had voted against the changes to the Voting Rights Act maintained their opposition. Here, Representative Goldwater, a California Republican and son of the famous Arizona senator and 1964

Republican presidential candidate, contends that the vote should not be extended to eighteen-year-olds.

Mr. Chairman, I would like to say a few words concerning the passage of House Joint Resolution 223, a constitutional amendment to lower the voting age to 18 in State and local elections.

When the 91st Congress voted last year to extend the Voting Rights Act, and to enfranchise 18-year-olds, I was opposed for a number of reasons. I felt that this enfranchisement was being rushed through the House without adequate debate, especially considering the seriousness of the issues involved. I also felt that, on the whole, the 18 to 21 age group was not responsible and socially aware enough to be given the vote. Studies have shown that even when enfranchised, the turnout of this age group tends to run about half of the normal voter turnout. Moreover, most of the States which had considered lowering the voting age had found that a majority of the people opposed this action in statewide referendums.

Now the Supreme Court has found that the enfranchisement is legal only for Federal elections, leaving a rather chaotic situation as regards State and local elections. In another mad rush we are attempting to remedy this situation—again without a really adequate exploration of the issues involved and debate on the floor of the House.

I am most concerned about this infringement on the expressed will of the American people, and the States' rights at this point. The high rejection rate of the 18-year-old vote at the State level is a clear mandate for the Congress, a mandate which we are now ignoring for the second time. How much further is this erosion of the will of the people going to continue?

I would like to reiterate my opposition to this measure. I have the greatest respect and admiration for the youth of America. I have found them consistently aware, knowledgeable, and concerned. But this particular combination is not necessarily conducive to the evolution of a politically and socially aware and responsible electorate—namely the fact that the voting turnout 21- to 30-year-olds is still markedly lower than the national average.

It takes more than education and idealistic principles to make a responsible American and a good voter. It takes a pragmatic knowledge of the working of our society, a knowledge that only comes through experience, maturity, and involvement. Paying taxes, raising children, seeing how the Federal Government acts upon our daily lives—I consider these more important requisites for good citizenship than an academic education. The anger with the Government which stems from experience with its red tape is a much more valid and productive anger than one based on negative idealism.

Therefore it is my sincere hope that the legislatures of the several States will be more responsive to the wishes and needs of the American people than this Congress has been, and will fail to ratify House Joint Resolution 223.

12

The Supreme Court's *Per Curiam* Opinion
in *Bush* v. *Gore* (2000)

Some recent disputes about the franchise have focused on how ballots—especially ones that may be improperly or imperfectly marked—are counted. This well-known and controversial case involves the recount of votes cast in the 2000 presidential election in Florida. The initial count showed Governor George W. Bush with a slim lead, so Vice President Al Gore sought a recount, hoping that reexamination of some ballots would result in additional votes for him, thus possibly changing the outcome of the Florida election and therefore the electoral college vote. Bush sued to stop the recount, complaining that Gore supporters in Democratic counties were examining the ballots according to arbitrary and changing standards intended only to shift enough votes for Gore to win. The Court in effect sided with Bush, thus ensuring his elevation to the presidency. It issued a "per curiam" opinion in the name of the Court as a whole with no single justice identified as its author. Per curiam opinions are used to create an appearance of unanimity on the Court, though the gesture was undermined in this case by the issuing of dissenting opinions by some of the justices.

The petition presents the following questions: whether the Florida Supreme Court established new standards for resolving Presidential election contests, thereby violating Art. II, §1, cl. 2, of the United States Constitution and failing to comply with 3 U.S.C. §5, and whether the use of standardless manual recounts violates the Equal Protection and Due Process Clauses. With respect to the equal protection question, we find a violation of the Equal Protection Clause. . . .

The individual citizen has no federal constitutional right to vote for electors for the President of the United States unless and until the state legislature chooses a statewide election as the means to implement its power to appoint members of the Electoral College. U.S. Const., Art. II, §1. This is the source for the statement in *McPherson* v. *Blacker* (1892), that the State legislature's power to select the manner for appointing electors is plenary; it may, if it so chooses, select the electors itself, which indeed was the manner used by State legislatures in several States for many years after the Framing of our Constitution. History has now favored the voter, and in each of the several States the citizens themselves vote for Presidential electors. When the state legislature vests the right to vote for President in its people, the right to vote as the legislature has prescribed is fundamental; and one source of its fundamental nature lies in the equal weight accorded to each vote and the equal dignity owed to each voter. The State, of course, after granting the franchise in the special context of Article II, can take back the power to appoint electors.

The right to vote is protected in more than the initial allocation of the franchise. Equal protection applies as well to the manner of its exercise. Having once granted the right to vote on equal terms, the State may not, by later arbitrary and disparate treatment, value one person's vote over that of another. It must be remembered that "the right of suffrage can be denied by a debasement or dilution of the weight of a citizen's vote just as effectively as by wholly prohibiting the free exercise of the franchise." *Reynolds* v. *Sims* (1964).

There is no difference between the two sides of the present controversy on these basic propositions. Respondents say that the very purpose of vindicating the right to vote justifies the recount procedures now at issue. The question before us, however, is whether the recount procedures the Florida Supreme Court has adopted are consistent with its obligation to avoid arbitrary and disparate treatment of the members of its electorate.

Much of the controversy seems to revolve around ballot cards designed to be perforated by a stylus but which, either through error or deliberate omission, have not been perforated with sufficient precision for a machine to count them. In some cases a piece of the card—a chad—is hanging, say by two corners. In other cases there is no separation at all, just an indentation.

The Florida Supreme Court has ordered that the intent of the voter be discerned from such ballots. For purposes of resolving the equal protection challenge, it is not necessary to decide whether the Florida Supreme Court had the authority under the legislative scheme for resolving election disputes to define what a legal vote is and to mandate a manual recount implementing that definition. The recount mechanisms implemented in response to the decisions of the Florida Supreme Court do not satisfy the minimum requirement for non-arbitrary treatment of voters necessary to secure the fundamental right. Florida's basic command for the count of legally cast votes is to consider the "intent of the voter." This is unobjectionable as an abstract proposition and a starting principle. The problem inheres in the absence of specific standards to ensure its equal application. The formulation of uniform rules to determine intent based on these recurring circumstances is practicable and, we conclude, necessary.

The law does not refrain from searching for the intent of the actor in a multitude of circumstances; and in some cases the general command to ascertain intent is not susceptible to much further refinement. In this instance, however, the question is not whether to believe a witness but how to interpret the marks or holes or scratches on an inanimate object, a piece of cardboard or paper which, it is said, might not have registered as a vote during the machine count. The factfinder confronts a thing, not a person. The search for intent can be confined by specific rules designed to ensure uniform treatment.

The want of those rules here has led to unequal evaluation of ballots in various respects. As seems to have been acknowledged at oral argument, the standards for accepting or rejecting contested ballots might vary not only from county to county but indeed within a single county from one recount team to another.

The record provides some examples. A monitor in Miami-Dade County testified at trial that he observed that three members of the county canvassing board applied different standards in defining a legal vote. And testimony at trial also revealed that at least one county changed its evaluative standards during the counting process. Palm Beach County, for example, began the process with a 1990 guideline which precluded counting completely attached chads, switched to a rule that considered a vote to be legal if any light could be seen through a chad, changed back to the 1990 rule, and then abandoned any pretense of a *per se* rule, only to have a court order that the county consider dimpled chads legal. This is not a process with sufficient guarantees of equal treatment. . . .

The State Supreme Court ratified this uneven treatment. It mandated that the recount totals from two counties, Miami–Dade and Palm Beach, be included in the certified total. The court also appeared to hold *sub silentio* that the recount totals from Broward County, which were not completed until after the original November 14 certification by the Secretary of State, were to be considered part of the new certified vote totals even though the county certification was not contested by Vice President Gore. Yet each of the counties used varying standards to determine what was a legal vote. Broward County used a more forgiving standard than Palm Beach County, and uncovered almost three times as many new votes, a result markedly disproportionate to the difference in population between the counties.

In addition, the recounts in these three counties were not limited to so-called undervotes but extended to all of the ballots. The distinction has real consequences. A manual recount of all ballots identifies not only those ballots which show no vote but also those which contain more than one, the so-called overvotes. Neither category will be counted by the machine. This is not a trivial concern. At oral argument, respondents estimated there are as many as 110,000 overvotes statewide. As a result, the citizen whose ballot was not read by a machine because he failed to vote for a candidate in a way readable by a machine may still have his vote counted in a manual recount; on the other hand, the citizen who marks two candidates in a way discernable by the machine will not have the same opportunity to have his vote count, even if a manual examination of the ballot would reveal the requisite indicia of intent. Furthermore, the citizen who marks two candidates, only one of which is discernable by the machine, will have his vote counted even though it should have been read as an invalid ballot. The State Supreme Court's inclusion of vote counts based on these variant standards exemplifies concerns with the remedial processes that were under way.

That brings the analysis to yet a further equal protection problem. The votes certified by the court included a partial total from one county, Miami–Dade. The Florida Supreme Court's decision thus gives no assurance that the recounts included in a final certification must be complete. Indeed, it is respondent's submission that it would be consistent with the rules of the recount procedures to include whatever partial counts are done by the time of final certification, and we interpret the Florida Supreme Court's decision to permit this. This accommodation no doubt results from the truncated contest period established by the Florida Supreme Court in *Bush I*, at respondents' own urging. The press of time does not diminish the constitutional concern. A desire for speed is not a general excuse for ignoring equal protection guarantees. In addition to these difficulties the actual process by which the votes were to be counted under the Florida Supreme Court's decision raises further concerns. That order did not specify who would recount the ballots. The county canvassing boards were forced to pull together ad hoc teams comprised of judges from various Circuits who had no previous training in handling and interpreting ballots. Furthermore, while others were permitted to observe, they were prohibited from objecting during the recount.

The recount process, in its features here described, is inconsistent with the minimum procedures necessary to protect the fundamental right of each voter in the special instance of a statewide recount under the authority of a single state judicial officer. Our consideration is limited to the present circumstances, for the problem of equal protection in election processes generally presents many complexities.

The question before the Court is not whether local entities, in the exercise of their expertise, may develop different systems for implementing elections. Instead, we are presented with a situation where a state court with the power to assure uniformity has ordered a statewide recount with minimal procedural safeguards. When a court orders a statewide remedy, there must be at least some assurance that the rudimentary requirements of equal treatment and fundamental fairness are satisfied. . . .

Upon due consideration of the difficulties identified to this point, it is obvious that the recount cannot be conducted in compliance with the requirements of equal protection and due process without substantial additional work. It would require not only the adoption (after opportunity for argument) of adequate statewide standards for determining what is a legal vote, and practicable procedures to implement them, but also orderly judicial review of any disputed matters that might arise. . . .

The Supreme Court of Florida has said that the legislature intended the State's electors to "participat[e] fully in the federal electoral process," as provided in 3 U.S.C. §5. . . . That date is upon us, and there is no recount procedure in place under the State Supreme Court's order that comports with minimal constitutional standards. Because it is evident that any recount seeking to meet the December 12 date will be unconstitutional for the reasons we have discussed, we reverse the judgment of the Supreme Court of Florida ordering a recount to proceed. . . .

None are more conscious of the vital limits on judicial authority than are the members of this Court, and none stand more in admiration of the Constitution's design to leave the selection of the President to the people, through their legislatures, and to the political sphere. When contending parties invoke the process of the courts, however, it becomes our unsought responsibility to resolve the federal and constitutional issues the judicial system has been forced to confront.

The judgment of the Supreme Court of Florida is reversed, and the case is remanded for further proceedings not inconsistent with this opinion.

13

Justice John Paul Stevens: Dissenting Opinion in *Bush* v. *Gore* (2000)

Justice Stevens here contends that the Court has improperly interfered in a state case and effectively disenfranchised a number of voters by stopping the recount.

The Constitution assigns to the States the primary responsibility for determining the manner of selecting the Presidential electors. See Art. II, §1, cl. 2. When questions arise about the meaning of state laws, including election laws, it is our settled practice to accept the opinions of the highest courts of the States as providing the final answers. On rare occasions, however, either federal statutes or the Federal Constitution may require federal judicial intervention in state elections. This is not such an occasion. The federal questions that ultimately emerged in this case are not substantial. Article II provides that "[e]ach *State* shall appoint, in such Manner as the Legislature *thereof* may direct, a Number of Electors." It does not create state legislatures out of whole cloth, but rather takes them as they come—as creatures born of, and constrained by, their state constitutions. Lest there be any doubt, we stated over 100 years ago in *McPherson* v. *Blacker* (1892) that "[w]hat is forbidden or required to be done by a State" in the Article II context "is forbidden or required of the legislative power under state constitutions as they exist." In the same vein, we also observed that "[t]he [State's] legislative power is the supreme authority except as limited by the constitution of the State." The legislative power in Florida is subject to judicial review pursuant to Article V of the Florida Constitution, and nothing in Article II of the Federal Constitution frees the state legislature from the constraints in the state constitution that created it. Moreover, the Florida Legislature's own decision to employ a unitary code for all elections indicates that it intended the Florida Supreme Court to play the same role in Presidential elections that it has historically played in resolving electoral disputes. The Florida Supreme Court's exercise of appellate jurisdiction therefore was wholly consistent with, and indeed contemplated by, the grant of authority in Article II. . . .

Nor are petitioners correct in asserting that the failure of the Florida Supreme Court to specify in detail the precise manner in which the "intent of the voter" is to be determined rises to the level of a constitutional violation. We found such a violation when individual votes within the same State were weighted unequally, see, *e.g.*, *Reynolds* v. *Sims* (1964), but we have never before called into question the substantive standard by which a State determines that a vote has been legally cast. And there is no reason to think that the guidance provided to the factfinders, specifically the various canvassing boards, by the "intent of the voter" standard is any less sufficient—or will lead to results any less uniform—than, for example, the "beyond a reasonable doubt" standard employed everyday by ordinary citizens in courtrooms across this country.

Admittedly, the use of differing substandards for determining voter intent in different counties employing similar voting systems may raise serious concerns. Those concerns are alleviated—if not eliminated—by the fact that a single impartial magistrate will ultimately adjudicate all objections arising from the recount process. Of course, as a general matter, "[t]he interpretation of constitutional principles must not be too literal. We must remember that the machinery of government would not work if it were not allowed a little play in its joints." *Bain Peanut Co. of Tex.* v. *Pinson* (1931) (Holmes, J.). If it were otherwise, Florida's decision to leave to each county the determination of what balloting system to employ—despite enormous differences in accuracy—might run afoul of equal protection. So, too, might the similar decisions of the vast majority of state legislatures to delegate to local authorities certain decisions with respect to voting systems and ballot design.

Even assuming that aspects of the remedial scheme might ultimately be found to violate the Equal Protection Clause, I could not subscribe to the majority's disposition of the case. As the majority explicitly holds, once a state legislature determines to select electors through a popular vote, the right to have one's vote counted is of constitutional stature. As the majority further acknowledges, Florida law holds that all ballots that reveal the intent of the voter constitute valid votes. Recognizing these principles, the majority nonetheless orders the termination of the contest proceeding before all such votes have been tabulated. Under their own reasoning, the appropriate course of action would be to remand to allow more specific procedures for implementing the legislature's uniform general standard to be established.

In the interest of finality, however, the majority effectively orders the disenfranchisement of an unknown number of voters whose ballots reveal their intent—and are therefore legal votes under state law—but were for some reason rejected by ballot-counting machines. It does so on the basis of the deadlines set forth in Title 3 of the United States Code. But . . . those provisions merely provide rules of decision for Congress to follow when selecting among conflicting slates of electors. They do not prohibit a State from counting what the majority concedes to be legal votes until a bona fide winner is determined. Indeed, in 1960, Hawaii appointed two slates of electors and Congress chose to count the one appointed on January 4, 1961, well after the Title 3 deadlines. Thus, nothing prevents the majority, even if it properly found an equal protection violation, from ordering relief appropriate to remedy that violation without depriving Florida voters of their right to have their votes counted. As the majority notes, "[a] desire for speed is not a general excuse for ignoring equal protection guarantees.". . .

What must underlie petitioners' entire federal assault on the Florida election procedures is an unstated lack of confidence in the impartiality and capacity of the state judges who would make the critical decisions if the vote count were to proceed. Otherwise, their position is wholly without merit. The endorsement of that position by the majority of this Court can only lend credence to the most cynical appraisal of the work of judges throughout the land. It is confidence in the men and women who administer the judicial system that is the true backbone of the rule of law. Time will one day heal the wound to that confidence that will be inflicted by today's decision. One thing, however, is certain. Although we may never know with complete certainty the identity of the winner of this year's Presidential election, the identity of the loser is perfectly clear. It is the Nation's confidence in the judge as an impartial guardian of the rule of law.

DISCUSSION QUESTIONS FOR CHAPTER 5

1. Contrast the arguments of Susan B. Anthony and Catharine Beecher. Is the extension of the vote to women a requirement of America's commitment to republican government, or does the involvement of women in political life merely distract them from more important domestic responsibilities?

2. Contrast the arguments of Representative Adair with those of Senator Warren. Can the people safely be entrusted with the election of senators, or does such a reform give them too much direct influence over government policy?

3. How does the position of Theodore Roosevelt differ from that of President Taft? Should voters be able to recall Court decisions or judges, or would this imperil the rights of individuals and minorities?

4. Discuss President Johnson's "We shall overcome" speech. What steps should the nation be prepared to take to ensure that the right to vote is available to all regardless of race?

5. Contrast the arguments of Justices Douglas and Harlan. Does republican government forbid that voters be required to pay a poll tax, or does such a notion show a preoccupation with absolute equality of political power that the founders would not have shared?

6. Contrast the speeches of Senator Percy and Representative Goldwater. Does fairness require that those at least eighteen years old be allowed to vote, or are people so young insufficiently experienced to exercise this right responsibly?

7. Explain the different conclusions reached by the Supreme Court and the dissenting justices in *Bush* v. *Gore*. Does the Court's opinion in that case uphold or deviate from America's commitment to republican government?

CHAPTER 6

Limited Government

1

Chief Justice Melville Fuller: Opinion of the Court in *U.S.* v. *E.C. Knight Company* (1895)

Essential to limited government is the Constitution's system of Federalism, according to which neither the federal government nor the states hold all power, but each is sovereign for some purposes or within its own sphere. In such a system, the precise limits of the federal power, or the exact dividing line between federal and state authority, is bound to be a matter of recurring controversy. American history bears this out. After the Civil War settled the question of whether the states could enforce their own understanding of limited government by seceding from the Union, it fell to the Supreme Court to decide disputes over the application of the principle of Federalism.

For a long period following the Civil War, the Supreme Court was very protective of state authority, and accordingly interpreted the powers of the federal government very narrowly. In the following case, which illustrates this tendency, the Court held that the federal government's power to regulate commerce among the states did not extend to a power to regulate a manufacturing monopoly, because manufacturing is different from commerce and only indirectly affects commerce. The Court's approach thus limited the federal government's ability to regulate the national economy.

The fundamental question is whether, conceding that the existence of a monopoly in manufacture is established by the evidence, that monopoly can be directly suppressed under the act of congress in the mode attempted by this bill.

It cannot be denied that the power of a state to protect the lives, health, and property of its citizens, and to preserve good order and the public morals, "the power to govern men and things within the limits of its dominion," is a power originally and always belonging to the states, not surrendered by them to the general government, nor directly restrained by the constitution of the United States, and essentially exclusive. The relief of the citizens of each state from the burden of monopoly and the evils resulting from the restraint of trade among such citizens was left with the states to deal with, and this court has recognized their possession of that power even to the extent of holding that an employment or business carried on by private individuals, when it becomes a matter of such public interest and importance as to create a common charge or burden upon the citizen—in other words, when it becomes a practical monopoly, to which the citizen is compelled to resort, and by means of which a tribute can be exacted from the community—is subject to regulation by state legislative power. On the other hand, the power of congress to regulate commerce among the several states is also exclusive. . . . That which belongs to commerce is within the jurisdiction of the United States, but that which does not belong to commerce is within the jurisdiction of the police power of the state. . . .

The argument is that the power to control the manufacture of refined sugar is a monopoly over a necessary of life, to the enjoyment of which by a large part of the population of the United States interstate commerce is indispensable, and that, therefore, the general government, in the exercise of the power to regulate commerce, may repress such monopoly directly, and set aside the instruments which have created it. But this argument cannot be confined to necessaries of life merely, and must include all articles of general consumption. Doubtless the power to control the manufacture of a given thing involves, in a certain sense, the control of its disposition, but this is a secondary, and not the primary, sense; and, although the exercise of that power may result in bringing the operation of commerce into play, it does not control it, and affects it only incidentally and indirectly. Commerce succeeds to manufacture, and is not a part of it. The power to regulate commerce is the power to prescribe the rule by which commerce shall be governed, and is a power independent of the power to suppress monopoly. But it may operate in repression of monopoly whenever that comes within the rules by which commerce is governed, or whenever the transaction is itself a monopoly of commerce. It is vital that the independence of the commercial power and of the police power, and the delimitation between them, however sometimes perplexing, should always be recognized and observed, for, while the one furnishes the strongest bond of union, the other is essential to the preservation of the autonomy of the states as required by our dual form of government; and acknowledged evils, however grave and urgent they may appear to be, had better be borne, than the risk be run, in the effort to suppress them, of more serious consequences by resort to expedients of even doubtful constitutionality.

It will be perceived how far-reaching the proposition is that the power of dealing with a monopoly directly may be exercised by the general government whenever interstate or international commerce may be ultimately affected. The regulation of commerce applies to the subjects of commerce, and not to matters of internal police. Contracts to buy, sell, or exchange goods to be transported among the several states, the transportation and its instrumentalities, and articles bought, sold, or exchanged for the purposes of such transit among the states, or put in the way of transit, may be regulated; but this is because they form part of interstate trade or commerce. The fact that an article is manufactured for export to another state does not of itself make it an article of interstate commerce, and the intent of the manufacturer does not determine the time when the article or product passes from the control of the state and belongs to commerce. . . .

It was in the light of well-settled principles that the act of July 2, 1890, was framed. Congress did not attempt thereby to assert the power to deal with monopoly directly as such; or to limit and restrict the rights of corporations created by the states or the citizens of the states in the acquisition, control, or disposition of property; or to regulate or prescribe the price or prices at which such property or the products thereof should be sold; or to make criminal the acts of persons in the acquisition and control of property which the states of their residence or creation sanctioned or permitted. Aside from the provisions applicable where congress might exercise municipal power, what the law struck at was combinations, contracts, and conspiracies to monopolize trade and commerce among the several states or with foreign nations; but the contracts and acts of the defendants related exclusively to the acquisition of the Philadelphia refineries and the business of sugar refining in Pennsylvania, and bore no direct relation to commerce between the states or with foreign nations. The object was manifestly private gain in the manufacture of the commodity, but not through the control of interstate or foreign commerce. It is true that the bill alleged that the products of these refineries were sold and distributed among the several states, and that all the companies were engaged in trade or commerce with the several states and with foreign nations; but this was no more than to say that trade and commerce served manufacture to fulfill its function. Sugar was refined for sale, and sales were probably made at Philadelphia for consumption, and undoubtedly for resale by the first purchasers throughout Pennsylvania and other states, and refined sugar was also forwarded by the companies to other states for sale. Nevertheless it does not follow that an attempt to monopolize, or the actual monopoly of, the manufacture was an attempt, whether executory or consummated, to monopolize commerce, even though, in order to dispose of the product, the instrumentality of commerce was necessarily invoked.

2

Justice Rufus Peckham: Opinion of the Court in *Lochner v. New York* (1905)

Even as the Supreme Court was limiting the federal government's power of economic regulation by a narrow reading of the commerce clause, it was also limiting the states' power of economic regulation by claiming that the Constitution protects the individual's "liberty of contract." There was little in the original Constitution and Bill of Rights in light of which the Court could limit the power of the states. This changed with the passage of the Fourteenth Amendment, which was intended to protect the rights of individuals from violation by the states. Part of the amendment, called the "due process" clause, prohibited states from depriving people of "life, liberty, or property without due process of law."

In the following case, the Court understands the "liberty" protected by the Fourteenth Amendment to include the liberty of contract and argues that this liberty limits the states' power to regulate the number of hours worked by laborers. Similar reasoning was used by the Court in other cases to strike down the minimum wage and other regulations designed to regulate the economy and protect the interests of workers.

The indictment, it will be seen, charges that the plaintiff in error violated the . . . labor law of the state of New York, in that he wrongfully and unlawfully required and permitted an employee working for him to work more than sixty hours in one week. There is nothing in any of the opinions delivered in this case, either in the supreme court or the court of appeals of the state, which construes the section, in using the word "required," as referring to any physical force being used to obtain the labor of an employee. It is assumed that the word means nothing more than the requirement arising from voluntary contract for such labor in excess of the number of hours specified in the statute. There is no pretense in any of the opinions that the statute was intended to meet a case of involuntary labor in any form. All the opinions assume that there is no real distinction, so far as this question is concerned, between the words "required" and "permitted." The mandate of the statute, that "no employee shall be required or permitted to work," is the substantial equivalent of an enactment that "no employee shall contract or agree to work," more than ten hours per day. . . . It is not an act merely fixing the number of hours which shall constitute a legal day's work, but an absolute prohibition upon the employer permitting, under any circumstances, more than ten hours' work to be done in his establishment. The employee may desire to earn the extra money which would arise from his working more than the prescribed time, but this statute forbids the employer from permitting the employee to earn it.

The statute necessarily interferes with the right of contract between the employer and employees, concerning the number of hours in which the latter may labor in the bakery of the employer. The general right to make a contract in relation to his business is part of the liberty of the individual protected by the 14th Amendment of the Federal Constitution. Under that provision no state can deprive any person of life, liberty, or property without due process of law. The right to purchase or to sell labor is part of the liberty protected by this amendment, unless there are circumstances which exclude the right. There are, however, certain powers, existing in the sovereignty of each state in the Union, somewhat vaguely termed police powers, the exact description and limitation of which have not been attempted by the courts. Those powers, broadly stated, and without, at present, any attempt at a more specific limitation, relate to the safety, health, morals, and general welfare of the public. Both property and liberty are held on such reasonable conditions as may be imposed by the governing power of the state in the exercise of those powers, and with such conditions the 14th Amendment was not designed to interfere.

The state, therefore, has power to prevent the individual from making certain kinds of contracts, and in regard to them the Federal Constitution offers no protection. If the contract be one which the state, in the legitimate exercise of its police power, has the right to prohibit, it is not prevented from prohibiting it by the 14th Amendment. Contracts in violation of a statute, either of the Federal or state government, or a contract to let one's property for immoral purposes, or to do any other unlawful act, could obtain no protection from the Federal Constitution, as coming under the liberty of person or of free contract. . . .

It must, of course, be conceded that there is a limit to the valid exercise of the police power by the state. There is no dispute concerning this general proposition. Otherwise the 14th Amendment would have no efficacy and the legislatures of the states would have unbounded power, and it would be enough to say that any piece of legislation was enacted to conserve the morals, the health, or the safety of the people; such legislation would be valid, no matter how absolutely without foundation the claim might be. The claim of the police power would be a mere pretext—become another and delusive name for the supreme sovereignty of the state to be exercised free from constitutional restraint. This is not contended for. In every case that comes before this court, therefore, where legislation of this character is concerned, and where the protection of the Federal Constitution is sought, the question necessarily arises: Is this a fair, reasonable, and appropriate exercise of the police power of the state, or is it an unreasonable, unnecessary, and arbitrary interference with the right of the individual to his personal liberty, or to enter into those contracts in relation to labor which may seem to him appropriate or necessary for the support of himself and his family? Of course the liberty of contract relating to labor includes both parties to it. The one has as much right to purchase as the other to sell labor.

This is not a question of substituting the judgment of the court for that of the legislature. If the act be within the power of the state it is valid, although the judgment of the court might be totally opposed to the enactment of such a law. But the question would still remain: Is it within the police power of the state? and that question must be answered by the court.

The question whether this act is valid as a labor law, pure and simple, may be dismissed in a few words. There is no reasonable ground for interfering with the liberty of person or the right of free contract, by determining the hours of labor, in the occupation of a baker. There is no contention that bakers as a class are not equal in intelligence and capacity to men in other trades or manual occupations, or that they are not able to assert their rights and care for themselves without the protecting arm of the state, interfering with their independence of judgment and of action. They are in no sense wards of the state. Viewed in the light of a purely labor law, with no reference whatever to the question of health, we think that a law like the one before us involves neither the safety, the morals, nor the welfare, of the public, and that the interest of the public is not in the slightest degree affected by such an act. The law must be upheld, if at all, as a law pertaining to the health of the individual engaged in the occupation of a baker. It does not affect any other portion of the public than those who are engaged in that occupation. Clean and wholesome bread does not depend upon whether the baker works but ten hours per day or only sixty hours a week. The limitation of the hours of labor does not come within the police power on that ground.

It is a question of which of two powers or rights shall prevail—the power of the state to legislate or the right of the individual to liberty of person and freedom of contract. The mere assertion that the subject relates, though but in a remote degree, to the public health, does not necessarily render the enactment valid. The act must have a more direct relation, as a means to an end, and the end itself must be appropriate and legitimate, before an act can be held to be valid which interferes with the general right of an individual to be free in his person and in his power to contract in relation to his own labor. . . .

We think the limit of the police power has been reached and passed in this case. There is, in our judgment, no reasonable foundation for holding this to be necessary or appropriate as a health law to safeguard the public health, or the health of the individuals who are following the trade of a baker. If this statute be valid, and if, therefore, a proper case is made out in which to deny the right of an individual . . . as employer or employee, to make contracts for the labor of the latter under the protection of the provisions of the Federal Constitution, there would seem to be no length to which legislation of this nature might not go. . . .

3

Chief Justice Charles Evans Hughes: Opinion of the Court in *National Labor Relations Board* v. *Jones and Laughlin Steel Corporation* (1937)

The Supreme Court held to its narrow reading of the federal government's commerce power well into the 1930s. During that period, however, the Court's efforts to limit federal regulation of the economy came into conflict with President Franklin Roosevelt's program to deal with the Great Depression. Initially the Court struck down important New Deal legislation. In the face of his threatened effort to "pack" the Court with his own appointees, however, the Court backed down. In this pivotal case it dispenses with its narrow interpretation of the commerce power, which it had wielded in the E.C. Knight case, and thus authorizes extensive government intervention in the economy.

The act is challenged in its entirety as an attempt to regulate all industry, thus invading the reserved powers of the States over their local concerns. It is asserted that the references in the act to interstate and foreign commerce are colorable at best; that the act is not a true regulation of such commerce or of matters which directly affect it, but on the contrary has the fundamental object of placing under the compulsory supervision of the federal government all industrial labor relations within the nation. . . .

The grant of authority to the Board does not purport to extend to the relationship between all industrial employees and employers. Its terms do not impose collective bargaining upon all industry regardless of effects upon interstate or foreign commerce. It purports to reach only what may be deemed to burden or obstruct that commerce and, thus qualified, it must be construed as contemplating the exercise of control within constitutional bounds. It is a familiar principle that acts which directly burden or obstruct interstate or foreign commerce, or its free flow, are within the reach of the congressional power. Acts having that effect are not rendered immune because they grow out of labor disputes. It is the effect upon commerce, not the source of the injury, which is the criterion. Whether or not particular action does affect commerce in such a close and intimate fashion as to be subject to federal control, and hence to lie within the authority conferred upon the Board, is left by the statute to be determined as individual cases arise. We are thus to inquire whether in the instant case the constitutional boundary has been passed. . . .

Respondent says that, whatever may be said of employees engaged in interstate commerce, the industrial relations and activities in the manufacturing department of respondent's enterprise are not subject to federal regulation. The argument rests upon the proposition that manufacturing in itself is not commerce. . . .

The congressional authority to protect interstate commerce from burdens and obstructions is not limited to transactions which can be deemed to be an essential part of a "flow" of interstate or foreign commerce. Burdens and obstructions may be due to injurious action springing from other sources. The fundamental principle is that the power to regulate commerce is the power to enact "all appropriate legislation" for its "protection or advancement"; to adopt measures "to promote its growth and insure its safety"; "to foster, protect, control, and restrain." That power is plenary and may be exerted to protect interstate commerce "no matter what the source of the dangers which threaten it." Although activities may be intrastate in character when separately considered, if they have such a close and substantial relation to interstate commerce that their control is essential or appropriate to protect that commerce from burdens and obstructions, Congress cannot be denied the power to exercise that control. Undoubtedly the scope of this power must be considered in the light of our dual system of government and may not be extended so as to embrace effects upon interstate commerce so indirect and remote that to embrace them, in view of our complex society, would effectually obliterate the distinction between what is national and what is local and create a completely centralized government. The question is necessarily one of degree. As the Court said in *Board of Trade of City of Chicago v. Olsen* . . . "Whatever amounts to more or less constant practice, and threatens to obstruct or unduly to burden the freedom of interstate commerce is within the regulatory power of Congress under the commerce clause, and it is primarily for Congress to consider and decide the fact of the danger and to meet it." . . .

[T]he stoppage of [Jones and Laughlin's] operations by industrial strife would have a most serious effect upon interstate commerce. In view of respondent's far-flung activities, it is idle to say that the effect would be indirect or remote. It is obvious that it would be immediate and might be catastrophic. We are asked to shut our eyes to the plainest facts of our national life and to deal with the question of direct and indirect effects in an intellectual vacuum. Because there may be but indirect and remote effects upon interstate commerce in connection with a host of local enterprises throughout the country, it does not follow that other industrial activities do not have such a close and intimate relation to interstate commerce as to make the presence of industrial strife a matter of the most urgent national concern. When industries organize themselves on a national scale, making their relation to interstate commerce the dominant factor in their activities, how can it be maintained that their industrial labor relations constitute a forbidden field into which Congress may not enter when it is necessary to protect interstate commerce from the paralyzing consequences of industrial war? . . .

4

Chief Justice Charles Evans Hughes: Opinion of the Court in *West Coast Hotel Company* v. *Parrish* (1937)

The Supreme Court's commitment to enforcing strict limits on government's ability to regulate the economy did not survive the Great Depression. In the same year that it abandoned the understanding of the "commerce" clause by which it had limited federal intervention, it also dropped the insistence on "liberty of contract" by which it had limited state intervention. In the following case, the Court upholds a Washington State minimum wage law and thus effectively rejects the reasoning of earlier cases such as Lochner *v.* New York.

The principle which must control our decision is not in doubt. The constitutional provision invoked is the due process clause of the Fourteenth Amendment governing the states . . . In [this] case the violation alleged by those attacking minimum wage regulation for women is deprivation of freedom of contract. What is this freedom? The Constitution does not speak of freedom of contract. It speaks of liberty and prohibits the deprivation of liberty without due process of law. In prohibiting that deprivation, the Constitution does not recognize an absolute and uncontrollable liberty. Liberty in each of its phases has its history and connotation. But the liberty safeguarded is liberty in a social organization which requires the protection of law against the evils which menace the health, safety, morals, and welfare of the people. Liberty under the Constitution is thus necessarily subject to the restraints of due process, and regulation which is reasonable in relation to its subject and is adopted in the interests of the community is due process. This essential limitation of liberty in general governs freedom of contract in particular. . . .

This power under the Constitution to restrict freedom of contract has had many illustrations. That it may be exercised in the public interest with respect to contracts between employer and employee is undeniable. Thus statutes have been sustained limiting employment in underground mines and smelters to eight hours a day; in requiring redemption in cash of store orders or other evidences of indebtedness issued in the payment of wages; in forbidding the payment of seamen's wages in advance; in making it unlawful to contract to pay miners employed at quantity rates upon the basis of screened coal instead of the weight of the coal as originally produced in the mine; in prohibiting contracts limiting liability for injuries to employees; in limiting hours of work of employees in manufacturing establishments; and in maintaining workmen's compensation laws. In dealing with the relation of employer and employed, the Legislature has necessarily a wide field of discretion in order that there may be suitable protection of health and safety, and that peace and good order may be promoted through regulations designed to insure wholesome conditions of work and freedom from oppression.

The point that has been strongly stressed that adult employees should be deemed competent to make their own contracts was decisively met nearly forty years ago in *Holden* v. *Hardy* . . . where we pointed out the inequality in the footing of the parties. We said . . . that the fact "that both parties are of full age, and competent to contract, does not necessarily deprive the state of the power to interfere, where the parties do not stand upon an equality, or where the public heath demands that one party to the contract shall be protected against himself." "The state still retains an interest in his welfare, however reckless he may be. The whole is no greater than the sum of all the parts, and when the individual health, safety, and welfare are sacrificed or neglected, the state must suffer."

It is manifest that this established principle is peculiarly applicable in relation to the employment of women in whose protection the state has a special interest. That phase of the subject received elaborate consideration in *Muller* v. *Oregon* (1908), where the constitutional authority of the state to limit the working hours of women was sustained. We emphasized the consideration that "woman's physical structure and the performance of maternal functions place her at a disadvantage in the struggle for subsistence" and that her physical well being "becomes an object of public interest and care in order to preserve the strength and vigor of the race." We emphasized the need of protecting women against oppression despite her possession of contractual rights. . . .

What can be closer to the public interest than the health of women and their protection from unscrupulous and overreaching employers? And if the protection of women is a legitimate end of the exercise of state power, how can it be said that the requirement of the payment of a minimum wage fairly fixed in order to meet the very necessities of existence is not an admissible means to that end? The Legislature of the state was clearly entitled to consider the situation of women in employment, the fact that they are in the class receiving the least pay, that their bargaining power is relatively weak, and that they are the ready victims of those who would take advantage of their necessitous circumstances. The Legislature was entitled to adopt measures to reduce the evils of the "sweating system," the exploiting of workers at wages so low as to be insufficient to meet the bare cost of living, thus making their very helplessness the occasion of a most injurious competition. The Legislature had the right to consider that its minimum wage requirements would be an important aid in carrying out its policy of protection. The adoption of similar requirements by many states evidences a deep-seated conviction both as to the presence of the evil and as to the means adapted to check it. Legislative response to that conviction cannot be regarded as arbitrary or capricious and that is all we have to decide. Even if the wisdom of the policy be regarded as debatable and its effects uncertain, still the Legislature is entitled to its judgment.

There is an additional and compelling consideration which recent economic experience has brought into a strong light. The exploitation of a class of workers who are in an unequal position with respect to bargaining power and are thus relatively defenseless against the denial of a living wage is not only detrimental to their health and well being, but casts a direct burden for their support upon the community. What these workers lose in wages the taxpayers are called upon to pay. The bare cost of living must be met. We may take judicial notice of the unparalleled demands for relief which arose during the recent period of depression and still continue to an alarming extent despite the degree of economic recovery which has been achieved. It is unnecessary to cite official statistics to establish what is of common knowledge through the length and breadth of the land. While in the instant case no factual brief has been presented, there is no reason to doubt that the state of Washington has encountered the same social problem that is present elsewhere. The community is not bound to provide what is in effect a subsidy for unconscionable employers. The community may direct its law-making power to correct the abuse which springs from their selfish disregard of the public interest. . . .

5

Justice Hugo Black: Opinion of the Court in *Korematsu* v. *United States* (1944)

War raises difficult questions about limited government and individual liberty. During war the government typically tries to exercise extraordinary powers over citizens, and many citizens typically object. Is the exercise of extraordinary powers justified by extreme public dangers, or should the government be held to a strict respect for rights even in times of war? This controversial case touches on these important questions. Here the

Court sustains the government's policy, during World War II, of excluding Japanese Americans from the West Coast. In times of war, Justice Black suggests in the majority opinion, the Court must defer to the military's judgment about what steps are necessary to protect the nation.

It should be noted, to begin with, that all legal restrictions which curtail the civil rights of a single racial group are immediately suspect. That is not to say that all such restrictions are unconstitutional. It is to say that courts must subject them to the most rigid scrutiny. Pressing public necessity may sometimes justify the existence of such restrictions; racial antagonism never can. . . .

Exclusion Order No. 34, which the petitioner knowingly and admittedly violated, was one of a number of military orders and proclamations, all of which were substantially based upon Executive Order No. 9066. That order, issued after we were at war with Japan, declared that "the successful prosecution of the war requires every possible protection against espionage and against sabotage to national-defense material, national-defense premises, and national-defense utilities. . . ."

One of the series of orders and proclamations, a curfew order, which like the exclusion order here was promulgated pursuant to Executive Order 9066, subjected all persons of Japanese ancestry in prescribed West Coast military areas to remain in their residences from 8 p.m. to 6 a.m. As is the case with the exclusion order here, that prior curfew order was designed as a "protection against espionage and against sabotage." In *Kiyoshi Hirabayashi v. United States* we sustained a conviction obtained for violation of the curfew order. The *Hirabayashi* conviction and this one thus rest on the same 1942 Congressional Act and the same basic executive and military orders, all of which orders were aimed at the twin dangers of espionage and sabotage.

The 1942 Act was attacked in the *Hirabayashi* case as an unconstitutional delegation of power; it was contended that the curfew order and other orders on which it rested were beyond the war powers of the Congress, the military authorities and of the President, as Commander in Chief of the Army; and finally that to apply the curfew order against none but citizens of Japanese ancestry amounted to a constitutionally prohibited discrimination solely on account of race. To these questions, we gave the serious consideration which their importance justified. We upheld the curfew order as an exercise of the power of the government to take steps necessary to prevent espionage and sabotage in an area threatened by Japanese attack.

In the light of the principles we announced in the *Hirabayashi* case, we are unable to conclude that it was beyond the war power of Congress and the Executive to exclude those of Japanese ancestry from the West Coast war area at the time they did. True, exclusion from the area in which one's home is located is a far greater deprivation than constant confinement to the home from 8 p.m. to 6 a.m. Nothing short of apprehension by the proper military authorities of the gravest imminent danger to the public safety can constitutionally justify either. But exclusion from a threatened area, no less than curfew, has a definite and close relationship to the prevention of espionage and sabotage. The military authorities, charged with the primary responsibility of defending our shores, concluded that curfew provided inadequate protection and ordered exclusion. They did so, as pointed out in our *Hirabayashi* opinion, in accordance with Congressional authority to the military to say who should, and who should not, remain in the threatened areas.

In this case the petitioner challenges the assumptions upon which we rested our conclusions in the *Hirabayashi* case. He also urges that by May 1942, when Order No. 34 was promulgated, all danger of Japanese invasion of the West Coast had disappeared. After careful consideration of these contentions we are compelled to reject them.

Here, as in the *Hirabayashi* case ". . . we cannot reject as unfounded the judgment of the military authorities and of Congress that there were disloyal members of that population, whose number and strength could not be precisely and quickly ascertained. We cannot say that the war-making branches of the Government did not have ground for believing that in a critical hour such persons could not readily be isolated and separately dealt with, and constituted a menace to the national defense and safety, which demanded that prompt and adequate measures be taken to guard against it."

Like curfew, exclusion of those of Japanese origin was deemed necessary because of the presence of an unascertained number of disloyal members of the group, most of whom we have no doubt were loyal to this country. It was because we could not reject the finding of the military authorities that it was impossible to bring about an immediate segregation of the disloyal from the loyal that we sustained the validity of the curfew order as applying to the whole group. In the instant case, temporary exclusion of the entire group was rested by the military on the same ground. The judgment that exclusion of the whole group was for the same reason a military imperative answers the contention that the exclusion was in the nature of group punishment based on antagonism to those of Japanese origin. That there were members of the group who retained loyalties to Japan has been confirmed by investigations made subsequent to the exclusion. Approximately five thousand American citizens of Japanese ancestry refused to swear unqualified allegiance to the United States and to renounce allegiance to the Japanese Emperor, and several thousand evacuees requested repatriation to Japan.

We uphold the exclusion order as of the time it was made and when the petitioner violated it. In doing so, we are not unmindful of the hardships imposed by it upon a large group of American citizens. But hardships are part of war, and war is an aggregation of hardships. All citizens alike, both in and out of uniform, feel the impact of war in greater or lesser measure. Citizenship has its responsibilities as well as its privileges, and in time of war the burden is always heavier. Compulsory exclusion of large groups of citizens from their homes, except under circumstances of direst emergency and peril, is inconsistent with our basic governmental institutions. But when under conditions of modern warfare our shores are threatened by hostile forces, the power to protect must be commensurate with the threatened danger. . . .

It is said that we are dealing here with the case of imprisonment of a citizen in a concentration camp solely because of his ancestry, without evidence or inquiry concerning his loyalty and good disposition towards the United States. Our task would be simple, our duty clear, were this a case involving the imprisonment of a loyal citizen in a concentration camp because of racial prejudice. Regardless of the true nature of the assembly and relocation centers—and we deem it unjustifiable to call them concentration camps with all the ugly connotations that term implies—we are dealing specifically with nothing but an exclusion order. To cast this case into outlines of racial prejudice, without reference to the real military dangers which were presented, merely confuses the issue. Korematsu was not excluded from the Military Area because of hostility to him or his race. He was excluded because we are at war with the Japanese Empire, because the properly constituted military authorities feared an invasion of our West Coast and felt constrained to take proper security measures, because they decided that the military urgency of the situation demanded that all citizens of Japanese ancestry be segregated from the West Coast temporarily, and finally, because Congress, reposing its confidence in this time of war in our military leaders—as inevitably it must—determined that they should have the power to do just this. There was evidence of disloyalty on the part of some, the military authorities considered that the need for action was great, and time was short. We cannot—by availing ourselves of the calm perspective of hindsight—now say that at that time these actions were unjustified.

6

Justice Frank Murphy: Dissenting Opinion in *Korematsu* v. *United States* (1944)

In his dissenting opinion, Justice Murphy advocates a more aggressive role for the Court in enforcing limited government even in time of war. He admits that the Court must show deference to the judgments of military officers, but at the same time he insists that those judgments must be reviewed by the Court lest constitutional rights be left unprotected.

This exclusion of "all persons of Japanese ancestry, both alien and non-alien," from the Pacific Coast area on a plea of military necessity in the absence of martial law ought not to be approved. Such exclusion goes over "the very brink of constitutional power" and falls into the ugly abyss of racism.

In dealing with matters relating to the prosecution and progress of a war, we must accord great respect and consideration to the judgments of the military authorities who are on the scene and who have full knowledge of the military facts. The scope of their discretion must, as a matter of necessity and common sense, be wide. And their judgments ought not to be overruled lightly by those whose training and duties ill-equip them to deal intelligently with matters so vital to the physical security of the nation.

At the same time, however, it is essential that there be definite limits to military discretion, especially where martial law has not been declared. Individuals must not be left impoverished of their constitutional rights on a plea of military necessity that has neither substance nor support. Thus, like other claims conflicting with the asserted constitutional rights of the individual, the military claim must subject itself to the judicial process of having its reasonableness determined and its conflicts with other interests reconciled. "What are the allowable limits of military discretion, and whether or not they have been overstepped in a particular case, are judicial questions."

The judicial test of whether the Government, on a plea of military necessity, can validly deprive an individual of any of his constitutional rights is whether the deprivation is reasonably related to a public danger that is so "immediate, imminent, and impending" as not to admit of delay and not to permit the intervention of ordinary constitutional processes to alleviate the danger. Civilian Exclusion Order No. 34, banishing from a prescribed area of the Pacific Coast "all persons of Japanese ancestry, both alien and non-alien," clearly does not meet that test. Being an obvious racial discrimination, the order deprives all those within its scope of the equal protection of the laws as guaranteed by the Fifth Amendment. It further deprives these individuals of their constitutional rights to live and work where they will, to establish a home where they choose and to move about freely. In excommunicating them without benefit of hearings, this order also deprives them of all their constitutional rights to procedural due process. Yet no reasonable relation to an "immediate, imminent, and impending" public danger is evident to support this racial restriction which is one of the most sweeping and complete deprivations of constitutional rights in the history of this nation in the absence of martial law.

It must be conceded that the military and naval situation in the spring of 1942 was such as to generate a very real fear of invasion of the Pacific Coast, accompanied by fears of sabotage and espionage in that area. The military command was therefore justified in adopting all reasonable means necessary to combat these dangers. In adjudging the military action taken in light of the then apparent dangers, we must not erect too high or too meticulous standards; it is necessary only that the action have some reasonable relation to the removal of the dangers of invasion, sabotage and espionage. But the exclusion, either temporarily or permanently, of all persons with Japanese blood in their veins has no such reasonable relation. And that relation is lacking because the exclusion order necessarily must rely for its reasonableness upon the assumption that all persons of Japanese ancestry may have a dangerous tendency to commit sabotage and espionage and to aid our Japanese enemy in other ways. It is difficult to believe that reason, logic or experience could be marshaled in support of such an assumption.

That this forced exclusion was the result in good measure of this erroneous assumption of racial guilt rather than bona fide military necessity is evidenced by the Commanding General's Final Report on the evacuation from the

Pacific Coast area. In it he refers to all individuals of Japanese descent as "subversive," as belonging to "an enemy race" whose "racial strains are undiluted," and as constituting "over 112,000 potential enemies . . . at large today" along the Pacific Coast. In support of this blanket condemnation of all persons of Japanese descent, however, no reliable evidence is cited to show that such individuals were generally disloyal, or had generally so conducted themselves in this area as to constitute a special menace to defense installations or war industries, or had otherwise by their behavior furnished reasonable ground for their exclusion as a group.

Justification for the exclusion is sought, instead, mainly upon questionable racial and sociological grounds not ordinarily within the realm of expert military judgment, supplemented by certain semi-military conclusions drawn from an unwarranted use of circumstantial evidence. Individuals of Japanese ancestry are condemned because they are said to be "a large, unassimilated, tightly knit racial group, bound to an enemy nation by strong ties of race, culture, custom and religion." They are claimed to be given to "emperor worshipping ceremonies" and to "dual citizenship." . . . Finally, it is intimated, though not directly charged or proved, that persons of Japanese ancestry were responsible for three minor isolated shellings and bombings of the Pacific Coast area, as well as for unidentified radio transmissions and night signaling.

The main reasons relied upon by those responsible for the forced evacuation, therefore, do not prove a reasonable relation between the group characteristics of Japanese Americans and the dangers of invasion, sabotage and espionage. The reasons appear, instead, to be largely an accumulation of much of the misinformation, half-truths and insinuations that for years have been directed against Japanese Americans by people with racial and economic prejudices—the same people who have been among the foremost advocates of the evacuation. A military judgment based upon such racial and sociological considerations is not entitled to the great weight ordinarily given the judgments based upon strictly military considerations. Especially is this so when every charge relative to race, religion, culture, geographical location, and legal and economic status has been substantially discredited by independent studies made by experts in these matters.

The military necessity which is essential to the validity of the evacuation order thus resolves itself into a few intimations that certain individuals actively aided the enemy, from which it is inferred that the entire group of Japanese Americans could not be trusted to be or remain loyal to the United States. No one denies, of course, that there were some disloyal persons of Japanese descent on the Pacific Coast who did all in their power to aid their ancestral land. Similar disloyal activities have been engaged in by many persons of German, Italian and even more pioneer stock in our country. But to infer that examples of individual disloyalty prove group disloyalty and justify discriminatory action against the entire group is to deny that under our system of law individual guilt is the sole basis for deprivation of rights. Moreover, this inference, which is at the very heart of the evacuation orders, has been used in support of the abhorrent and despicable treatment of minority groups by the dictatorial tyrannies which this nation is now pledged to destroy. To give constitutional sanction to that inference in this case, however well-intentioned may have been the military command on the Pacific Coast, is to adopt one of the cruelest of the rationales used by our enemies to destroy the dignity of the individual and to encourage and open the door to discriminatory actions against other minority groups in the passions of tomorrow. No adequate reason is given for the failure to treat these Japanese Americans on an individual basis by holding investigations and hearings to separate the loyal from the disloyal, as was done in the case of persons of German and Italian ancestry. It is asserted merely that the loyalties of this group "were unknown and time was of the essence." Yet nearly four months elapsed after Pearl Harbor before the first exclusion order was issued; nearly eight months went by until the last order was issued; and the last of these "subversive" persons was not actually removed until almost eleven months had elapsed. Leisure and deliberation seem to have been more of the essence than speed. And the fact that conditions were not such as to warrant a declaration of martial law adds strength to the belief that the factors of time and military necessity were not as urgent as they have been represented to be. . . .

I dissent, therefore, from this legalization of racism. Racial discrimination in any form and in any degree has no justifiable part whatever in our democratic way of life. It is unattractive in any setting but it is utterly revolting among a free people who have embraced the principles set forth in the Constitution of the United States. All residents of this nation are kin in some way by blood or culture to a foreign land. Yet they are primarily and necessarily a part of the new and distinct civilization of the United States. They must accordingly be treated at all times as the heirs of the American experiment and as entitled to all the rights and freedoms guaranteed by the Constitution.

7

Chief Justice Fred Vinson: Opinion of the Court in *Dennis* v. *United States* (1951)

World War II was followed by the "Cold War," a long period of tension and ideological competition between the United States and the Soviet Union. This period saw serious government fears about, and consequently serious attempts to restrict the activities of, possible Soviet sympathizers within the United States. Thus the Cold War also caused arguments about the proper limits of government power in relation to individual liberties like freedom of speech. In this case, the Supreme Court upheld the Smith Act, which prohibited organizing for the purpose of advocating the violent overthrow of the government.

The obvious purpose of the statute is to protect existing Government, not from change by peaceable, lawful and constitutional means, but from change by violence, revolution and terrorism. That it is within the power of the Congress to protect the Government of the United States from armed rebellion is a proposition which requires little discussion. . . . The question with which we are concerned here is not whether Congress has such power, but whether the means which it has employed conflict with the First and Fifth Amendments to the Constitution.

One of the bases for the contention that the means which Congress has employed are invalid takes the form of an attack on the face of the statute on the grounds that by its terms it prohibits academic discussion of the merits of Marxism-Leninism, that it stifles ideas and is contrary to all concepts of a free speech and a free press. . . .

The very language of the Smith Act negates the interpretation which petitioners would have us impose on that Act. It is directed at advocacy, not discussion. Thus, the trial judge properly charged the jury that they could not convict if they found that petitioners did "no more than pursue peaceful studies and discussions or teaching and advocacy in the realm of ideas." . . .

In this case we are squarely presented with the application of the "clear and present danger" test, and must decide what that phrase imports. We first note that many of the cases in which this Court has reversed convictions by use of this or similar tests have been based on the fact that the interest which the State was attempting to protect was itself too insubstantial to warrant restriction of speech. . . . Overthrow of the Government by force and violence is certainly a substantial enough interest for the Government to limit speech. Indeed, this is the ultimate value of any society, for if a society cannot protect its very structure from armed internal attack, it must follow that no subordinate value can be protected. If, then, this interest may be protected, the literal problem which is presented is what has been meant by the use of the phrase "clear and present danger" of the utterances bringing about the evil within the power of Congress to punish.

Obviously, the words cannot mean that before the Government may act, it must wait until the putsch is about to be executed, the plans have been laid and the signal is awaited. If Government is aware that a group aiming at its overthrow is attempting to indoctrinate its members and to commit them to a course whereby they will strike when the leaders feel the circumstances permit, action by the Government is required. The argument that there is no need for Government to concern itself, for Government is strong, it possesses ample powers to put down a rebellion, it may defeat the revolution with ease needs no answer. For that is not the question. Certainly an attempt to overthrow the Government by force, even though doomed from the outset because of inadequate numbers of power of the revolutionists, is a sufficient evil for Congress to prevent. The damage which such attempts create both physically and politically to a nation makes it impossible to measure the validity in terms of the probability of success, or the immediacy of a successful attempt. In the instant case the trial judge charged the jury that they could not convict unless they found that petitioners intended to overthrow the Government "as speedily as circumstances would permit." This does not mean, and could not properly mean, that they would not strike until there was certainty of success. What was meant was that the revolutionists would strike when they thought the time was ripe. We must therefore reject the contention that success or probability of success is the criterion. . . .

[W]e are in accord with the court below, which affirmed the trial court's finding that the requisite danger existed. The mere fact that from the period 1945 to 1948 petitioners' activities did not result in an attempt to overthrow the Government by force and violence is of course no answer to the fact that there was a group that was ready to make the attempt. The formation by petitioners of such a highly organized conspiracy, with rigidly disciplined members subject to call when the leaders, these petitioners, felt that the time had come for action, coupled with the inflammable nature of world conditions, similar uprisings in other countries, and the touch-and-go nature of our relations with countries with whom petitioners were in the very least ideologically attuned, convince us that their convictions were justified on this score. And this analysis disposes of the contention that a conspiracy to advocate, as distinguished from the advocacy itself, cannot be constitutionally restrained, because it comprises only the preparation. It is the existence of the conspiracy which creates the danger. . . .

We hold that . . . the Smith Act do[es] not inherently, or as construed or applied in the instant case, violate the First Amendment and other provisions of the Bill of Rights, or the First and Fifth Amendments because of indefiniteness. Petitioners intended to overthrow the Government of the United States as speedily as the circumstances would permit. Their conspiracy to organize the Communist Party and to teach and advocate the overthrow of the Government of the United States by force and violence created a "clear and present danger" of an attempt to overthrow the Government by force and violence. They were properly and constitutionally convicted for violation of the Smith Act. The judgments of conviction are Affirmed.

8

Justice William O. Douglas: Dissenting Opinion in *Dennis* v. *United States* (1951)

In his dissent Justice Douglas argues for a more strict application of the "clear and present danger" test and, accordingly, for a more permissive understanding of freedom of speech. Although the Court upheld the conviction in this case, in the 1960s it returned to a policy of allowing punishment of speech only when the danger it threatened is imminent.

Free speech has occupied an exalted position because of the high service it has given our society. Its protection is essential to the very existence of a democracy.

The airing of ideas releases pressures which otherwise might become destructive. When ideas compete in the market for acceptance, full and free discussion exposes the false and they gain few adherents. Full and free discussion
even of ideas we hate encourages the testing of our own prejudices and pre-
conceptions. Full and free discussion keeps a society from becoming stagnant
and unprepared for the stresses and strains that work to tear all civilizations
apart. Full and free discussion has indeed been the first article of our faith. We
have founded our political system on it. It has been the safeguard of every religious, political, philosophical, economic, and racial group amongst us. We have
counted on it to keep us from embracing what is cheap and false; we have
trusted the common sense of our people to choose the doctrine true to our
genius and to reject the rest. This has been the one single outstanding tenet
that has made our institutions the symbol of freedom and equality. We have
deemed it more costly to liberty to suppress a despised minority than to let
them vent their spleen. We have above all else feared the political censor. We
have wanted a land where our people can be exposed to all the diverse creeds
and cultures of the world.

There comes a time when even speech loses its constitutional immunity.
Speech innocuous one year may at another time fan such destructive flames
that it must be halted in the interests of the safety of the Republic. That is the
meaning of the clear and present danger test. When conditions are so critical
that there will be no time to avoid the evil that the speech threatens, it is time
to call a halt. Otherwise, free speech which is the strength of the Nation will
be the cause of its destruction.

Yet free speech is the rule, not the exception. The restraint to be constitutional must be based on more than fear, on more than passionate opposition
against the speech, on more than a revolted dislike for its contents. There must
be some immediate injury to society that is likely if speech is allowed. . . . This
record . . . contains no evidence whatsoever showing that the acts charged,
viz., the teaching of the Soviet theory of revolution with the hope that it will
be realized, have created any clear and present danger to the Nation. The
Court, however, rules to the contrary. It says, "The formation by petitioners of
such a highly organized conspiracy, with rigidly disciplined members subject
to call when the leaders, these petitioners, felt that the time had come for
action, coupled with the inflammable nature of world conditions, similar uprisings in other countries, and the touch-and-go nature of our relations with
countries with whom petitioners were in the very least ideologically attuned,
convince us that their convictions were justified on this score."

That ruling is in my view not responsive to the issue in the case. We might
as well say that the speech of petitioners is outlawed because Soviet Russia and
her Red Army are a threat to world peace. The nature of Communism as a
force on the world scene would, of course, be relevant to the issue of clear and
present danger of petitioners' advocacy within the United States. But the primary consideration is the strength and tactical position of petitioners and their
converts in this country. On that there is no evidence in the record. If we are
to take judicial notice of the threat of Communists within the nation, it should

not be difficult to conclude that as a political party they are of little conse-quence. Communists in this country have never made a respectable or serious showing in any election. I would doubt that there is a village, let alone a city or county or state, which the Communists could carry. Communism in the world scene is no bogeyman; but Communism as a political faction or party in this country plainly is. Communism has been so thoroughly exposed in this country that it has been crippled as a political force. Free speech has destroyed it as an effective political party. It is inconceivable that those who went up and down this country preaching the doctrine of revolution which petitioners espouse would have any success. In days of trouble and confusion, when bread lines were long, when the unemployed walked the streets, when people were starving, the advocates of a short-cut by revolution might have a chance to gain adherents. But today there are no such conditions. The coun-try is not in despair; the people know Soviet Communism; the doctrine of Soviet revolution is exposed in all of its ugliness and the American people want none of it.

How it can be said that there is a clear and present danger that this advo-cacy will succeed is, therefore, a mystery. Some nations less resilient than the United States, where illiteracy is high and where democratic traditions are only budding, might have to take drastic steps and jail these men for merely speaking their creed. But in America they are miserable merchants of unwanted ideas; their wares remain unsold. The fact that their ideas are abhor-rent does not make them powerful.

The political impotence of the Communists in this country does not, of course, dispose of the problem. Their numbers; their positions in industry and government; the extent to which they have in fact infiltrated the police, the armed services, transportation, stevedoring, power plants, munitions works, and other critical places—these facts all bear on the likelihood that their advo-cacy of the Soviet theory of revolution will endanger the Republic. But the record is silent on these facts. If we are to proceed on the basis of judicial notice, it is impossible for me to say that the Communists in this country are so potent or so strategically deployed that they must be suppressed for their speech. I could not so hold unless I were willing to conclude that the activities in recent years of committees of Congress, of the Attorney General, of labor unions, of state legislatures, and of Loyalty Boards were so futile as to leave the country on the edge of grave peril. To believe that petitioners and their fol-lowing are placed in such critical positions as to endanger the Nation is to believe the incredible. It is safe to say that the followers of the creed of Soviet Communism are known to the F.B.I.; that in case of war with Russia they will be picked up overnight as were all prospective saboteurs at the commence-ment of World War II; that the invisible army of petitioners is the best known, the most beset, and the least thriving of any fifth column in history. Only those held by fear and panic could think otherwise. . . .

The First Amendment provides that "Congress shall make no law . . . abridging the freedom of speech." The Constitution provides no exception. This does not mean, however, that the Nation need hold its hand until it is in such weakened condition that there is no time to protect itself from incitement to revolution. Seditious conduct can always be punished. But the command of the First Amendment is so clear that we should not allow Congress to call a halt to free speech except in the extreme case of peril from the speech itself. . . . Unless and until extreme and necessitous circumstances are shown, our aim should be to keep speech unfettered and to allow the processes of law to be invoked only when the provocateurs among us move from speech to action.

Vishinsky wrote in 1938 in *The Law of the Soviet State*, "In our state, naturally, there is and can be no place for freedom of speech, press, and so on for the foes of socialism."

Our concern should be that we accept no such standard for the United States. Our faith should be that our people will never give support to these advocates of revolution, so long as we remain loyal to the purposes for which our Nation was founded.

9

Justice Harry Blackmun: Opinion of the Court in *Roe* v. *Wade* (1973)

In recent decades the Supreme Court has added a new element to the American understanding of limited government: the notion that there is a right to privacy that neither the federal government nor the states may invade without compelling reasons. In this case, the Court holds that the right to privacy includes the right to procure an abortion.

Three reasons have been advanced to explain historically the enactment of criminal abortion laws in the 19th century and to justify their continued existence. It has been argued occasionally that these laws were the product of a Victorian social concern to discourage illicit sexual conduct. Texas, however, does not advance this justification in the present case, and it appears that no court or commentator has taken the argument seriously. . . .

A second reason is concerned with abortion as a medical procedure. When most criminal abortion laws were first enacted, the procedure was a hazardous one for the woman. . . . Thus, it has been argued that a State's real concern in enacting a criminal abortion law was to protect the pregnant woman, that is, to restrain her from submitting to a procedure that placed her life in serious jeopardy.

Modern medical techniques have altered this situation. Appellants . . . refer to medical data indicating that abortion in early pregnancy, that is, prior to the end of the first trimester, although not without its risk, is now relatively safe. Mortality rates for women undergoing early abortions, where the procedure is legal, appear to be as low as or lower than the rates for normal childbirth.

Consequently, any interest of the State in protecting the woman from an inherently hazardous procedure, except when it would be equally dangerous for her to forgo it, has largely disappeared. . . .

The third reason is the State's interest—some phrase it in terms of duty—in protecting prenatal life. Some of the argument for this justification rests on the theory that a new human life is present from the moment of conception. The State's interest and general obligation to protect life then extends, it is argued, to prenatal life. Only when the life of the pregnant mother herself is at stake, balanced against the life she carries within her, should the interest of the embryo or fetus not prevail. Logically, of course, a legitimate state interest in this area need not stand or fall on acceptance of the belief that life begins at conception or at some other point prior to live birth. In assessing the State's interest, recognition may be given to the less rigid claim that as long as at least potential life is involved, the State may assert interests beyond the protection of the pregnant woman alone. . . .

It is with these interests, and the weight to be attached to them, that this case is concerned. The Constitution does not explicitly mention any right of privacy. In a line of decisions, however, going back perhaps as far as *Union Pacific R. Co.* v. *Botsford* (1891), the Court has recognized that a right of personal privacy, or a guarantee of certain areas or zones of privacy, does exist under the Constitution. In varying contexts, the Court or individual Justices have, indeed, found at least the roots of that right in the First Amendment; in the Fourth and Fifth Amendments; in the penumbras of the Bill of Rights; in the Ninth Amendment; or in the concept of liberty guaranteed by the first section of the Fourteenth Amendment. These decisions make it clear that only personal rights that can be deemed "fundamental" or "implicit in the concept of ordered liberty" are included in this guarantee of personal privacy. They also make it clear that the right has some extension to activities relating to marriage, procreation, contraception, family relationships, and child rearing and education.

This right of privacy, whether it be founded in the Fourteenth Amendment's concept of personal liberty and restrictions upon state action, as we feel it is, or, as the District Court determined, in the Ninth Amendment's reservation of rights to the people, is broad enough to encompass a woman's decision whether or not to terminate her pregnancy. The detriment that the State would impose upon the pregnant woman by denying this choice altogether is apparent. Specific and direct harm medically diagnosable even in early pregnancy may be involved. Maternity, or additional offspring, may force upon the woman a distressful life and future. Psychological harm may be imminent. Mental and physical health may be taxed by child care. There is also the distress, for all concerned, associated with the unwanted child, and there is the problem of bringing a child into a family already unable, psychologically and otherwise, to care for it. In other cases, as in this one, the additional difficulties and continuing stigma of unwed motherhood may be involved. All these are factors the woman and her responsible physician necessarily will consider in consultation. . . .

Texas urges that . . . life begins at conception and is present throughout pregnancy, and that, therefore, the State has a compelling interest in protecting that life from and after conception. We need not resolve the difficult question of when life begins. When those trained in the respective disciplines of medicine, philosophy, and theology are unable to arrive at any consensus, the judiciary, at this point in the development of man's knowledge, is not in a position to speculate as to the answer.

It should be sufficient to note briefly the wide divergence of thinking on this most sensitive and difficult question. There has always been strong support for the view that life does not begin until live birth. This was the belief of the Stoics. It appears to be the predominant, though not the unanimous, attitude of the Jewish faith. It may be taken to represent also the position of a large segment of the Protestant community, insofar as that can be ascertained; organized groups that have taken a formal position on the abortion issue have generally regarded abortion as a matter for the conscience of the individual and her family. As we have noted, the common law found greater significance in quickening. Physicians and their scientific colleagues have regarded that event with less interest and have tended to focus either upon conception, upon live birth, or upon the interim point at which the fetus becomes "viable," that is, potentially able to live outside the mother's womb, albeit with artificial aid. Viability is usually placed at about seven months (28 weeks) but may occur earlier, even at 24 weeks. The Aristotelian theory of "mediate animation," that held sway throughout the Middle Ages and the Renaissance in Europe, continued to be official Roman Catholic dogma until the 19th century, despite opposition to this "ensoulment" theory from those in the Church who would recognize the existence of life from the moment of conception. The latter is now, of course, the official belief of the Catholic Church. As one brief amicus discloses, this is a view strongly held by many non-Catholics as well, and by many physicians. Substantial problems for precise definition of this view are posed, however, by new embryological data that purport to indicate that conception is a "process" over time, rather than an event, and by new medical techniques such as menstrual extraction, the "morning-after" pill, implantation of embryos, artificial insemination, and even artificial wombs. . . .

In areas other than criminal abortion, the law has been reluctant to endorse any theory that life, as we recognize it, begins before live birth or to accord legal rights to the unborn except in narrowly defined situations and except when the rights are contingent upon live birth. . . . In short, the unborn have never been recognized in the law as persons in the whole sense.

In view of all this, we do not agree that, by adopting one theory of life, Texas may override the rights of the pregnant woman that are at stake.

10

Justice Byron White:
Dissenting Opinion in *Doe* v. *Bolton* (1973)

The Supreme Court's introduction of a right to privacy limiting the government's ability to regulate certain personal decisions has proven to be a source of continuing controversy. In his dissenting opinion in the companion case to Roe, *Justice White contends that the Court has simply invented a new right without a sufficient constitutional basis. It has therefore arbitrarily invalidated the will of the people manifested in law enacted through the democratic political process.*

At the heart of the controversy in these cases are those recurring pregnancies that pose no danger whatsoever to the life or health of the mother but are, nevertheless, unwanted for any one or more of a variety of reasons— convenience, family planning, economics, dislike of children, the embarrassment of illegitimacy, etc. The common claim before us is that for any one of such reasons, or for no reason at all, and without asserting or claiming any threat to life or health, any woman is entitled to an abortion at her request if she is able to find a medical advisor willing to undertake the procedure.

The Court for the most part sustains this position: During the period prior to the time the fetus becomes viable, the Constitution of the United States values the convenience, whim, or caprice of the putative mother more than the life or potential life of the fetus; the Constitution, therefore, guarantees the right to an abortion as against any state law or policy seeking to protect the fetus from an abortion not prompted by more compelling reasons of the mother.

With all due respect, I dissent. I find nothing in the language or history of the Constitution to support the Court's judgment. The Court simply fashions and announces a new constitutional right for pregnant mothers and, with scarcely any reason or authority for its action, invests that right with sufficient substance to override most existing state abortion statutes. The upshot is that the people and the legislatures of the 50 States are constitutionally disentitled to weigh the relative importance of the continued existence and development of the fetus, on the one hand, against a spectrum of possible impacts on the mother, on the other hand. As an exercise of raw judicial power, the Court perhaps has authority to do what it does today; but in my view its judgment is an improvident and extravagant exercise of the power of judicial review that the Constitution extends to this Court.

The Court apparently values the convenience of the pregnant mother more than the continued existence and development of the life or potential life that she carries. Whether or not I might agree with that marshaling of values, I can in no event join the Court's judgment because I find no constitutional warrant for imposing such an order of priorities on the people and legislatures of the States. In a sensitive area such as this, involving as it does issues over which reasonable men may easily and heatedly differ, I cannot accept the Court's exercise of its clear power of choice by interposing a constitutional barrier to state efforts to protect human life and by investing mothers and doctors with the constitutionally protected right to exterminate it. This issue, for the most part, should be left with the people and to the political processes the people have devised to govern their affairs.

11

Justice Anthony Kennedy: Opinion of the Court in *Lawrence* v. *Texas* (2003)

In some recent cases the Supreme Court has continued to develop the notion that the Constitution protects a realm of privacy into which the government may not intrude. Here the Court strikes down a Texas law punishing acts of homosexual sodomy. The Court argues that the Constitution prohibits state regulation of private, consensual sexual acts between adults.

Liberty protects the person from unwarranted government intrusions into a dwelling or other private places. In our tradition the State is not omnipresent in the home. And there are other spheres of our lives and existence, outside the home, where the State should not be a dominant presence. Freedom extends beyond spatial bounds. Liberty presumes an autonomy of self that includes freedom of thought, belief, expression, and certain intimate conduct. The instant case involves liberty of the person both in its spatial and more transcendent dimensions. . . .

We conclude the case should be resolved by determining whether the petitioners were free as adults to engage in the private conduct in the exercise of their liberty under the Due Process Clause of the Fourteenth Amendment to the Constitution. For this inquiry we deem it necessary to reconsider the Court's holding in *Bowers v. Hardwick* (1985). . . .

The Court began its substantive discussion in *Bowers* as follows: "The issue presented is whether the Federal Constitution confers a fundamental right upon homosexuals to engage in sodomy and hence invalidates the laws of the many States that still make such conduct illegal and have done so for a very long time." That statement, we now conclude, discloses the Court's own failure to appreciate the extent of the liberty at stake. To say that the issue in *Bowers* was simply the right to engage in certain sexual conduct demeans the claim the individual put forward, just as it would demean a married couple were it to be said marriage is simply about the right to have sexual intercourse.

The laws involved in *Bowers* and here are, to be sure, statutes that purport to do no more than prohibit a particular sexual act. Their penalties and purposes, though, have more far-reaching consequences, touching upon the most private human conduct, sexual behavior, and in the most private of places, the home. The statutes do seek to control a personal relationship that, whether or not entitled to formal recognition in the law, is within the liberty of persons to choose without being punished as criminals.

This, as a general rule, should counsel against attempts by the State, or a court, to define the meaning of the relationship or to set its boundaries absent injury to a person or abuse of an institution the law protects. It suffices for us to acknowledge that adults may choose to enter upon this relationship in the confines of their homes and their own private lives and still retain their dignity as free persons. When sexuality finds overt expression in intimate conduct with another person, the conduct can be but one element in a personal bond that is more enduring. The liberty protected by the Constitution allows homosexual persons the right to make this choice. . . .

[T]he Court in *Bowers* was making the broader point that for centuries there have been powerful voices to condemn homosexual conduct as immoral. The condemnation has been shaped by religious beliefs, conceptions of right and acceptable behavior, and respect for the traditional family. For many persons these are not trivial concerns but profound and deep convictions accepted as ethical and moral principles to which they aspire and which thus determine the course of their lives. These considerations do not answer the question before us, however. The issue is whether the majority may use the power of the State to enforce these views on the whole society through operation of the criminal law. "Our obligation is to define the liberty of all, not to mandate our own moral code." *Planned Parenthood of Southeastern Pa. v. Casey* (1992).

Chief Justice Burger joined the opinion for the Court in *Bowers* and further explained his views as follows: "Decisions of individuals relating to homosexual conduct have been subject to state intervention throughout the history of Western civilization. Condemnation of those practices is firmly rooted in Judeo-Christian moral and ethical standards.". . . [W]e think [however] that our laws and traditions in the past half century are of most relevance here. These references show an emerging awareness that liberty gives substantial protection to adult persons in deciding how to conduct their private lives in matters pertaining to sex. . . .

This emerging recognition should have been apparent when *Bowers* was decided. . . .

In *Bowers* the Court referred to the fact that before 1961 all 50 States had outlawed sodomy, and that at the time of the Court's decision 24 States and the District of Columbia had sodomy laws. Justice Powell pointed out that these prohibitions often were being ignored, however. Georgia, for instance, had not sought to enforce its law for decades.

The sweeping references by Chief Justice Burger to the history of Western civilization and to Judeo-Christian moral and ethical standards did not take account of other authorities pointing in an opposite direction. A committee advising the British Parliament recommended in 1957 repeal of laws punishing homosexual conduct.

Of even more importance, almost five years before *Bowers* was decided the European Court of Human Rights considered a case with parallels to *Bowers* and to today's case. An adult male resident in Northern Ireland alleged he was a practicing homosexual who desired to engage in consensual homosexual conduct. The laws of Northern Ireland forbade him that right. He alleged that he had been questioned, his home had been searched, and he feared criminal prosecution. The court held that the laws proscribing the conduct were invalid under the European Convention on Human Rights. Authoritative in all countries that are members of the Council of Europe (21 nations then, 45 nations now), the decision is at odds with the premise in *Bowers* that the claim put forward was insubstantial in our Western civilization.

In our own constitutional system the deficiencies in *Bowers* became even more apparent in the years following its announcement. The 25 States with laws prohibiting the relevant conduct referenced in the *Bowers* decision are reduced now to 13, of which 4 enforce their laws only against homosexual conduct. In those States where sodomy is still proscribed, whether for same-sex or heterosexual conduct, there is a pattern of nonenforcement with respect to consenting adults acting in private. The State of Texas admitted in 1994 that as of that date it had not prosecuted anyone under those circumstances. . . .

Bowers was not correct when it was decided, and it is not correct today. It ought not to remain binding precedent. *Bowers* v. *Hardwick* should be and now is overruled.

The present case does not involve minors. It does not involve persons who might be injured or coerced or who are situated in relationships where consent might not easily be refused. It does not involve public conduct or prostitution. It does not involve whether the government must give formal recognition to any relationship that homosexual persons seek to enter. The case does involve two adults who, with full and mutual consent from each other, engaged in sexual practices common to a homosexual lifestyle. The petitioners are entitled to respect for their private lives. The State cannot demean their existence or control their destiny by making their private sexual conduct a crime. Their right to liberty under the Due Process Clause gives them the full right to engage in their conduct without intervention of the government. "It is a promise of the Constitution that there is a realm of personal liberty which the government may not enter." The Texas statute furthers no legitimate state interest which can justify its intrusion into the personal and private life of the individual.

Had those who drew and ratified the Due Process Clauses of the Fifth Amendment or the Fourteenth Amendment known the components of liberty in its manifold possibilities, they might have been more specific. They did not presume to have this insight. They knew times can blind us to certain truths and later generations can see that laws once thought necessary and proper in fact serve only to oppress. As the Constitution endures, persons in every generation can invoke its principles in their own search for greater freedom.

12

Justice Antonin Scalia:
Dissenting Opinion in *Lawrence* v. *Texas* (2003)

Here Justice Scalia criticizes the Court for striking down the Texas statute prohibiting homosexual sodomy. He contends that the Court's decision limits, without any constitutional basis, the power of states to regulate the conduct of citizens through democratically enacted laws. He also contends that the Court's reasoning undermines the constitutionality of all state legislation to regulate morals and lays the foundation for a court-imposed legitimization of homosexual marriage. His reference, in the second sentence in this reading, to "laws prohibiting . . . working more than 60 hours a week" is to Lochner v. New York. *That decision is now commonly regarded as an act of questionable judicial activism, so Justice Scalia is implying that in* Lawrence *the Court is not interpreting the Constitution so much as substituting its own values for those of the people and legislators of Texas.*

Texas Penal Code Ann. §21.06(a) (2003) undoubtedly imposes constraints on liberty. So do laws prohibiting prostitution, recreational use of heroin, and, for that matter, working more than 60 hours per week in a bakery. But there is no right to "liberty" under the Due Process Clause, though today's opinion repeatedly makes that claim. The Fourteenth Amendment *expressly allows* States to deprive their citizens of "liberty," *so long as "due process of law" is provided.* . . .

Our opinions applying the doctrine known as "substantive due process" hold that the Due Process Clause prohibits States from infringing *fundamental* liberty interests, unless the infringement is narrowly tailored to serve a compelling state interest. We have held repeatedly, in cases the Court today does not overrule, that *only* fundamental rights qualify for this so-called "heightened scrutiny" protection—that is, rights which are "deeply rooted in this Nation's history and tradition." All other liberty interests may be abridged or abrogated pursuant to a validly enacted state law if that law is rationally related to a legitimate state interest.

Bowers held, first, that criminal prohibitions of homosexual sodomy are not subject to heightened scrutiny because they do not implicate a "fundamental right" under the Due Process Clause. Noting that "[p]roscriptions against that conduct have ancient roots," that "[s]odomy was a criminal offense at common law and was forbidden by the laws of the original 13 States when they ratified the Bill of Rights," and that many States had retained their bans on sodomy, *Bowers* concluded that a right to engage in homosexual sodomy was not "deeply rooted in this Nation's history and tradition."

The Court today does not overrule this holding. Not once does it describe homosexual sodomy as a "fundamental right" or a "fundamental liberty interest," nor does it subject the Texas statute to strict scrutiny. Instead, having failed to establish that the right to homosexual sodomy is "deeply rooted in this

Nation's history and tradition," the Court concludes that the application of Texas's statute to petitioners' conduct fails the rational-basis test, and overrules *Bowers'* holding to the contrary. "The Texas statute furthers no legitimate state interest which can justify its intrusion into the personal and private life of the individual." . . .

[T]he Court . . . says: "[W]e think that our laws and traditions in the past half century are of most relevance here. These references show *an emerging awareness* that liberty gives substantial protection to adult persons in deciding how to conduct their private lives *in matters pertaining to sex*." Apart from the fact that such an "emerging awareness" does not establish a "fundamental right," the statement is factually false. States continue to prosecute all sorts of crimes by adults "in matters pertaining to sex": prostitution, adult incest, adultery, obscenity, and child pornography. Sodomy laws, too, have been enforced "in the past half century," in which there have been 134 reported cases involving prosecutions for consensual, adult, homosexual sodomy. . . .

In any event, an "emerging awareness" is by definition not "deeply rooted in this Nation's history and tradition[s]," as we have said "fundamental right" status requires. Constitutional entitlements do not spring into existence because some States choose to lessen or eliminate criminal sanctions on certain behavior. . . .

I turn now to the ground on which the Court squarely rests its holding: the contention that there is no rational basis for the law here under attack. This proposition is so out of accord with our jurisprudence—indeed, with the jurisprudence of *any* society we know—that it requires little discussion.

The Texas statute undeniably seeks to further the belief of its citizens that certain forms of sexual behavior are "immoral and unacceptable"—the same interest furthered by criminal laws against fornication, bigamy, adultery, adult incest, bestiality, and obscenity. *Bowers* held that this *was* a legitimate state interest. The Court today reaches the opposite conclusion. The Texas statute, it says, "furthers *no legitimate state interest* which can justify its intrusion into the personal and private life of the individual." The Court embraces instead *Justice Stevens'* declaration in his *Bowers* dissent, that "the fact that the governing majority in a State has traditionally viewed a particular practice as immoral is not a sufficient reason for upholding a law prohibiting the practice." This effectively decrees the end of all morals legislation. If, as the Court asserts, the promotion of majoritarian sexual morality is not even a *legitimate* state interest, none of the above-mentioned laws can survive rational-basis review. . . .

Today's opinion is the product of a Court, which is the product of a law-profession culture, that has largely signed on to the so-called homosexual agenda, by which I mean the agenda promoted by some homosexual activists directed at eliminating the moral opprobrium that has traditionally attached to homosexual conduct. I noted in an earlier opinion the fact that the American Association of Law Schools (to which any reputable law school *must* seek to belong) excludes from membership any school that refuses to ban from its job-interview facilities a law firm (no matter how small) that does not wish to hire as a prospective partner a person who openly engages in homosexual conduct.

One of the most revealing statements in today's opinion is the Court's grim warning that the criminalization of homosexual conduct is "an invitation to subject homosexual persons to discrimination both in the public and in the private spheres." It is clear from this that the Court has taken sides in the culture war, departing from its role of assuring, as neutral observer, that the democratic rules of engagement are observed. Many Americans do not want persons who openly engage in homosexual conduct as partners in their business, as scoutmasters for their children, as teachers in their children's schools, or as boarders in their home. They view this as protecting themselves and their families from a lifestyle that they believe to be immoral and destructive. The Court views it as "discrimination" which it is the function of our judgments to deter. So imbued is the Court with the law profession's anti-anti-homosexual culture, that it is seemingly unaware that the attitudes of that culture are not obviously "mainstream"; that in most States what the Court calls "discrimination" against those who engage in homosexual acts is perfectly legal; that proposals to ban such "discrimination" under Title VII have repeatedly been rejected by Congress. . . .

Let me be clear that I have nothing against homosexuals, or any other group, promoting their agenda through normal democratic means. Social perceptions of sexual and other morality change over time, and every group has the right to persuade its fellow citizens that its view of such matters is the best. That homosexuals have achieved some success in that enterprise is attested to by the fact that Texas is one of the few remaining States that criminalize private, consensual homosexual acts. But persuading one's fellow citizens is one thing, and imposing one's views in absence of democratic majority will is something else. I would no more *require* a State to criminalize homosexual acts—or, for that matter, display *any* moral disapprobation of them—than I would *forbid* it to do so. What Texas has chosen to do is well within the range of traditional democratic action, and its hand should not be stayed through the invention of a brand-new "constitutional right" by a Court that is impatient of democratic change. It is indeed true that "later generations can see that laws once thought necessary and proper in fact serve only to oppress"; and when that happens, later generations can repeal those laws. But it is the premise of our system that those judgments are to be made by the people, and not imposed by a governing caste that knows best.

One of the benefits of leaving regulation of this matter to the people rather than to the courts is that the people, unlike judges, need not carry things to their logical conclusion. The people may feel that their disapprobation of homosexual conduct is strong enough to disallow homosexual marriage, but not strong enough to criminalize private homosexual acts—and may legislate accordingly. The Court today pretends that it possesses a similar freedom of action, so that that we need not fear judicial imposition of homosexual marriage, as has recently occurred in Canada. At the end of its opinion—after having laid waste the foundations of our rational-basis jurisprudence—the Court says that the present case "does not involve whether the government must give formal recognition to any relationship that homosexual persons seek to enter."

Do not believe it. More illuminating than this bald, unreasoned disclaimer is the progression of thought displayed by an earlier passage in the Court's opinion, which notes the constitutional protections afforded to "personal decisions relating to *marriage*, procreation, contraception, family relationships, child rearing, and education," and then declares that "[p]ersons in a homosexual relationship may seek autonomy for these purposes, just as heterosexual persons do." Today's opinion dismantles the structure of constitutional law that has permitted a distinction to be made between heterosexual and homosexual unions, insofar as formal recognition in marriage is concerned. If moral disapprobation of homosexual conduct is "no legitimate state interest" for purposes of proscribing that conduct; and if, as the Court coos (casting aside all pretense of neutrality), "[w]hen sexuality finds overt expression in intimate conduct with another person, the conduct can be but one element in a personal bond that is more enduring," what justification could there possibly be for denying the benefits of marriage to homosexual couples exercising "[t]he liberty protected by the Constitution"? Surely not the encouragement of procreation, since the sterile and the elderly are allowed to marry. This case "does not involve" the issue of homosexual marriage only if one entertains the belief that principle and logic have nothing to do with the decisions of this Court. Many will hope that, as the Court comfortingly assures us, this is so.

DISCUSSION QUESTIONS FOR CHAPTER 6

1. Contrast the arguments of Justice Fuller with those of Chief Justice Hughes (in reading 3). Does respect for Federalism require that the national government's regulation of the economy be strictly limited, or does the complexity of the modern economy require national oversight?

2. Contrast the arguments of Justice Peckham with those of Chief Justice Hughes (in reading 4). Is there a liberty of contract that limits the rights of state governments to intervene in the economy, or does the state have a right to regulate work and trade in order to enforce the majority's understanding of the common good?

3. Explain the differences between Justices Black and Murphy in the *Korematsu* case. Should the Court have intervened to stop the government's detention policy, or was the Court correct to defer to the judgment of the military and political authorities?

4. Explain the differences between Chief Justice Vinson and Justice Douglas in the *Dennis* case. Does the government have the authority to suppress the speech of those who would advocate its overthrow, or does freedom of speech require that even the most radical political opinions be unregulated by law?

5. Contrast the position of Justice Blackmun in *Roe* v. *Wade* to Justice White's opinion in *Doe* v. *Bolton*. Is there a right to privacy protecting the right to have an abortion, or do states have the right to forbid abortion in order to protect the lives of human fetuses?

6. Contrast the arguments of Justices Kennedy and Scalia in *Lawrence* v. *Texas*. Does the Constitution protect the right of individuals to engage in consensual sexual conduct without being regulated by law, or does the majority in a democracy have the right to enforce its moral convictions through legislation?

CHAPTER 7

Economic Liberty

1

William Graham Sumner: Testimony to Congress on an Ailing Economy (1878)

In 1873, the American economy endured one of several severe depression of the era that limited the ability of citizens to find jobs and left thousands destitute and hopelessly impoverished. By the late nineteenth century, the federal government as well as most economists and educated elite had embraced the laissez-faire concept of free market capitalism. In the following reading, Yale professor William Graham Sumner testifies before a House of Representatives committee that had begun to investigate the boom and bust cycle of the American economy. Sumner, a free trade advocate, argues that the federal government should limit any attempt to regulate the nation's economy.

The Chairman: Have you given any special attention to the condition of labor and of business generally at the present time in the United States?

Mr. Sumner: That is within the range of my professional studies. I have studied it and given all the attention I could to it, and I have availed myself of all the means that I know of for forming ideas about it. I should like to say that the means of forming ideas about it on the part of professional economists are very meager and unsatisfactory. It is exceedingly difficult for any person, however well trained he may be, to embrace this whole subject of the causes of the present depression in the United States; and he would be a very bold man indeed who should claim that he had sounded the whole question. I am certainly not in that position before this committee. I should think that that question ought to be carefully considered in two different points of view. There has been very great industrial reaction over the whole world during the last five or six years, and the United States have, of course, participated in the general state of industry and commerce over the whole world. They have had their share of it. There have been other local and peculiar circumstances in the United States which should be considered by themselves as combining with and intensifying here the effects produced by general causes the world over. Now, I do not know anyone in the world who has undertaken to study the whole question of the present commercial crisis over the world in all its bearings, or who has ventured to publish his opinion as to what the cause of this general depression may be, because I am sure that any professional economist would regard that as a subject of enormous magnitude, and would be very timid about any of his conclusions in regard to it. I do not care to enter into that. . . .

The Chairman: I do not know whether you are ready to take up the question of remedies. Do you think that there is any remedy that may be applied by legislation or otherwise to relieve labor from the consequences of this speculative era?

Mr. Sumner: And every one must do the best he can.

The Chairman: Can legislation do anything toward relieving this accumulation of labor by transferring it to some other place where labor is in request or can be utilized?

Mr. Sumner: Legislation might do a great deal of mischief, but nothing else. . . . Of course, I have not any remedy to offer for such a state of things as this. The only answer I can give to a question like that would be the application of simple sound doctrine and sound principles to the case in point. I do not know of anything that the government can do that is at all specific to assist labor—to assist non–capitalists. The only things that the government can do are general things, such as are in the province of a government. The general things that a government can do to assist the non–capitalist in the accumulation of capital (for that is what he wants) are two things. The first thing is to give him the greatest possible measure of liberty in the directing of his own energies for his own development, and the second is to give him the greatest possible security in the possession and use of the products of his own industry. I do not see anything more than that that a government can do in the premises. . . .

The Chairman: The grievance complained of is that, in the operations of society, certain persons, who are just as deserving as others, find it impossible to get any employment at all. They say that society owes them a living; that, if they cannot get work at private hands, the public should intervene for the time being and provide some place where their labor could be employed, and where they could get a livelihood. They claim that they are just as industrious and meritorious as other citizens; and the proposition is for government to intervene and provide them with employment. What have you got to say to that? Can that be done?

Mr. Sumner: Sir. The moment that government provided work for one, it would have to provide work for all, and there would be no end whatever possible. Society does not owe any man a living. In all the cases that I have ever known of young men who claimed that society owed them a living, it has turned out that society paid them—in the State prison. I do not see any other result. Society does not owe any man a living. The fact that a man is here is no demand upon other people that they shall keep him alive and sustain him. He has got to fight the battle with nature as every other man has; and if he fights it with the same energy and enterprise and skill and industry as any other man, I cannot imagine his failing—that is, misfortune apart.

2

Andrew Carnegie: "Wealth" (1889)

By the late nineteenth century a small number of aggressive businessmen and financiers had amassed huge quantities of wealth through various means, both ethical and unethical. The most noted capitalists of the era, such as J. Piermont Morgan, John D. Rockefeller, and Andrew Carnegie, sought to utilize the advantages of a nonintrusive federal government to dominate their particular business interests. Carnegie, specifically, was able to virtually monopolize the steel industry and became one of the wealthiest men in America through a pattern of corporate fiscal discipline and the sound management of facilities. In 1889, amid growing cries that capitalism was an oppressive economic system, Carnegie published the following article, which defends capitalism but acknowledges that the wealthy benefactors of such an economic structure were obligated to be good stewards of society's collective wealth.

. . . The price which society pays for the law of competition, like the price it pays for cheap comforts and luxuries, is also great; but the advantages of this law are also greater still, for it is to this law that we owe our wonderful material development, which brings improved conditions in its train. But, whether the law be benign or not, we must say of it, as we say of the change in the conditions of men to which we have referred: It is here; we cannot evade it; no substitutes for it have been found; and while the law may be sometimes hard for the individual, it is best for the race, because it insures the survival of the fittest in every department. We accept and welcome, therefore, as conditions to which we must accommodate ourselves, great inequality of environment, the concentration of business, industrial and commercial, in the hands of a few, and the law of competition between these, as being not only beneficial, but essential for the future progress of the race. Having accepted these, it follows that there must be great scope for the exercise of special ability in the merchant and in the manufacturer who has to conduct affairs upon a great scale. That this talent for organization and management is rare among men is proved by the fact that it invariably secures for its possessor enormous rewards, no matter where or under what laws or conditions. The experienced in affairs always rate the MAN whose services can be obtained as a partner as not only the first consideration, but such as to render the question of his capital scarcely worth considering, for such men soon create capital; while, without the special talent required, capital soon takes wings. Such men become interested in firms or corporations using millions; and estimating only simple interest to be made upon the capital invested, it is inevitable that their income must exceed their expenditures, and that they must accumulate wealth. Nor is there any middle ground which such men can occupy, because the great manufacturing or commercial concern which does not earn at least interest upon its capital soon becomes bankrupt. It must either go forward or fall behind: to stand still is impossible. It is a condition essential for its successful operation that it should be thus far profitable, and even that, in addition to interest on capital, it should make profit. It is a law, as certain as any of the others named, that men possessed of this peculiar talent for affairs, under the free play of economic forces, must, of necessity, soon be in receipt of more revenue than can be judiciously expended upon themselves; and this law is as beneficial for the race as the others.

Objections to the foundations upon which society is based are not in order, because the condition of the race is better with these than it has been with any others which have been tried. Of the effect of any new substitutes proposed we cannot be sure. The Socialist or Anarchist who seeks to overturn present conditions is to be regarded as attacking the foundation upon which civilization itself rests, for civilization took its start from the day that the capable, industrious workman said to his incompetent and lazy fellow, "If thou dost not sow, thou shalt no reap," and thus ended primitive Communism by separating the drones from the bees. One who studies this subject will soon be brought face to face with the conclusion that upon the sacredness of property civilization itself depends—the right of the laborer to his hundred dollars in the savings bank, and equally the legal right of the millionaire to his millions. To those who propose to substitute Communism for this intense Individualism the answer, therefore, is: The race has tried that. All progress from that barbarous day to the present time has resulted from its displacement. Not evil, but good, has come to the race from the accumulation of wealth by those who have the ability and energy that produce it. . . . This is not evolution, but revolution. It necessitates the changing of human nature itself—a work of eons, even if it were good to change it, which we cannot know. It is not practicable in our day or in our age. Even if desirable theoretically, it belongs to another and long-succeeding sociological stratum. . . . Individualism, Private Property, the Law of Accumulation of Wealth, and the Law of Competition; for these are the highest results of human experience, the soil in which society so far has produced the best fruit. Unequally or unjustly, perhaps, as these laws sometimes operate, and imperfect as they appear to the Idealist, they are, nevertheless, like the highest type of man, the best and most valuable of all that humanity has yet accomplished. . . .

This, then, is held to be the duty of the man of Wealth: First, to set an example of modest, unostentatious living, shunning display or extravagance; to provide moderately for the legitimate wants of those dependent upon him; and after doing so to consider all surplus revenues which come to him simply as trust funds, which he is called upon to administer, and strictly bound as a matter of duty to administer in the manner which, in his judgment, is best calculated to produce the most beneficial results for the community—the man of wealth thus becoming the mere agent and trustee for his poorer brethren, bringing to their service his superior wisdom, experience, and ability to administer, doing for them better than they would or could do for themselves. . . .

In bestowing charity, the main consideration should be to help those who will help themselves; to provide part of the means by which those who desire to improve may do so; to give those who desire to rise the aids by which they may rise; to assist, but rarely or never to do all. Neither the individual nor the race is improved by alms-giving. Those worthy of assistance, except in rare cases, seldom require assistance. The really valuable men of the race never do, except in cases of accident or sudden change. Every one has, of course, cases of individuals brought to his own knowledge where temporary assistance can do genuine good, and these he will not overlook. But the amount which can be wisely given by the individual for individuals is necessarily limited by his lack of knowledge of the circumstances connected with each. He is the only true reformer who is as careful and as anxious not to aid the unworthy as he is to aid the worthy, and, perhaps, even more so, for in alms-giving more injury is probably done by rewarding vice than by relieving virtue. . . .

Thus is the problem of Rich and Poor to be solved. The laws of accumulation will be left free; the laws of distribution free. Individualism will continue, but the millionaire will be but a trustee for the poor; intrusted for a season with a great part of the increased wealth of the community, but administering it for the community far better than it could or would have done for itself. The best minds will thus have reached a stage in the development of the race in which it is clearly seen that there is no mode of disposing of surplus wealth creditable to thoughtful and earnest men into whose hands it flows save by using it year by year for the general good. This day already dawns. But a little while, and although, without incurring the pity of their fellows, men may die sharers in great business enterprises from which their capital cannot be or has not been withdrawn, and is left chiefly at death for public uses, yet the man who dies leaving behind him millions of available wealth, which was his to administer during life, will pass away "unwept, unhonored, and unsung," no matter to what uses he leaves the dross which he cannot take with him. Of such as these the public verdict will then be: "The man who dies thus rich dies disgraced."

Such, in my opinion, is the true Gospel concerning Wealth, obedience to which is destined some day to solve the problem of the Rich and the Poor, and to bring "Peace on earth, among men Good-Will."

3

President Theodore Roosevelt: Speech to Congress on the Threat of Trusts (1901)

Because of the domination of certain industries by a small number of individuals and groups, by the late nineteenth century the federal government, led by individuals such as Teddy Roosevelt, began taking an active role in eliminating threats to the economic liberty of Americans. The emergence of trusts as a legal mechanism for corporate consolidation posed a threat to the natural order of free market capitalism and, thus, beginning in the 1890s, the federal government supported a series of legislative acts to combat the trend. In the following reading, Roosevelt issues a warning on the destructive nature of trusts and illustrates some of his main concerns about their proliferation.

The tremendous and highly complex industrial development which went on with ever accelerated rapidity during the latter half of the nineteenth century brings us face to face, at the beginning of the twentieth, with very serious social problems. The old laws, and the old customs which had almost the binding force of law, were once quite sufficient to regulate the accumulation and distribution of wealth. Since the industrial changes which have so enormously increased the productive power of mankind, they are no longer sufficient.

The growth of cities has gone beyond comparison faster than the growth of the country, and the upbuilding of the great industrial centres has meant a startling increase, not merely in the aggregate of wealth, but in the number of very large individual, and especially of very large corporate, fortunes. The creation of these great corporate fortunes has not been due to natural causes in the business world, operating in other countries as they operate in our own. . . .

The mechanism of modern business is so delicate that extreme care must be taken not to interfere with it in a spirit of rashness or ignorance. Many of those who have made it their vocation to denounce the great industrial combinations which are popularly, although with technical inaccuracy, known as "trusts," appeal especially to hatred and fear. There are precisely the two emotions, particularly when combined with ignorance, which unfit men for the exercise of cool steady judgment. In facing new industrial conditions, the whole history of the world shows that legislation will generally be both unwise and ineffective unless undertaken after calm inquiry and with sober self-restraint. Much of the legislation directed at the trusts would have been exceedingly mischievous had it not also been entirely ineffective. In accordance with a well-known sociological law, the ignorant or reckless agitator has been the really effective friend of the evils which he has been nominally opposing. In dealing with business interests, for the Government to undertake by crude and ill-considered legislation to do what may turn out to be bad, would be to incur the risk of such far-reaching national disaster that it would be preferable to undertake nothing at all. . . .

All this is true; and yet it is also true that there are real and grave evils, one of the chief being over-capitalization because of its many baleful consequences; and a resolute and practical effort must be made to correct these evils.

There is a widespread conviction in the minds of the American people that the great corporations known as trusts are in certain of their features and tendencies hurtful to the general welfare. This springs from no spirit of envy or uncharitableness, nor a lack of pride in the great industrial achievements that have placed this country at the head of the nations struggling for commercial supremacy. It does not rest upon a lack of intelligent appreciation of the necessity of meeting changing and changed conditions of trade with new methods, nor upon ignorance of the fact that combination of capital in the effort to accomplish great things is necessary when the world's progress demands that great things be done. It is based upon sincere conviction that combination and concentration should be, not prohibited, but supervised and within reasonable limits controlled; and in my judgment this conviction is right.

It is no limitation upon property rights or freedom of contract to require that when men receive from Government the privilege of doing business under corporate form, which frees them from individual responsibility, and enables them to call into their enterprises the capital of the public, they shall do so upon absolutely truthful representations as to the value of the property in which the capital is to be invested. Corporations engaged in interstate commerce should be regulated if they are found to exercise a license working to the public injury. It should be as much the aim of those who seek for social betterment to rid the business world of crimes of cunning as to rid the entire body politic of crimes of violence. Great corporations exist only because they are created and safeguarded by our institutions; and it is therefore our right and our duty to see that they work in harmony with these institutions.

The first essential in determining how to deal with the great industrial combinations is knowledge of the facts—publicity. In the interest of the public, the Government should have the right to inspect and examine the workings of the great corporations engaged in interstate business. Publicity is the only sure remedy which we can now invoke. What further remedies are needed in the way of governmental regulation, or taxation, can only be determined after publicity has been obtained, by process of law, and in the course of administration. The first requisite is knowledge, full and complete knowledge which may be public to the world.

Artificial bodies, such as corporations and joint-stock or other associations, depending upon any statutory law for their existence or privileges, should be subject to proper governmental supervision, and full and accurate information as to their operations should be made public regularly at reasonable intervals. The large corporations, commonly called trusts, though organized in one State, always do business in many States, often doing very little business in the state where they are incorporated. There is utter lack of uniformity in the State laws about them; and as no State has any exclusive interest in or power over their acts, it has in practice proved impossible to get adequate regulation through State action. Therefore, in the interest of the whole people, the Nation should, without interfering with the power of the States in the matter itself, also assume power of supervision and regulation over all corporations doing an interstate business. . . .

There should be created a Cabinet officer, to be known as the Secretary of Commerce and Industries, as provided in the bill introduced at the last session of the Congress. It should be his province to deal with commerce in its broadest sense; including among many other things whatever concerns labor and all matters affecting the great business corporations and our merchant marine.

The course proposed is one phase of what should be a comprehensive and far-reaching scheme of constructive statesmanship for the purpose of broadening our markets, securing our business interests on a safe basis, and making firm our new position in the international industrial world; while scrupulously safeguarding the rights of wage worker and capitalist, of investor and private citizen, so as to secure equity as between man and man in this Republic.

4

Thorstein Veblen:
The Theory of the Leisure Class (1902)

Even with restrictions on trusts and monopolies, by the turn of the twentieth century the wealthiest Americans controlled more relative wealth than in previous generations, and the overall economic disparity between the classes was growing. This rise in income for the wealthy allowed them to enjoy extravagant lifestyles and capitalize on the freedoms inherent in American society related to pursuing their own, unencumbered interests. In this famous analysis of the "leisure class," economist and sociologist Thorstein Veblen characterizes the fabulously wealthy in the United States.

. . . As wealth accumulates, the leisure class develops further in function and structure, and there arises a differentiation within the class. There is a more or less elaborate system of rank and grades. This differentiation is furthered by the inheritance of wealth and the consequent inheritance of gentility. With the inheritance of gentility goes the inheritance of obligatory leisure; and gentility of a sufficient potency to entail a life of leisure may be inherited without the complement of wealth required to maintain a dignified leisure. Gentle blood may be transmitted without goods enough to afford a reputably free consumption at one's ease. Hence results a class of impecunious gentlemen of leisure, incidentally referred to already. These half-caste gentlemen of leisure fall into a system of hierarchical gradations. Those who stand near the higher and the highest grades of the wealthy leisure class, in point of birth, or in point of wealth, or both, outrank the remoter-born and the pecuniarily weaker. These lower grades, especially the impecunious, or marginal, gentlemen of leisure, affiliate themselves by a system of dependence or fealty to the great ones; by so doing they gain an increment of repute, or of the means with which to lead a life of leisure, from their patron. They become his courtiers or retainers, servants; and being fed and countenanced by their patron they are indices of his rank and vicarious consumers of his superfluous wealth. Many of these affiliated gentlemen of leisure are at the same time lesser men of substance in their own right; so that some of them are scarcely at all, others only partially, to be rated as vicarious consumers. So many of them, however, as make up the retainers and hangers-on of the patron may be classed as vicarious consumers without qualification. Many of these again, and also many of the other aristocracy of less degree, have in turn attached to their persons a more or less comprehensive group of vicarious consumers in the persons of their wives and children, their servants, retainers, etc.

With the disappearance of servitude, the number of vicarious consumers attached to any one gentleman tends, on the whole, to decrease. The like is of course true, and perhaps in a still higher degree, of the number of dependents who perform vicarious leisure for him. . . .

And here occurs a curious inversion. It is a fact of common observation that in this lower middle class there is no pretence of leisure on the part of the head of the household. Through force of circumstances it has fallen into disuse. But the middle-class wife still carries on the business of vicarious leisure, for the good name of the household and its master. In descending the social scale in any modern industrial community, the primary fact—the conspicuous leisure of the master of the household—disappears at a relatively high point. The head of the middle-class household has been reduced by economic circumstances to turn his hand to gaining a livelihood by occupations which often partake largely of the character of industry, as in the case of the ordinary business man of today. But the derivative fact—the vicarious leisure and consumption rendered by the wife, and the auxiliary vicarious performance of leisure by menials—remains in vogue as a conventionality which the demands of reputability will not suffer to be slighted. It is by no means an uncommon spectacle to find a man applying himself to work with the utmost assiduity, in order that his wife may in due form render for him that degree of vicarious leisure which the common sense of the time demands. . . .

The requirement of vicarious consumption at the hands of the wife continues in force even at a lower point in the pecuniary scale than the requirement of vicarious leisure. At a point below which little if any pretence of wasted effort, in ceremonial cleanness and the like, is observable, and where there is assuredly no conscious attempt at ostensible leisure, decency still requires the wife to consume some goods conspicuously for the reputability of the household and its head. So that, as the latter-day outcome of this evolution of an archaic institution, the wife, who was at the outset the drudge and chattel of the man, both in fact and in theory,—the producer of goods for him to consume,—has become the ceremonial consumer of goods which he produces. But she still quite unmistakably remains his chattel in theory; for the habitual rendering of vicarious leisure and consumption is the abiding mark of the unfree servant. . . .

The observance of these standards, in some degree of approximation, becomes incumbent upon all classes lower in the scale. In modern civilized communities the lines of demarcation between social classes have grown vague and transient, and wherever this happens the norm of reputability imposed by the upper class extends its coercive influence with but slight hindrance down through the social structure to the lowest strata. The result is that the members of each stratum accept as their ideal of decency the scheme of life in vogue in the next higher stratum, and bend their energies to live up to that ideal. On pain of forfeiting their good name and their self-respect in case of failure, they must conform to the accepted code, at least in appearance. . . .

It is also noticeable that the serviceability of consumption as a means of repute, as well as the insistence on it as an element of decency, is at its best in those portions of the community where the human contact of the individual is widest and the mobility of the population is greatest. Conspicuous consumption claims a relatively larger portion of the income of the urban than of the rural population, and the claim is also more imperative. The result is that, in order to keep up a decent appearance, the former habitually live hand-to-mouth to a greater extent than the latter. So it comes, for instance, that the American farmer and his wife and daughters are notoriously less modish in their dress, as well as less urbane in their manners, than the city artisan's family with an equal income. It is not that the city population is by nature much more eager for the peculiar complacency that comes of a conspicuous consumption, nor has the rural population less regard for pecuniary decency. But the provocation to this line of evidence, as well as its transient effectiveness, are more decided in the city. This method is therefore more readily resorted to, and in the struggle to outdo one another the city population push their normal standard of conspicuous consumption to a higher point, with the result that a relatively greater expenditure in this direction is required to indicate a given degree of pecuniary decency in the city. The requirement of conformity to this higher conventional standard becomes mandatory. The standard of decency is higher, class for class, and this requirement of decent appearance must be lived up to on pain of losing caste. . . .

Throughout the entire evolution of conspicuous expenditure, whether of goods or of services or human life, runs the obvious implication that in order to effectually mend the consumer's good fame it must be an expenditure of superfluities. In order to be reputable it must be wasteful. No merit would accrue from the consumption of the bare necessaries of life, except by comparison with the abjectly poor who fall short even of the subsistence minimum; and no standard of expenditure could result from such a comparison, except the most prosaic and unattractive level of decency. A standard of life would still be possible which should admit of invidious comparison in other respects than that of opulence; as, for instance, a comparison in various directions in the manifestation of moral, physical, intellectual, or aesthetic force. Comparison in all these directions is in vogue to-day; and the comparison made in these respects is commonly so inextricably bound up with the pecuniary comparison as to be scarcely distinguishable from the latter. This is especially true as regards the current rating of expressions of intellectual and aesthetic force or proficiency; so that we frequently interpret as aesthetic or intellectual a difference which in substance is pecuniary only. . . .

5

Dawes Severalty Act (1887)

By the 1880s the destruction of Native American culture was nearly complete following almost three centuries of gradual encroachment by outside forces. Confined in most areas to reservations, the dismal plight of Native Americans became the focal point for some reformers during the late nineteenth century who advocated assimilation. Thus, Congress passed the Dawes Severalty Act, which allocated land to individuals and families and removed the authority from tribes. Although intended to alleviate the suffering of Native Americans by allowing them to achieve economic freedom, the act caused millions of acres of land to be removed from Native American control through the exercise of Section 5, which allowed for the purchase of excess reservation land after the allotments were completed.

. . .Be it enacted by the Senate and House of Representatives of the United States of America in Congress assembled, That in all cases where any tribe or band of Indians has been, or shall hereafter be, located upon any reservation created for their use, either by treaty stipulation or by virtue of an act of Congress or executive order setting apart the same for their use, the President of the United States be, and he hereby is, authorized, whenever in his opinion any reservation or any part thereof of such Indians is advantageous for agricultural and grazing purposes, to cause said reservation, or any part thereof, to be surveyed, or resurveyed if necessary, and to allot the lands in said reservation in severalty to any Indian located thereon in quantities as follows:

To each head of a family, one-quarter of a section;

To each single person over eighteen years of age, one-eighth of a section;

To each orphan child under eighteen years of age, one-eighth of a section; and

To each other single person under eighteen years now living, or who may be born prior to the date of the order of the President directing an allotment of the lands embraced in any reservation, one-sixteenth of a section:

Provided, That in case there is not sufficient land in any of said reservations to allot lands to each individual of the classes above named in quantities as above provided, the lands embraced in such reservation or reservations shall be allotted to each individual of each of said classes pro rata in accordance with the provisions of this act: And provided further, That where the treaty or act of Congress setting apart such reservation provides the allotment of lands in severalty in quantities in excess of those herein provided, the President, in making allotments upon such reservation, shall allot the lands to each individual Indian belonging thereon in quantity as specified in such treaty or act: And provided further, That when the lands allotted are only valuable for grazing purposes, an additional allotment of such grazing lands, in quantities as above provided, shall be made to each individual.

Sec. 2.   That all allotments set apart under the provisions of this act shall be selected by the Indians, heads of families selecting for their minor children, and the agents shall select for each orphan child, and in such manner as to embrace the improvements of the Indians making the selection. Where the improvements of two or more Indians have been made on the same legal subdivision of land, unless they shall otherwise agree, a provisional line may be run dividing said lands between them, and the amount to which each is entitled shall be equalized in the assignment of the remainder of the land to which they are entitled under his act. . . .

Sec. 4.   That where any Indian not residing upon a reservation, or for whose tribe no reservation has been provided by treaty, act of Congress, or executive order, shall make settlement upon any surveyed or unsurveyed lands of the United States not otherwise appropriated, he or she shall be entitled, upon application to the local land-office for the district in which the lands arc located, to have the same allotted to him or her, and to his or her children, in quantities and manner as provided in this act for Indians residing upon reservations; and when such settlement is made upon unsurveyed lands, the grant to such Indians shall be adjusted upon the survey of the lands so as to conform thereto; and patents shall be issued to them for such lands in the manner and with the restrictions as herein provided. And the fees to which the officers of such local land-office would have been entitled had such lands been entered under the general laws for the disposition of the public lands shall be paid to them, from any moneys in the Treasury of the United States not otherwise appropriated, upon a statement of an account in their behalf for such fees by the Commissioner of the General Land Office, and a certification of such account to the Secretary of the Treasury by the Secretary of the Interior.

Sec. 5.   That upon the approval of the allotments provided for in this act by the Secretary of the Interior, he shall cause patents to issue therefore in the name of the allottees, which patents shall be of the legal effect, and declare that the United States does and will hold the land thus allotted, for the period of twenty-five years, in trust for thc solc use and benefit of the Indian to whom such allotment shall have been made, or, in case of his decease, of his heirs according to the laws of the State or Territory where such land is located, and that at the expiration of said period the United States will convey the same by patent to said Indian, or his heirs as aforesaid, in fee, discharged of said trust and free of all charge or incumbrance whatsoever: . . . And provided further, That at any time after lands have been allotted to all the Indians of any tribe as herein provided, or sooner if in the opinion of the President it shall be for the best interests of said tribe, it shall be lawful for the Secretary of the Interior to negotiate with such Indian tribe for the purchase and release by said tribe, in conformity with the treaty or statute under which such reservation is held, of such portions of its reservation not allotted as such tribe shall, from time to time, consent to sell, on such terms and conditions as shall be considered just and equitable between the United States and said tribe of Indians, which purchase shall not be complete until ratified by Congress, and the form and manner of executing such release prescribed by Congress. . . .

Sec. 6. That upon the completion of said allotments and the patenting of the lands to said allottees, each and every member of the respective bands or tribes of Indians to whom allotments have been made shall have the benefit of and be subject to the laws, both civil and criminal, of the State or Territory in which they may reside; and no Territory shall pass or enforce any law denying any such Indian within its jurisdiction the equal protection of the law. And every Indian born within the territorial limits of the United States to whom allotments shall have been made under the provisions of this act, or under any law or treaty, and every Indian born within the territorial limits of the United States who has voluntarily taken up, within said limits, his residence separate and apart from any tribe of Indians therein, and has adopted the habits of civilized life, is hereby declared to be a citizen of the United States, and is entitled to all the rights, privileges, and immunities of such citizens, whether said Indian has been or not, by birth or otherwise, a member of any tribe of Indians within the territorial limits of the United States without in any manner affecting the right of any such Indian to tribal or other property. . . .

Sec. 8. That the provisions of this act shall not extend to the territory occupied by the Cherokees, Creeks, Choctaws, Chickasaws, Seminoles, and Osage, Miamies and Peorias, and Sacs and Foxes, in the Indian Territory, nor to any of the reservations of the Seneca Nation of New York Indians in the State of New York, nor to that strip of territory in the State of Nebraska adjoining the Sioux Nation on the south added by executive order.

Sec. 9. That for the purpose of making the surveys and resurveys mentioned in section two of this act, there be, and hereby is, appropriated, out of any moneys in the Treasury not otherwise appropriated, the sum of one hundred thousand dollars, to be repaid proportionately out of the proceeds of the sales of such land as may be acquired from the Indians under the provisions of this act.

Sec. 10. That nothing in this act contained shall be so construed to affect the right and power of Congress to grant the right of way through any lands granted to an Indian, or a tribe of Indians, for railroads or other highways, or telegraph lines, for the public use, or condemn such lands to public uses, upon making just compensation.

Sec. 11. That nothing in this act shall be so construed as to prevent the removal of the Southern Ute Indians from their present reservation in Southwestern Colorado to a new reservation by and with consent of a majority of the adult male members of said tribe.

6

Pauline Newman: Letter About Working Conditions at the Triangle Shirtwaist Factory (1951)

In 1911 the Triangle Shirtwaist Factory caught fire, resulting in the deaths of nearly 150 employees. The victims were mainly girls and young women who worked in sweatshop conditions for relatively little pay. Though little changed in the immediate aftermath of the fire, the tragedy did heighten public awareness of dangerous working conditions and reveal the need for reform. In 1951, a former Triangle Shirtwaist employee, Pauline Newman, reminisced about her time at the factory, openly expressing her disdain for the job and her resentment at being, in her opinion, exploited.

One day a relative of mine who was employed by the now infamous Triangle Shirt Waist Co., the largest manufacturers of shirt waists in New York City, got me a job with that firm. The day I left the Jackson street shop the foreman told me that I was very lucky to have gotten a job with that concern because there is work all year round and that I will no longer have to look for another job. I found later that workers were actually eager to work for this company because there was steady employment. For me this job differed in many respects from the previous ones. The Triangle Waist Co. was located at Green Street and Washington Place. This was quite a distance from my home. Since the day's work began at seven thirty it meant that I had to leave home at six forty. . . .

The day's work was supposed to end at six in the afternoon. But, during most of the year we youngsters worked overtime until 9 p.m. every night except Fridays and Saturdays. No, we did not get additional pay for overtime. At this point it is worth recording the generocity [sic] of the Triangle Waist Co. by giving us a piece of apple pie for supper instead of additional pay! Working men and women of today who receive time and one half and at times double time for overtime will find it difficult to understand and to believe that the workers of those days were evidently willing to accept such conditions of labor without protest. However, the answer is quite simple—we were not organized and we knew that individual protest amounted to the loss of one's job. No one in those days could afford the luxory [sic] of changing jobs—there

Reprinted with permission of the Kheel Center for Labor-Management Documentation and Archives at Cornell University.

was no unemployment insurance, there was nothing better than to look for another job which will not be better than the one we had. Therefore, we were, due to our ignorance and poverty, helpless against the power of the exploiters.

As you will note, the days were long and the wages low—my starting wage was just one dollar and a half a week—a long week—consisting more often than not, of seven days. Especially was this true during the season, which in those days were longer than they are now. I will never forget the sign which on Saturday afternoons was posted on the wall near the elevator stating—"if you don't come in on Sunday you need not come in on Monday"! What choice did we have except to look for another job on Monday morning. We did not relish the thought of walking the factory district in search of another job. And would we find a better one? We did not like it. As a matter of fact we looked forward to the one day on which we could sleep a little longer, go to the park and get to see one's friends and relatives. It was a bitter disappointment.

My job, like that of the other kids was not strenous [sic]. It consisted of trimming off the threads left on the shirt waists by the operators. We were called "cleaners." Hundreds of dozens of shirt waists were carried from the machines to the "children's corner" and put into huge cases. When these were trimmed they were put in similar empty case ready for the examiners to finish the job. By the way, these cases were used for another purpose which served the employers very well indeed. You see, boys, these cases were high enough and deep enough for us kids to hide in, so that when a factory inspector came to inspect the factory he found no violation of the child labor law, because he did not see any children at work—we were all hidden in the cases and covered with shirt waists! Clever of them, was it not? Somehow the employers seemed to have known when the inspector would come and had time enough to arrange for our hiding place. . . .

The deductions for being late was stricktly [sic] enforced because deductions even for a few minutes from several hundred people must have meant quite a sum of money. And since it was money the Triangle Waist Co. employers were after this was an easy way to get it. That these deductions meant less food for the worker's children bothered the employers not at all. If they had a conscience it apparently did not function in that direction. As I look back to those years of actual slavery I am quite certain that the conditions under which we worked and which existed in the factory of the Triangle Waist Co. were the acme of exploitation perpetrated by humans upon defenceless [sic] men women and children—a sort of punishment for being poor and docile.

Despite these inhuman working conditions the workers—including myself—continued to work for this firm. What good would it do to change jobs since similar conditions existed in all garment factories of that era? There were other reasons why we did not change jobs—call them psychological, if you will. One gets used to a place even if it is only a work shop. One gets to know the people you work with. You are no longer a stranger and alone. You have a feeling of belonging which helps to make life in a factory a bit easier to endure. Very often friendships are formed and a common understanding established. These among other factors made us stay put, as it were. . . .

7

Eugene V. Debs: Statement to the Court (1918)

By the early portion of the twentieth century, the negative components of a largely unbri-dled capitalistic economic system as well as substantial immigration from socialistic-inclined eastern and southern Europe led many American laborers to embrace various radical ideologies. In 1918, labor leader and socialist Eugene V. Debs criticized U.S. entry into World War I and eventually received a ten-year jail sentence for his subver-sive activities. In his statement to the court during the subsequent proceedings, Debs used the occasion to opine on the oppressive nature of American society and the absence of collective economic liberty in the United States.

Your Honor, years ago I recognized my kinship with all living beings, and I made up my mind that I was not one bit better than the meanest on earth. I said then, and I say now, that while there is a lower class, I am in it, and while there is a criminal element I am of it, and while there is a soul in prison, I am not free. I listened to all that was said in this court in support and justification of this prosecution, but my mind remains unchanged. I look upon the Espionage Law as a despotic enactment in flagrant conflict with democratic principles and with the spirit of free institutions. . . .

Your Honor, I have stated in this court that I am opposed to the social sys-tem in which we live; that I believe in a fundamental change—but if possible by peaceable and orderly means. . . .

Standing here this morning, I recall my boyhood. At fourteen I went to work in a railroad shop; at sixteen I was firing a freight engine on a railroad. I remember all the hardships and privations of that earlier day, and from that time until now my heart has been with the working class. I could have been in Congress long ago. I have preferred to go to prison. . . .

I am thinking this morning of the men in the mills and the factories; of the men in the mines and on the railroads. I am thinking of the women who for a paltry wage are compelled to work out their barren lives; of the little children who in this system are robbed of their childhood and in their tender years are seized in the remorseless grasp of Mammon and forced into the industrial dungeons, there to feed the monster machines while they them-selves are being starved and stunted, body and soul. I see them dwarfed and diseased and their little lives broken and blasted because in this high noon of Christian civilization money is still so much more important than the flesh and blood of childhood. In very truth gold is god today and rules with pitiless sway in the affairs of men. In this country—the most favored beneath the bending skies—we have vast areas of the richest and most fertile soil, material resources in inexhaustible abundance, the most marvelous productive machin-ery on earth, and millions of eager workers ready to apply their labor to that machinery to produce in abundance for every man, woman, and child—and if there are still vast numbers of our people who are the victims of poverty and whose lives are an unceasing struggle all the way from youth to old age, until at last death comes to their rescue and lulls these hapless victims to dreamless sleep, it is not the fault of the Almighty: it cannot be charged to nature, but it is due entirely to the outgrown social system in which we live that ought to be abolished not only in the interest of the toiling masses but in the higher interest of all humanity. . . .

I believe, Your Honor, in common with all Socialists, that this nation ought to own and control its own industries. I believe, as all Socialists do, that all things that are jointly needed and used ought to be jointly owned—that industry, the basis of our social life, instead of being the private property of a few and operated for their enrichment, ought to be the common property of all, democratically administered in the interest of all. . . .

I am opposing a social order in which it is possible for one man who does absolutely nothing that is useful to amass a fortune of hundreds of millions of dollars, while millions of men and women who work all the days of their lives secure barely enough for a wretched existence. This order of things cannot always endure. I have registered my protest against it. I recognize the feebleness of my effort, but, fortunately, I am not alone. There are multiplied thousands of others who, like myself, have come to realize that before we may truly enjoy the blessings of civilized life, we must reorganize society upon a mutual and cooperative basis; and to this end we have organized a great economic and political movement that spreads over the face of all the earth. There are today upwards of sixty millions of Socialists, loyal, devoted adherents to this cause, regardless of nationality, race, creed, color, or sex. They are all making common cause. They are spreading with tireless energy the propaganda of the new social order. They are waiting, watching, and working hopefully through all the hours of the day and the night. They are still in a minority. But they have learned how to be patient and to bide their time. The feel—they know, indeed—that the time is coming, in spite of all opposition, all persecution, when this emancipating gospel will spread among all the peoples, and when this minority will become the triumphant majority and, sweeping into power, inaugurate the greatest social and economic change in history. In that day we shall have the universal commonwealth—the harmonious cooperation of every nation with every other nation on earth. . . .

Your Honor, I ask no mercy and I plead for no immunity. I realize that finally the right must prevail. I never so clearly comprehended as now the great struggle between the powers of greed and exploitation on the one hand and upon the other the rising hosts of industrial freedom and social justice. I can see the dawn of the better day for humanity. The people are awakening. In due time they will and must come to their own. . . .

8

Calvin Coolidge: Inaugural Address (1925)

The 1920s were an era of unprecedented prosperity for most Americans—buying power increased, many modern conveniences appeared, and new forms of entertainment allowed individuals to spend disposable income in a variety of ways. The 1920s also witnessed the tenure of arguably the most inactive president in modern history. Calvin Coolidge was thrust into the presidency following the death of Warren Harding amid the exposure of scandal from the previous administration and attempted to restore dignity to the office. As evidenced by the following reading, Coolidge believed in a federal government that encouraged the economic liberty of its citizens by reducing taxes and encouraging rights of private ownership.

. . . When the country has bestowed its confidence upon a party by making it a majority in the Congress, it has a right to expect such unity of action as will make the party majority an effective instrument of government. This Administration has come into power with a very clear and definite mandate from the people. The expression of the popular will in favor of maintaining our constitutional guarantees was overwhelming and decisive. There was a manifestation of such faith in the integrity of the courts that we can consider that issue rejected for some time to come. Likewise, the policy of public ownership of railroads and certain electric utilities met with unmistakable defeat. The people declared that they wanted their rights to have not a political but a judicial determination, and their independence and freedom continued and supported by having the ownership and control of their property, not in the Government, but in their own hands. As they always do when they have a fair chance, the people demonstrated that they are sound and are determined to have a sound government.

When we turn from what was rejected to inquire what was accepted, the policy that stands out with the greatest clearness is that of economy in public expenditure with reduction and reform of taxation. The principle involved in this effort is that of conservation. The resources of this country are almost beyond computation. No mind can comprehend them. But the cost of our combined governments is likewise almost beyond definition. Not only those who are now making their tax returns, but those who meet the enhanced cost of existence in their monthly bills, know by hard experience what this great burden is and what it does. No matter what others may want, these people want a drastic economy. They are opposed to waste. They know that extravagance lengthens the hours and diminishes the rewards of their labor. I favor the policy of economy, not because I wish to save money, but because I wish to save people. The men and women of this country who toil are the ones who bear the cost of the Government. Every dollar that we carelessly waste means that their life will be so much the more meager. Every dollar that we prudently save means that their life will be so much the more abundant. Economy is idealism in its most practical form.

If extravagance were not reflected in taxation, and through taxation both directly and indirectly injuriously affecting the people, it would not be of so much consequence. The wisest and soundest method of solving our tax problem is through economy. Fortunately, of all the great nations this country is best in a position to adopt that simple remedy. We do not any longer need wartime revenues. The collection of any taxes which are not absolutely required, which do not beyond reasonable doubt contribute to the public welfare, is only a species of legalized larceny. Under this republic the rewards of industry belong to those who earn them. The only constitutional tax is the tax which ministers to public necessity. The property of the country belongs to the people of the country. Their title is absolute. They do not support any privileged class; they do not need to maintain great military forces; they ought not to be burdened with a great array of public employees. They are not required to make any contribution to Government expenditures except that which they voluntarily assess upon themselves through the action of their own representatives. Whenever taxes become burdensome a remedy can be applied by the people; but if they do not act for themselves, no one can be very successful in acting for them.

The time is arriving when we can have further tax reduction, when, unless we wish to hamper the people in their right to earn a living, we must have tax reform. The method of raising revenue ought not to impede the transaction of business; it ought to encourage it. I am opposed to extremely high rates, because they produce little or no revenue, because they are bad for the country, and, finally, because they are wrong. We can not finance the country, we can not improve social conditions, through any system of injustice, even if we attempt to inflict it upon the rich. Those who suffer the most harm will be the poor. This country believes in prosperity. It is absurd to suppose that it is envious of those who are already prosperous. The wise and correct course to follow in taxation and all other economic legislation is not to destroy those who have already secured success but to create conditions under which every one will have a better chance to be successful. The verdict of the country has been given on this question. That verdict stands. We shall do well to heed it.

These questions involve moral issues. We need not concern ourselves much about the rights of property if we will faithfully observe the rights of persons. Under our institutions their rights are supreme. It is not property but the right to hold property, both great and small, which our Constitution guarantees. All owners of property are charged with a service. These rights and duties have been revealed, through the conscience of society, to have a divine sanction. The very stability of our society rests upon production and conservation. For individuals or for governments to waste and squander their resources is to deny these rights and disregard these obligations. The result of economic dissipation to a nation is always moral decay. These policies of better international understandings, greater economy, and lower taxes have contributed largely to peaceful and prosperous industrial relations. Under the helpful influences of restrictive immigration and a protective tariff, employ-ment is plentiful, the rate of pay is high, and wage earners are in a state of con-tentment seldom before seen. Our transportation systems have been gradually recovering and have been able to meet all the requirements of the service. Agriculture has been very slow in reviving, but the price of cereals at last indi-cates that the day of its deliverance is at hand. . . .

9

Huey P. Long: The "Share Our Wealth" Plan (1935)

The continuation and even deepening of the Great Depression during the mid-1930s led many Americans to flirt with theretofore radical ideas to alleviate deteriorating eco-nomic conditions. First as the governor of Louisiana and later as senator from the state, the charismatic demagogue Huey Long was part of the increasing chorus urging drastic economic reforms in American society. In the speech transcribed here, Long describes to listeners his plan for restoring economic liberty to American citizens.

WE have nothing more for which we should ask the Lord. He has allowed this land to have too much of everything that humanity needs.

So in this land of God's abundance we propose laws, viz.:

1. The fortunes of the multimillionaires and billionaires shall be reduced so that no one person shall own more than a few million dollars to the person. We would do this by a capital levy tax. On the first mil-lion that a man was worth, we would not impose any tax. We would say, "All right for your first million dollars, but after you get that rich you will have to start helping the balance of us." So we would not levy and capital levy tax on the first million one owned. But on the second million a man owns, we would tax that 1 percent, so that every year the man owned the second million dollars he would be taxed $10,000. On the third million we would impose a tax of 2 per-cent. On the fourth million we would impose a tax of 4 percent. On the fifth million we would impose a tax of 16 percent. On the sev-enth million we would impose a tax of 32 percent. On the eighth million we would impose a tax of 64 percent; and on all over the eight million we would impose a tax of 100 percent.

    What this would mean is that the annual tax would bring the biggest fortune down to $3 or $4 million to the person because no one could pay taxes very long in the higher brackets. But $3 or $4 million is enough for any one person and his children and his chil-dren's children. We cannot allow one to have more than that because it would not leave enough for the balance to have something.

2. We propose to limit the amount any one man can earn in one year or inherit to $1 million to the person.

3. Now, by limiting the size of the fortunes and incomes of the big men, we will throw into the government Treasury the money and property from which we will care for the millions of people who have nothing; and with this money we will provide a home and the comforts of home, with such common conveniences as radio and automobile, for every family in America, free of debt.

4. We guarantee food and clothing and employment for everyone who should work by shortening the hours of labor to thirty hours per week, maybe less, and to eleven months per year, maybe less. We would have the hours shortened just so much as would give work to everybody to produce enough for everybody; and if we were to get them down to where they were too short, then we would lengthen them again. As long as all the people working can produce enough of automobiles, radios, homes, schools, and theatres for everyone to have that kind of comfort and convenience, then let us all have work to do and have that much of heaven on earth.

5. We would provide education at the expense of the states and the United States for every child, not only through grammar school and high school but through to a college and vocational education. We would simply extend the Louisiana plan to apply to colleges and all people. Yes, we would have to build thousands of more colleges and employ 100,000 more teachers; but we have materials, men, and women who are ready and available for the work. Why have the right to a college education depend upon whether the father or mother is so well-to-do as to send a boy or girl to college? We would give every child the right to education and a living at birth.

6. We would give a pension to all persons above sixty years of age in an amount sufficient to support them in comfortable circumstances, expecting those who earn $1,000 per year or who are worth $10,000.

7. Until we could straighten things out—and we can straighten things out in two months under our program—we would grant a moratorium on all debts which people owe that they cannot pay.

And now you have our program, none too big, none too little, but every man a king.

We owe debts in America today, public and private, amounting to $252 billion. That means that every child is born with a $2,000 debt tied around his neck to hold him down before he gets started. Then, on top of that, the wealth is locked in a vise owned by a few people. We propose that children shall be born in a land of opportunity, guaranteed a home, food, clothes, and the other things that make for living, including the right to education.

Our plan would injure no one. It would not stop us from having millionaires—it would increase them ten-fold, because so many more people could make

$1 million if they had the chance our plan gives them. Our plan would not break up big concerns. The only difference would be that maybe 10,000 people would own a concern instead of 10 people owning it.

But, my friends, unless we do share our wealth, unless we limit the size of the big man so as to give something to the little man, we can never have a happy or free people. God said so! He ordered it. We have everything our people need. Too much of food, clothes, and houses—why not let all have their fill and lie down in the ease and comfort God has given us? Why not? Because a few own everything—the masses own nothing.

I wonder if any of you people who are listening to me were ever at a barbecue! We used to go there—sometimes 1,000 people or more. If there were 1,000 people, we would put enough meat and bread and everything else on the table for 1,000 people. Then everybody would be called and everyone would eat all they wanted. But suppose at one of these barbecues for 1,000 people that one man took 90 percent of the food and ran off with it and ate until he got sick and let the balance rot. Then 999 people would have only enough for 100 to eat and there would be many to starve because of the greed of just one person for something he couldn't eat himself.

Well, ladies and gentlemen, America, all the people of America, have been invited to a barbecue. God invited us all to come and eat and drink all we wanted. He smiled on our land; we grew crops of plenty to eat and wear. He showed us in the earth the iron and other things to make everything we wanted. He unfolded to us the secrets of science so that our work might be easy. God called: "Come to my feast."

Then what happened? Rockefeller, Morgan, and their crowd stepped up and took enough for 120 million people and left only enough for 5 million for all the other 125 million to eat. And so many million must go hungry and without these good things God gave us unless we call on them to put some of it back.

10

President Lyndon B. Johnson: The State of the Union Address (1964)

Despite the relatively prosperous era of the 1950s, the United States still was burdened with a significant number of its citizens living below the poverty line and unable to support themselves or their family by the time President Lyndon Johnson took office in 1963. Waging his famous "War on Poverty," Johnson was intent on restoring the economic liberty of the hopelessly impoverished and, as detailed here, advocated an active federal government for that end.

. . . This administration today, here and now, declares unconditional war on poverty in America. I urge this Congress and all Americans to join with me in that effort.

It will not be a short or easy struggle, no single weapon or strategy will suffice, but we shall not rest until that war is won. The richest Nation on earth can afford to win it. We cannot afford to lose it. One thousand dollars invested in salvaging an unemployable youth today can return $40,000 or more in his lifetime.

Poverty is a national problem, requiring improved national organization and support. But this attack, to be effective, must also be organized at the State and the local level and must be supported and directed by State and local efforts.

For the war against poverty will not be won here in Washington. It must be won in the field, in every private home, in every public office, from the courthouse to the White House.

The program I shall propose will emphasize this cooperative approach to help that one-fifth of all American families with incomes too small to even meet their basic needs.

Our chief weapons in a more pinpointed attack will be better schools, and better health, and better homes, and better training, and better job opportunities to help more Americans, especially young Americans, escape from squalor and misery and unemployment rolls where other citizens help to carry them.

Very often a lack of jobs and money is not the cause of poverty, but the symptom. The cause may lie deeper in our failure to give our fellow citizens a fair chance to develop their own capacities, in a lack of education and training, in a lack of medical care and housing, in a lack of decent communities in which to live and bring up their children.

But whatever the cause, our joint Federal-local effort must pursue poverty, pursue it wherever it exists—in city slums and small towns, in sharecropper shacks or in migrant worker camps, on Indian Reservations, among whites as well as Negroes, among the young as well as the aged, in the boom towns and in the depressed areas.

Our aim is not only to relieve the symptom of poverty, but to cure it and, above all, to prevent it. No single piece of legislation, however, is going to suffice.

We will launch a special effort in the chronically distressed areas of Appalachia.

We must expand our small but our successful area redevelopment program.

We must enact youth employment legislation to put jobless, aimless, hopeless youngsters to work on useful projects.

We must distribute more food to the needy through a broader food stamp program.

We must create a National Service Corps to help the economically handicapped of our own country as the Peace Corps now helps those abroad.

We must modernize our unemployment insurance and establish a high-level commission on automation. If we have the brain power to invent these machines, we have the brain power to make certain that they are a boon and not a bane to humanity.

We must extend the coverage of our minimum wage laws to more than 2 million workers now lacking this basic protection of purchasing power.

We must, by including special school aid funds as part of our education program, improve the quality of teaching, training, and counseling in our hardest hit areas.

We must build more libraries in every area and more hospitals and nursing homes under the Hill–Burton Act, and train more nurses to staff them.

We must provide hospital insurance for our older citizens financed by every worker and his employer under Social Security, contributing no more than $1 a month during the employee's working career to protect him in his old age in a dignified manner without cost to the Treasury, against the devastating hardship of prolonged or repeated illness.

We must, as a part of a revised housing and urban renewal program, give more help to those displaced by slum clearance, provide more housing for our poor and our elderly, and seek as our ultimate goal in our free enterprise system a decent home for every American family.

We must help obtain more modern mass transit within our communities as well as low-cost transportation between them.

Above all, we must release $11 billion of tax reduction into the private spending stream to create new jobs and new markets in every area of this land.

These programs are obviously not for the poor or the underprivileged alone. Every American will benefit by the extension of social security to cover the hospital costs of their aged parents. Every American community will benefit from the construction or modernization of schools, libraries, hospitals, and nursing homes, from the training of more nurses and from the improvement of urban renewal in public transit. And every individual American taxpayer and every corporate taxpayer will benefit from the earliest possible passage of the pending tax bill from both the new investment it will bring and the new jobs that it will create.

That tax bill has been thoroughly discussed for a year. Now we need action. The new budget clearly allows it. Our taxpayers surely deserve it. Our economy strongly demands it. And every month of delay dilutes its benefits in 1964 for consumption, for investment, and for employment.

For until the bill is signed, its investment incentives cannot be deemed certain, and the withholding rate cannot be reduced—and the most damaging and devastating thing you can do to any businessman in America is to keep him in doubt and to keep him guessing on what our tax policy is. And I say that we should now reduce to 14 percent instead of 15 percent our withholding rate.

I therefore urge the Congress to take final action on this bill by the first of February, if at all possible. For however proud we may be of the unprecedented progress of our free enterprise economy over the last 3 years, we should not and we cannot permit it to pause.

In 1963, for the first time in history, we crossed the 70 million job mark, but we will soon need more than 75 million jobs. In 1963 our gross national product reached the $600 billion level—$100 billion higher than when we took office. But it easily could and it should be still $30 billion higher today than it is. Wages and profits and family income are also at their highest levels in history—but I would remind you that 4 million workers and 13 percent of our industrial capacity are still idle today.

We need a tax cut now to keep this country moving. For our goal is not merely to spread the work. Our goal is to create more jobs. I believe the enactment of a 35-hour week would sharply increase costs, would invite inflation, would impair our ability to compete, and merely share instead of creating employment. But I am equally opposed to the 45- or 50-hour week in those industries where consistently excessive use of overtime causes increased unemployment.

So, therefore, I recommend legislation authorizing the creation of a tripartite industry committee to determine on an industry-by-industry basis as to where a higher penalty rate for overtime would increase job openings without unduly increasing costs, and authorizing the establishment of such higher rates. . . .

11

Stokely Carmichael: Testimony Before Congress on the Evils of Capitalism (1967)

One of the most radical black activists of the 1960s, Stokely Carmichael maintained the opinion that assimilation was a useless exercise for African Americans because of the exploitative nature of capitalism. In the following reading, excerpted from a Senate subcommittee record, Carmichael expresses clearly his belief that the United States had deprived African Americans of their economic liberty.

. . . Economically speaking, we want our people to be able to enjoy a life and to get all the things they need to have a decent life without having to struggle as hard as they now do because they're economically exploited by the imperialist power structure of the United States, just as the colonies outside are economically able to divide those resources among the people of the—backward—communities. We do not want to set up, for example, a black capitalist system. We want to economically destroy capitalism because capitalism goes hand in hand with racism and exploitation. Wherever capitalism has gone, those two characteristics are sure to follow, racism and exploitation, so we must destroy the capitalistic system which enslaves us on the inside and the people of the third world on the outside. . . .

In order for capitalism to exist it must make the people they conquer, make them feel ashamed of themselves, ashamed of their culture. And what we want to do is to make our people not ashamed . . . so that they can feel that they're equal to anybody else, psychologically, physically, and morally. . . .

The Black people who are living in the North are first generation people; that is to say, it is the first generation of Black people that have been born in the North. Most of the people in the North migrated from the South right after World War II. They migrated from the South because racial discrimination was the (worst) and most brutal in the South and they were told that in the North people didn't care about the color of your skin. It didn't matter. You could get an opportunity and good job if you just worked hard.

And we believed that nonsense and packed up our bags and went north. But what we found when we got north was that life was the same. So . . . [what] we found in the North was that there's nowhere in the United States where you can go under the capitalistic system and enjoy a decent way of life. So that you have now people who do not have hope in any of the legal systems. . . . So that the relationship has become very strong because the people from the South no longer look to the North as an escape, and we now see that the only way that we're going to get out of our, of the capitalistic system, and get our liberation is that both of us join hands and see ourselves as one people. . . .

Most of the poor whites, the white working class in the United States, when they organize, their fight is never a fight for the redistribution of land. Their fight is a fight for more money. All they want is more money. They do not have any concept of the distribution of wealth because they are so capitalistic in their own approach. So what happens is that the ruling class of America then begins to exploit other countries in the third world and make more money. When they get more of those profits, they share those profits with the white working class.

But the ruling class never cuts down on its profits. It makes more, as a matter of fact. Once it begins to share its profits with the working class, the working class becomes part and parcel of the capitalistic system and they enjoy blood money. They enjoy the money that is exploiting other people, so that they are then incapable of fighting the very system, because they become a part of it by accepting the blood money. So it's hard to develop a white working class revolutionary consciousness. What you have then is white people who are fighting to save their money. . . .

And finally, I think that what people outside the United States recognize is that unlike any other people, we were the only people who were made slaves inside the continent of the people who were exploiting us. Other people were slaves in their own countries, so that when they fought they could develop a nationalistic concept as a point of unity to come together. We were brought inside the United States, which is the most vicious thing that the United States could have done. So we cannot develop a nationalistic concept. Our concept must be around our color, because it was our color around which they decided to make us slaves. . . .

12

Ronald Reagan: Speech to the Conservative Political Action Conference (1974)

*The 1970s was a difficult time for the American economy—oil embargoes, unemploy-
ment, and rising inflation all eroded the confidence that many citizens had in a regulated capitalistic economic system. Given that he was ascending into national prominence,
the speech transcribed here encapsulated future president Ronald Reagan's economic
policies. Note especially his effusive praise for business interests and the benefits that economic expansion and development have brought to the American people.*

. . . For the second time in this century, capitalism and the free enterprise are
under assault. Privately owned business is blamed for spoiling the environment, exploiting the worker and seducing, if not outright raping, the customer.
Those who make the charge have the solution, of course—government regulation and control. We may never get around to explaining how citizens who
are so gullible that they can be suckered into buying cereal or soap that they
don't need and would not be good for them, can at the same time be astute
enough to choose representatives in government to which they would entrust
the running of their lives.

Not too long ago, a poll was taken on 2,500 college campuses in this country. Thousands and thousands of responses were obtained. Overwhelmingly,
65, 70, and 75 percent of the students found business responsible, as I have said
before, for the things that were wrong in this country. That same number said
that government was the solution and should take over the management and
the control of private business. Eighty percent of the respondents said they
wanted government to keep its paws out of their private lives.

We are told every day that the assembly-line worker is becoming a dull-
witted robot and that mass production results in standardization. Well, there
isn't a socialist country in the world that would not give its copy of Karl Marx
for our standardization.

Standardization means production for the masses and the assembly line
means more leisure for the worker—freedom from backbreaking and mind-
dulling drudgery that man had known for centuries past. Karl Marx did not
abolish child labor or free the women from working in the coal mines in
England; the steam engine and modern machinery did that.

Unfortunately, the disciples of the new order have had a hand in determining too much policy in recent decades. Government has grown in size and
power and cost through the New Deal, the Fair Deal, the New Frontier and
the Great Society. It costs more for government today than a family pays for
food, shelter and clothing combined. Not even the Office of Management and
Budget knows how many boards, commissions, bureaus and agencies there are
in the federal government, but the federal registry, listing their regulations, is
just a few pages short of being as big as the Encyclopedia Britannica.

During the Great Society we saw the greatest growth of this government. There were eight cabinet departments and 12 independent agencies to administer the federal health program. There were 35 housing programs and 20 transportation projects. Public utilities had to cope with 27 different agencies on just routine business. There were 192 installations and nine departments with 1,000 projects having to do with the field of pollution.

One Congressman found the federal government was spending 4 billion dollars on research in its own laboratories but did not know where they were, how many people were working in them, or what they were doing. One of the research projects was "The Demography of Happiness," and for 249,000 dollars we found that "people who make more money are happier than people who make less, young people are happier than old people, and people who are healthier are happier than people who are sick." For 15 cents they could have bought an Almanac and read the old bromide, "It's better to be rich, young and healthy, than poor, old and sick."

The course that you have chosen is far more in tune with the hopes and aspirations of our people than are those who would sacrifice freedom for some fancied security.

Standing on the tiny deck of the Arabella in 1630 off the Massachusetts coast, John Winthrop said, "We will be as a city upon a hill. The eyes of all people are upon us, so that if we deal falsely with our God in this work we have undertaken and so cause Him to withdraw His present help from us, we shall be made a story and a byword throughout the world." Well, we have not dealt falsely with our God, even if He is temporarily suspended from the classroom.

When I was born my life expectancy was 10 years less than I have already lived—that's a cause of regret for some people in California, I know. Ninety percent of Americans at that time lived beneath what is considered the poverty line today, three-quarters lived in what is considered substandard housing. Today each of those figures is less than 10 percent. We have increased our life expectancy by wiping out, almost totally, diseases that still ravage mankind in other parts of the world. I doubt if the young people here tonight know the names of some of the diseases that were commonplace when we were growing up. We have more doctors per thousand people than any nation in the world. We have more hospitals that any nation in the world.

When I was your age, believe it or not, none of us knew that we even had a racial problem. When I graduated from college and became a radio sports announcer, broadcasting major league baseball, I didn't have a Hank Aaron or a Willie Mays to talk about. The Spaulding Guide said baseball was a game for Caucasian gentlemen. Some of us then began editorializing and campaigning against this. Gradually we campaigned against all those other areas where the constitutional rights of a large segment of our citizenry were being denied. We have not finished the job. We still have a long way to go, but we have made more progress in a few years than we have made in more than a century.

One-third of all the students in the world who are pursuing higher education are doing so in the United States. The percentage of our young Negro community that is going to college is greater than the percentage of whites in any other country in the world.

One-half of all the economic activity in the entire history of man has taken place in this republic. We have distributed our wealth more widely among our people than any society known to man. Americans work less hours for a higher standard of living than any other people. Ninety-five percent of all our families have an adequate daily intake of nutrients—and a part of the five percent that don't are trying to lose weight! Ninety-nine percent have gas or electric refrigeration, 92 percent have televisions, and an equal number have telephones. There are 120 million cars on our streets and highways—and all of them are on the street at once when you are trying to get home at night. But isn't this just proof of our materialism—the very thing that we are charged with? Well, we also have more churches, more libraries, we support voluntarily more symphony orchestras, and opera companies, non-profit theaters, and publish more books than all the other nations of the world put together.

Somehow America has bred a kindliness into our people unmatched anywhere, as has been pointed out in that best-selling record by a Canadian journalist. We are not a sick society. A sick society could not produce the men that set foot on the moon, or who are now circling the earth above us in the Skylab. A sick society bereft of morality and courage did not produce the men who went through those years of torture and captivity in Vietnam. Where did we find such men? They are typical of this land as the Founding Fathers were typical. We found them in our streets, in the offices, the shops and the working places of our country and on the farms.

We cannot escape our destiny, nor should we try to do so. The leadership of the free world was thrust upon us two centuries ago in that little hall of Philadelphia. In the days following World War II, when the economic strength and power of America was all that stood between the world and the return to the dark ages, Pope Pius XII said, "The American people have a great genius for splendid and unselfish actions. Into the hands of America God has placed the destinies of an afflicted mankind."

We are indeed, and we are today, the last best hope of man on earth.

13

George H. W. Bush: Acceptance Speech at the Republican National Convention (1988)

In 1988 the enormously popular President Reagan was finishing his second term in the White House, and his logical successor was his Vice President, George H. W. Bush. The American economy had rebounded significantly from the depths of the 1970s, though both outgoing President Reagan and presidential-hopeful Bush advocated for further improvement in economic conditions, primarily through the reduction of taxes. In the following reading, George H. W. Bush, on his way to ultimately being elected, expounds on the economic successes of Reagan and utters the infamous phrase that will ultimately prove to be his downfall: "Read my lips, no new taxes."

. . . Consider the size of our triumph: A record high percentage of Americans with jobs, a record high rate of new businesses—a record high rate of real personal income.

These are the facts. And one way you know our opponents know the facts is that to attack the record they have to misrepresent it. They call it a Swiss cheese economy. Well, that's the way it may look to the three blind mice. But when they were in charge it was all holes and no cheese.

Inflation was 12 percent when we came in. We got it down to four. Interest rates were more than 21. We cut them in half. Unemployment was up and climbing, now it's the lowest in 14 years.

My friends, eight years ago this economy was flat on its back—intensive care. We came in and gave it emergency treatment: Got the temperature down by lowering regulation, got the blood pressure down when we lowered taxes. Pretty soon the patient was up, back on his feet, and stronger than ever.

And now who do we hear knocking on the door but the doctors who made him sick. And they're telling us to put them in charge of the case again. My friends, they're lucky we don't hit them with a malpractice suit!

We've created seventeen million new jobs in the past five years—more than twice as many as Europe and Japan combined. And they're good jobs. The majority of them created in the past six years paid an average of more than $22,000 a year. Someone better take 'a message to [Democratic opponent Michael Dukakis]: Tell him we've been creating good jobs at good wages. The fact is, they talk—we deliver. They promise—we perform.

There are millions of young Americans in their 20's who barely remember the days of gas lines and unemployment lines. Now they're marrying and starting careers. To those young people I say "You have the opportunity you deserve—and I'm not going to let them take it away from you."

There are millions of older Americans who were brutalized by inflation. We arrested it—and we're not going to let it out on furlough. We're going to keep the social security trust fund sound, and out of reach of the big spenders. To America's elderly I say, "Once again you have the security that is your right—and I'm not going to let them take it away from you."

I know the liberal democrats are worried about the economy. They're worried it's going to remain strong. And they're right, it is. With the right leadership.

But let's be frank. Things aren't perfect in this country. There are people who haven't tasted the fruits of the expansion. I've talked to farmers about the bills they can't pay. I've been to the factories that feel the strain of change. I've seen the urban children who play amidst the shattered glass and shattered lives. And there are the homeless. And you know, it doesn't do any good to debate endlessly which policy mistake of the '70's is responsible. They're there. We have to help them.

But what we must remember if we are to be responsible—and compassionate—is that economic growth is the key to our endeavors.

I want growth that stays, that broadens, and that touches, finally, all Americans, form the hollows of Kentucky to the sunlit streets of Denver, from the suburbs of Chicago to the broad avenues of New York, from the oil fields of Oklahoma to the farms of the great plains.

Can we do it? Of course we can. We know how. We've done it. If we continue to grow at our current rate, we will be able to produce 30 million jobs in the next eight years. We will do it—by maintaining our commitment to free and fair trade, by keeping government spending down, and by keeping taxes down. Our economic life is not the only test of our success, overwhelms all the others, and that is the issue of peace. . . .

My opponent won't rule out raising taxes. But I will. The Congress will push me to raise taxes, and I'll say no, and they'll push, and I'll say no, and they'll push again, and I'll say to them, "Read my lips: no new taxes."

DISCUSSION QUESTIONS FOR CHAPTER 7

1. According to Sumner, what regulates an unchecked capitalistic economy? How does Carnegie justify supporting an unchecked capitalistic economy? Is his argument that wealthy industrialists should be the stewards of society's wealth a valid one? Does Veblen seem positively or negatively disposed toward the "leisure class"? Is it immoral for society to allow for huge disparities in wealth?

2. How does the Dawes Severalty Act represent a step toward providing economic liberty for Native Americans? Why was this ineffective? If conditions for laborers in the United States were as bad as expressed by Newman and Debs, why did millions of immigrants continue to come to the United States?

3. Compare and contrast the views of Calvin Coolidge and Huey Long. Who had a stronger argument regarding the right of Americans to acquire and accumulate wealth? What are the pros and cons to low taxations levels? What are the pros and cons to high taxation levels?

4. Compare and contrast the views of Johnson and Carmichael on poverty. Why does Johnson seem so optimistic that the government can alleviate the suffering of the masses, whereas Carmichael had virtually no faith in public aid? Is it possible for a capitalistic society to be devoid of exploitation?

5. What reasons do Reagan and Bush offer for minimizing taxes and cultivating the expansion of business and industry? Are corporate taxes counterproductive to stimulating the economy? Why are tax increases often inevitable?

Index